FOX AND I

FOX AND I

An Uncommon Friendship

CATHERINE RAVEN

Spiegel and Grau

S&G

SPIEGEL & GRAU

Copyright © 2021 by Catherine Raven

Published in the United States by Spiegel & Grau, New York
www.spiegelandgrau.com

Jacket design by Strick&Williams; Jacket Illustration by June Glasson
Interior design by Meighan Cavanaugh

Library of Congress Cataloging-in-Publication Data Available Upon Request

ISBN 978-1-954118-00-3 (HC)
ISBN 978-1-954118-01-0 (eBook)

Printed in the United States on 30% post consumer recycled paper

First Edition
10 9 8 7 6 5 4 3 2 1

The stories in this book reflect the author's recollection of events. Some names, locations, and identifying characteristics have been changed to protect the privacy of those depicted. Some of the dialogue has been recreated from memory.

For Fox

FOX AND I

A double rainbow had changed the course of my relationship with the fox. I had been jogging when I realized that he would live only a few years in this harsh country. At the time, I believed that making an emotional investment in a short-lived creature was a fool's game. Before the jog ended, a rainbow appeared in front of me. One end of the rainbow slipped through an island of tall dead poplars drowning in gray sky, their crowns splitting and spraying into each other. I stopped. A second rainbow arched over the poplars. How many rainbows had I seen in this one valley? A hundred easy, and I always paused to watch. I realized that a fox, like a rainbow and every other gift from Nature, had an intrinsic value that was quite independent of its longevity. After that, whenever I questioned devoting so much time to an animal whose lifespan barely exceeded the blink of an eye, I remembered rainbows.

SAINT-EX'S BOA

For twelve consecutive days, the fox had appeared at my cottage. At no more than one minute after the sun capped the western hill, he lay down in a spot of dirt among the powdery blue bunchgrasses. Tucking the tip of his tail under his chin and squinting his eyes, he pretended to sleep. I sat on a camp chair with stiff spikes of bunchgrass poking into the canvas. Opening a book, I pretended to read. Nothing but two meters and one spindly forget-me-not lay between us. Someone may have been watching us—a dusky shrew, a field mouse, a rubber boa—but it felt like we were alone with the world to ourselves.

On the thirteenth day, at around three thirty and no later than four o'clock, I bundled up in more clothing than necessary to stay comfortably warm and went outside. Pressing my hands together as if praying, I pushed them between my knees while I sat with my feet tapping the ground. I was waiting for the fox and hoping he wouldn't show.

Two miles up a gravel road in an isolated mountain valley and sixty miles from the nearest city, the cottage was not an appropriate arrangement for a girl on her own. My street was unnamed, so I didn't have an address. Living in this remote spot left me without access to reasonable employment. I was many miles beyond reach of cell phone towers, and if a rattlesnake bit me, or if I slipped climbing the rocky cliff behind the cottage, no one would hear me cry for help. Of course, this saved me the trouble of crying in the first place.

I had purchased this land three years earlier. Until then I had been living up valley, renting a cabin that the owner had "winterized," in the sense that if I wore a down parka and mukluks to bed, I wouldn't succumb to frostbite overnight. That was what I could afford with the money I'd earned guiding backcountry hikers and teaching field classes part-time. When a university offered me a one-year research position, you might think I would have jumped at the chance to leave. Not just because I was dodging icicles when entering the shower, but because riding the postdoc train was the next logical step for a biologist. But I didn't jump. I made the university wait until after I had bought this land. Then I accepted and rented a speck of a dormitory room at the university, 130 miles away. Every weekend, through snowstorms and over icy roads, I drove back here to camp. Perching on a small boulder, listening to my propane stove hissing and the pinging sound of grasshoppers flying headfirst into my tent's taut surface, I felt like I was part of my land. I had never felt part of anything before. When the university position ended, I camped full-time while arranging for contractors to develop the land and build the cottage.

Outside the cottage, from where I sat waiting for the fox, the view was beautiful. Few structures marred my valley; full rainbows were common. The ends of the rainbows touched down in the rolling fields below me, no place green enough to hide a leprechaun but a fair swap for living with rattlers. Still, I was torn. Even a full double rainbow couldn't give me what a city could: a chance to interact with people, immerse myself in culture, and find a real job to keep me so busy doing responsible work that I wouldn't have time for chasing a fox down a hole. I had sacrificed plenty to earn my PhD in biology: I had slept in abandoned buildings and mopped floors at the university. In exchange for which I had learned that the scientific method is the foundation for knowledge and that wild foxes do not have personalities.

When Fox padded toward me, a flute was playing a faint, hypnotic melody like the Pied Piper's song in my favorite fairy tale. You remember: a colorfully dressed stranger appears in town, enticing children with his music to a land of alpine lakes and snowy peaks. When the fox curled up beside me and squinted, I opened my book. The music was still playing. No, it wasn't the Pied Piper at all. It was just a bird—a faraway thrush.

❧

H aving slept since midmorning in the shade of his favorite boulder, the fox woke to the heat of a sinking sun. Pointing his butt skyward and his nose windward, he stretched his neck along a foreleg that was naked as a newborn mouse. The fur wasn't actually gone, just misdirected. Turning tailward, he discovered his fur blowing flat back, leaving the hide on the front of his legs exposed but warm.

A mouse was scraping through the gravelly soil with footsteps as heavy and hesitant as a pregnant female's. The mouse was almost close enough when a wind whip cracked the dried grasses and wiped out the soundtrack. *Weasel pee!* And his day was just starting. Below, on Alfalfa Flat, the wind was not blowing. A tangle of mice tumbled under a shadow of shrubs, and partridge bustled in the hedgerows. But not for him. The flat belonged to his mother, and she permitted access to only her mate and their freshly weaned kits. Her permission, however, rarely got in the way of the fox's plans. He was a yearling now, with agility enough to test her vigilance. In fact, trespassing forays frequently topped his agenda.

For now, he planned to avoid his mother's territory and visit the house with the shiny blue roof. The house perched on the hillside below his den and above his mother's. Its roof appeared to sit directly on the ground, with sagebrush and juniper spilling over its north and south flanks.

In fact, it was situated much like his own den. Both homes burrowed into the same mountainside and exposed themselves fully to the rising and setting sun. Both faced the curvy, glinting river and hid from the cold north wind.

He scanned the hillside, checking possible routes that led to the house. The dry channel was noisy, but he wasn't on a covert mission and it presented fewer challenges overall. Picking up the channel trail required traversing a windy ridge. Ahead of the wind, a gigantic cloud was colliding with Round Hill. Crouching between a couple of chin-high cactus blades, he nearly stopped breathing to keep their spines from poking his chest. Fair price to watch a cloud performance. After crashing into the hill, the cloud burst open and flew into pieces. *On plan!*

Thick clumps of perennial grasses rattled in the dry channel, their stalks bending under the weight of ripe seed heads. Long and thin as fish bones, grass seeds matted his fur and pierced his hide. Stopping at a small rose bush, he combed himself against the thorns. Now lighter, he skipped down the draw, tilting side to side as if he were a vole-thieving hawk on low glide.

Cactuses, wind whips, fish-bone seeds: these were not optimal digs. The Alfalfa Flat foxes were probably half-asleep on their green field, mouths open, waiting for some errant mice to run blindly across the short soft grasses and impale themselves on undeserving canines. Those were optimal digs. Well, they would be if you were one of those foxes whose only purpose in life was commanding a hunting ground with a high density of dimwitted mice.

🔺

Stuffing my backcountry Therm-a-Rest sleeping pad into a canvas cover, I converted it into a camp chair. The pad had accompanied me during hundreds of nights in the wilderness, and, like a racehorse retired to a riding saddle, it bucked domestication. No matter how I threw it down, the pad landed on the most distressing piece of ground. Fox trotted into the shade of the cottage, then curled up and flattened down like a rug, nothing but two meters and that one forget-me-not between us. He waited motionless on his smooth spot while I floundered around on the soft, spineless chair that left me off-balance and rocking. "*The Little Prince*," I said, opening a waxy-covered paperback, "by Antoine Saint-Exupéry."

For a long while, my life had been a skunk's tail. A question mark. Now that I had decided to leave this place, the question wasn't what to do, but why I wasn't doing it. The answer, I am ashamed to say, had something to do with the fox.

We had been zigzagging along for months—the fox and I—before arriving at our current level of comfort. I had not bothered to map out our exact route, but a reconnoitering was on the horizon, and in wild, open country, the horizon is hard to avoid.

"The little prince asks Saint-Ex to draw him a sheep. Saint-Ex obliges because . . . well, I think it's about graciousness, Fox." I had fallen into a pattern of reading and talking to Fox, and then looking at him in silence for fifteen seconds. The fifteen-second pause simulated his turn to speak.

"Prince doesn't like any of the sheep drawings, so Saint-Ex hands him a drawing of a box and tells him there's a sheep inside." I shrugged. "It works. An invisible boxed sheep. All along, Fox, a sheep in a box." Then it was his turn for a fifteen-second count.

People buy, cage, license, and leash all kinds of animals. The animals live in boxes like the prince's sheep. Whoever holds the box imposes their imagination on the confined animals. They can humanize or dehumanize their boxed animals, depending on their own discretion or indiscretion.

I pulled a clump of dry wheatgrass out of the ground with one bare hand. The stalks split and splintered into my palm. Fox opened his eyes wide, staring while I shook out my injured hand. We had almost reached his average sitting time of eighteen minutes. He tilted his head back in a wide yawn and poked out a tongue, rubbery and pink like an old-school eraser.

Would you listen attentively for eighteen minutes while a duck quacked? A cow mooed? A dog barked? Those feelings are mutual. We animals recognize distinct vocal signals from our own species and relegate the sounds of other species to background noise. Mostly they hear "blah blah blah" and we hear "quack quack quack."

Mostly. Even before meeting the fox, I suspected that red foxes might be an exceptional case. Dr. Dmitri Belyaev, a Russian scientist, spent fifty years taming red foxes to respond to human voice commands. His experiments suggested that foxes, like dogs, distinguished discrete human sounds. In other words, foxes could identify the differences between *zzz*, *mmm*, *shhh*, and so on. If Belyaev was correct, Fox heard words but did not understand them. Like me at the opera.

The unboxed fox and I were still reading when the landline interrupted. I tried ignoring it, but I didn't own an answering machine and my caller had limitless patience. After listening to about a dozen rings, I went inside and picked up the downstairs phone, leaving the door open so I could keep an eye on Fox. Jenna, my supervisor from the local college's continuing education program, wanted to review details about my upcoming wildlife class. The job, thirty miles away, kept me employed for about ten weeks a year. But what to do about the fox? I had never walked away from him before. Our times together had always ended by his choosing. He left first; that was our custom. And yet, there he sat, seven meters away, beyond the possibility of eye contact, beyond visiting distance in any culture, pulling the blue forget-me-not forward with one paw and rubbing his nose back and forth across the captive stalk.

To create the impression that I was not abandoning him, I stepped closer to the door, shouldering the handset so Jenna couldn't hear me tell

Fox that I wouldn't be long and that he should wait. When I put the receiver back to my ear, Jenna was asking who I was talking to.

"Nobody. It's just me here. How many students do I have?" Fox released his fading flower and scanned the ground for an insect to menace.

"Didn't I just tell you? Thirty-two. So, you have a pet."

"I do not. I am here alone. You know I mutter and talk to myself." Fox turned around to see if anything more interesting was happening on his butt.

"Do you know that when you talk to yourself you *don't* mutter?"

By the time the call ended, Fox was "mousing," by which I mean hunting for both mice and voles, two distinct species that are indistinguishable when viewed from a propitious distance. A gifted hunter, Fox couldn't eat everything he caught. He scattered caches about, thoughtfully including the area around my camp chair. A week after Fox decided to become a regular visitor, I built a cobblestone wall to delineate a mouse-free zone (MFZ) around my sitting area. I planned the MFZ as an area free from the burial of mutilated, flat-dead, stinking mice and, more importantly (at least in my presence), their exhumation.

Fox had different ideas. When he buried a carcass inside the MFZ, I pointed to the Lilliputian cobblestone wall and explained that mummified rodents were not copacetic. Then I discussed the meaning of *copacetic*. Sensing that I was not saying anything entertaining, he translated it all as "blah blah blah." Although the little wall did not change Fox's behavior, it did on one occasion mitigate the embarrassment of my harboring a fox.

"There's a putrid rodent festering on your walkway here." The UPS driver handed me my monthly office supplies.

"Another mouse? Geez. Some animal . . ." I shook my head and looked down at my bare toes curling up at me. "It's been happening for a while." I looked straight at the driver. "Maybe . . . ahhh . . . skunk?"

"Oh, no, it's fox. Nothing but fox."

Like all country people, I was resourceful. Out here there weren't any trash-removal or snow-clearing services. My sheriff lived thirty miles away. We all took care of our own houses, lawns, and roads. But we did not deliver mail. Neither did the US government. Apparently, our isolation made mailboxes impractical. The UPS driver kicked the ground, and a puff of dried clay exploded onto his cordovan dress shoe. "Tear up the place and stink. I sure wouldn't allow any fox on my place."

Without waiting for him to finish shaking his head, I pointed to the cobblestone wall. "I do *not* allow him. It. Allow whatever it is. I don't."

THE NEXT DAY, while waiting for Fox's 4:15 appearance, I thought about our upcoming milestone: fifteen consecutive days spent reading together—six months in fox time. Many foxes had visited before him; some had been born a minute's walk from my back door. All of them remained furtive. Against all odds, and over several months, Fox and I had created a relationship by carefully navigating a series of sundry and haphazard events. We had achieved something worth celebrating. *But how to celebrate?*

I decided to ditch him.

I poured coffee grounds from a red can into a pot of boiling water, waited to decant cowboy coffee, and thought about how to lose the fox. Maybe he wouldn't come by anymore. I opened the door of the fridge. "Have I mistaken a coincidence for a commitment?"

The refrigerator had no answer and very little food. But it gave me an idea. I drew up a list of grocery items and enough chores to keep me busy until long after 4:15 p.m. and headed out. The supermarket was in a small town thirty miles down valley, and I had to drive with my blue southern sky behind me. Ahead, black-bottomed clouds with white faces chased each other into the eastern mountains. Below, in the revolving shade, Angus cattle, lambing ewes, and rough horses conspired to render each passing mile indistinguishable from the one before. Usually, I tracked my location counting bends in the snaky river, my time watching the clouds shift, and my fortune spotting golden eagles. (Seven was my record; four earned a journal entry.) Not today.

Now that I was free to be anywhere I wanted at 4:15 p.m., I returned to my mercurial habits and drove too fast to tally eagles. Imagine a straight open road with no potholes and not another rig in sight. Shifting into fifth gear, I straddled the centerline to correct the bevel toward the borrow pit and accelerated into triple digits. Never mind the adjective, I *was* mercury: quicksilver, Hg, *hydrargyrum*, ore of cinnabar, resistant to herding, incapable of assuming a fixed form. The steering wheel vibrated in agreement.

The privilege of consorting with a fox cost more than I had already paid. The previous week, while I was in town collecting my groceries, I got a wild hair to stop at the gym. The only person lifting weights was Bill, a scientist whom I had worked with in the park service. I mentioned that a fox "might" be visiting me. "As long as you're not anthropomorphizing," he responded. Six words and a wink left me mortified, and I slunk away. Anthropomorphism describes the unacceptable act of humanizing animals, imagining that they have qualities only people should have, and admitting foxes into your social circle. Anyone could get away with humanizing animals they owned—horses, hawks, or even leashed skunks. But for someone like me, teaching natural history, anthropomorphizing *wild* animals was corny and very uncool.

You don't need much imagination to see that society has bulldozed a gorge between humans and wild, unboxed animals, and it's far too wide and deep for anyone who isn't foolhardy to risk the crossing. As for making yourself unpopular, you might as well show up to a university lecture wearing Christopher Robin shorts and white bobby socks as be accused of anthropomorphism. Only Winnie-the-Pooh would associate with you.

Why suffer such humiliation? Better to stay on your own side of the gorge. As for me, I was bushed from climbing in, crossing over, and climbing out so many times. Sometimes, I wasn't climbing in and out so much as falling. Was I imagining Fox's personality? My notion of anthropomorphism kept changing as I spent time with him. At this point, at the beginning of our relationship, I was mostly overcome with curiosity.

I GRIPPED A COUPLE OF firm white mushrooms in one hand and reached for one of those slippery plastic sacks with the other. The Timex face flashed on my exposed inner wrist. Forty-five minutes shy of 4:15 p.m. The fox! Meeting a fox that I wanted to jettison suddenly felt more important than mushrooms for which I was driving sixty miles round trip. I shook the bag several times, but it refused to open, so I jammed the mushrooms back onto the shelf between some oranges and pushed my full cart to the registers. While calculating the time needed to drive home through a gauntlet of white-tailed deer along a two-lane road, I somehow ended up in the empty express-checkout lane. A cowboy rolled in behind me. The clerk observed my cart, raised her eyebrows, smiled, and said nothing. She was supposed to ask if I had found everything I was looking for; she wanted to ask if I could count to eight.

"Yes. Thank you," I answered the unasked question, "but I regret abandoning some mushrooms at the last minute."

Her eyebrows dropped. Eyes rolled.

I pulled a wallet out of my back pocket. "Shame about the mushrooms," I said, flipping through the cash. Then I turned to the cowboy and noticed he was about 110 years old.

"Goodness. Just a little bunch of bananas." I bent over his cart and peered inside. Nothing. Just bananas. "Didn't even need a cart for that, did you?"

"Needed something to hold me up," he said, "while waiting."

For a moment I considered the remark, wondering if it had some underlying message. The cue hadn't been in the cowboy's words, but in his flinty-eyed stare. He'd expected an apology. Halfway home, I realized that he was annoyed that I was in the wrong checkout lane. I hated missing social cues. For every cue I caught too late, I worried about another few flying right over my head.

But more so, I worried about not being home when the fox came visiting. He was an uninvited guest and I couldn't keep him waiting. Uninvited guests are quite unlike invited guests, whose entitlement (I imagine) allows them to overlook their host's temporary tardiness. Invited guests will call, "Yoo-hoo!" and without waiting to see if "yoo" is even home, they will let themselves in. They will saunter over to the fridge and grab a drink. But uninvited guests are fragile, and you need to greet them punctually to minimize the discomfort inherent in their ambiguous status. Most problematic is the uninvited guest who knows he's expected.

Unless I was home in forty minutes, a red fox would trot his reasonable expectation of hospitality down to my cottage, scratch the dirt, sniff the air, feign preoccupation, and expend his tiny reserves of patience and humility. Then he would slip away in a dreadful sulk. This could not be explained to a 110-year-old cowboy propped up by a five-banana cart, but it was true nonetheless.

Motoring down the driveway, I scanned the chubby hill across the draw. A vertical cliff with a sassy tilt to the north lay on top of the hill like an elegant pillbox hat. In the middle of the cliff, on a ledge tucked into a shaded pleat, a golden eagle rose from its nest. I ran upstairs, leaned onto the window ledge, and searched for the fox. When the tip of his tail breached the wheatgrasses, I led him with binoculars as though he were a grouse ahead of my 20-gauge. Leading, a traditional hunting skill, requires hunters to anticipate an animal's speed and direction, keeping the barrel, sights, or scope just ahead of the moving target. Fox was an easy lead. His tail bobbed brazenly down the fall line. My college textbook claimed that wild animals instinctively elude their natural enemies. That may be true for a generic fox, but this specific fox was not eluding the golden eagle; he was bounding down the hill to the tune of the "William Tell Overture."

A s the golden eagle rose from its nest, a hundred feet below it a tiny dog fox was journeying down the draw. Just as the fox reached a blue-roofed house, the garage door roared shut and he turned sharply to run along the only clear path to the river, a dirt road adjacent to a rivulet lined with cottonwoods. An alfalfa field as green and neat as a pheasant's neckband stretched along one side of the rivulet. Dry hummocks as mottled and messy as a pheasant's tail pushed against the other side.

Across the river, fields bounced into hills, hills rose into forests, forests slid off steep cliffs, cliffs tucked underneath snowcaps. Beyond the snowcaps, rows of mountain ridges stretched endlessly. Where the mountains ended, or if they ended at all, the eagle could not know. After watching the fox disappear into the thick leafless willows along the river's edge, the eagle flew upriver, where newborn lambs dotted the nearby fields.

The fox crept under the shrubs until his front paws dipped into the river. He stared at a newly exposed sand island glowing in the sun. The fox could swim, but he preferred not to. In any case, the river, almost at high water, was muddy and tumbling wide, drowning last autumn's braided channels, spits, and gravel shoals. Not even a moose would try to cross. And today? Today a girl might be waiting for him.

Later, the eagle saw two animals outside the blue-roofed house: a fox moving west toward the sagebrush hills, and a person heading east toward the river. Quartering lower, the eagle decided they were not going in separate directions; they were walking—the two animals—toward each other.

I left *The Little Prince* and an iced tea next to my camp chair and went looking for Fox. I spotted him trotting back from the river, following a trail that swung below my cottage. He could have either stayed the course and avoided me altogether or broken trail and marched uphill to meet me at the rendezvous site. I walked directly toward him, tripping over pits and mounds where the skunks had been digging, stubbing my toes on mud-mired rocks the size of melons, fighting through thigh-high pea thickets. Clover vines clawed at my burr-covered shoelaces. When he was about nine meters away, he stopped and watched me. Had I wandered around obstacles instead of through them, turned my gaze toward the singing meadowlark, or stooped to pull a weed, he would not have understood that I was expecting him. Standing at the meadow's edge, I wrapped my arms around my chest and squatted like a frog, tucking my torso between my knees. He saw me waiting and started for his regular spot next to the forget-me-not. I followed.

I continued reading out loud from where we'd left off the day before. After two paragraphs, I held up the open book and showed him a prince with hair as blond and spiky as an antelope fawn. Switching from reading to summarizing, I continued, "The little prince lives on an asteroid—it's a miniature planet. The planet has one flower—a rose. She's vain. Her petals . . ." I planed a hand like a 737 on takeoff (just for emphasis), "flat. Like a face-lift. Never wrinkled. Yeah, I know, Fox." I nodded. "But the prince loves the rose." My throat, prone to laryngitis, tightened against the hot, dry wind.

Like all domestic roses, the prince's rose was high-maintenance. "Here she is, swollen with water"—I held up an imaginary beach ball— "sending . . . *demanding* that the prince fetch more water." I tossed the beach ball over Fox's head and reached for the glass of iced tea sweating next to me. Fox's eyes followed the glass. He twitched and startled; I set the tea down without drinking. "He polished her single thorn just to appease her vanity."

Fox winked and stared intermittently. I coughed without looking away from him, silently counted to fifteen, including the "one thousand" pauses in the middle, coughed again. "I know what you are thinking, Fox. The rose is not in love with the prince. He is wasting his time."

Fox sat up and cocked his head in the classic pose of canine inquisitiveness. This encouraged me to continue summarizing. I pointed to the single-flowered forget-me-not and explained that a rose, like the forget-me-not, is a plant: a small, sessile autotroph with a short life span and limited emotive capabilities.

"This obviates the question about whether the rose is really in love, Fox."

I paused and counted. He showed no sign that he had found that last comment flippant, so I continued recapping the plot. "The prince propels off his planet, travels all over the universe, and ends up on Earth. He wanders through the Sahara." I told Fox that the prince stumbles upon the delusional Saint-Exupéry, who is trying to patch a broken airplane and a relationship with a woman he's left behind. "The woman, like the rose, is spoiled and vain."

At the time I was reading to Fox, there were fifty million copies of *The Little Prince* in circulation. You could read it in 160 languages. The book's author, Antoine Saint-Exupéry, a pioneer in the field of aviation, had written the international bestselling novella *Night Flight*, winner of the Prix Femina, and *Wind, Sand and Stars*, a memoir that the National Geographic Society considered the world's third best adventure book. During Saint-Ex's heyday—the 1930s and '40s—the world's rich and cultured elite rolled out their welcome mats for him.

But he preferred places where he was not welcome. The Sahara, for example. Saint-Ex could do without civilization and maintained a desultory relationship with it all his life. Despite having access to the world's most sophisticated people, he preferred talking to baobab trees, roses, foxes, and God.

You mean he talked to himself?

No. I mean he talked to baobab trees, roses, foxes, and God. I imagine he also talked to himself. He socialized with people, plants, and wild animals who were unashamed or unaware of their eccentric appearance: lopsided haircuts, wilted leaves, rumpled trousers, mouse tails stuck on their upper lips. Saint-Ex didn't care about social facades. He liked being around people who imagined widely and with a hint of magic—like a child. And so he wrote a book in which he vets potential companions by showing them a copy of a child's drawing, a beast in situ, and asking them to identify it. Everyone quickly and confidently identifies the beast—as a hat.

The "hat" turns out to be a boa constrictor digesting an elephant. Only the little prince correctly identifies the drawing, and he's an extraterrestrial. In other words, Saint-Ex—French war hero and fearless explorer of the Sahara—had imaginary friends.

In 1935, Saint-Ex's single-engine plane exploded over the Sahara. He leapt from the cockpit to safety. Able to walk, but without communication, food, or water, he became a self-described "prisoner of the sand." When death became imminent, he occupied himself by observing the survival strategies of animals. He interpreted the activities of foxes—when they hunted, ate, and paired—from their signs. Eventually, he found their den. He could save himself if he killed a fox and drank its blood. He didn't. Instead, he thanked the foxes for their friendship in his dying hours.

Eventually rescued by nomads, Saint-Ex survived the desert but not the Second World War; his P-38 Lockheed Lightning reconnaissance plane crashed into the Mediterranean Sea in 1944.

AFTER HUNTING, THE FOX stretched himself into a long thin line on the gravel driveway, stomach down, shoulders and both front legs stretched back toward his hips, pads up. The wind licked his gray fur cross—one streak down his back and one the length of his shoulders—into calico. When he finished sunbathing, we hiked to his den. Despite the presence of a well-worn route, he gerrymandered the trail to avoid facing the sun. He was already inside the den when I said goodbye. I told him I was off to teach a wildlife class in Yellowstone and would return in half a fortnight.

The next day, I arrived at class hoarse. "Talking the ears off a visitor," I told the students. Luckily, no one asked if my visitor had talked back, because Fox, the runt of his litter, had been born mute. When he opened his mouth, only one faint sound escaped—*qwah*—like the last gasp of a dying duck.

Our field campus, built as a vacation resort, was comprised of a semi-circle of shiny, varnished log cabins stuck together two by two, each pair surrounded by freshly mowed lawn. A lodge with a great high ceiling and windows all around served as our auditorium and dining hall. Separating the lawn from the river was a cobblestone beach, where carnelian-stemmed coyote willows waved with the slightest breeze. Outside the cabins: long wooden decks. Inside: rough-hewn pine furniture, wildlife-patterned upholstery, TV sets, and thirty-two students looking to augment their knowledge of natural history.

After dinner, I showed slides and told stories about wildlife, starting with the three species we could see from the cabins: pronghorn antelope, Rocky Mountain elk, and bison. In the first story, an antelope harem is placidly feeding in a tight group when one doe makes a lightning-fast run for freedom. The dominant buck chases down the escapee, rounds her off, and trots her back to his harem. Almost immediately, a second doe charges for the hinterlands. The buck responds as with the first. While the second runaway resumes feeding, a third female flees. I showed a slide of a panting buck facing the camera. I interpreted his look as "total exasperation" and heard stifled laughing. I moved on to elk without pausing.

With their heads upright, a group of cow elk are sitting with their butts together. When photographed from the hillside above, they look like spokes on a wagon wheel. On another hillside in deep snow, two bull elk sit tail to tail, rotating their heads to enjoy 360-degree vigilance in an area dense with wolves. In the next slide, wolf tracks surround a bloody bull carcass. "Males are more likely than females to be killed by wolves. In fact, even where there aren't wolves around, bulls don't live as long as cows. Why?" Students stir. I shake my head. "No. Don't even try that joke. I've heard it so many times: Why do men die before their wives?" I pause before the hackneyed punch line, "Because they want to." I tell them that cows live longer than bulls because they are mammals. Among mammals, the gender responsible for child-rearing lives longest. I return to the pair of bulls. In the next slide, one of them has shirked his responsibility. Instead of being on the lookout for wolves, he has placed his head in the snow and fallen asleep. "Males engage in activities," I tell them, "that are not evolutionarily stable." They laugh at my interpretation because they think I'm talking about people. Tomorrow we'll watch a biker without a helmet cross a double yellow, pass an RV around a blind curve, and edge his Kawasaki along a 300-foot cliff face. Following what sounds like a collective gasp, I'll hear "not evolutionarily stable" recited by a chorus of voices.

The last in the series of bison stories starts with a herdlet meandering around thinly frozen ponds. One adult cow falls through the ice and descends into freezing water. She buoys herself up, dog-paddles to where she fell in, secures both front legs on the snowy edge of the hole, and, with her backbone twisting like a black python, she strains to pull herself over the lip. She almost makes it. Exhaling loudly, she slips backward. Another adult cow stands sentinel at the hole's slippery edge, watching for three hours until the drowning cow finally sinks. I ask the class whether the sentinel cow is loyal or stupid.

I lecture while the students shuffle and scribble, point while they lean and whisper, pause while they cough and sneeze. Each time, after asking a question, I count to fifteen. For most of my life, except for these sporadic lectures, I spoke in soliloquy or not at all.

Uncomfortable with dialogue—let alone group conversations—I blocked out the extemporaneous noise filling the auditorium. Instead, I listened to the inherent rhythm of the sounds around me: the stories I told, spoken slowly and steadily with intermission for questions, and the fast, jerky speech in response. No one answered my question about the sentinel bison, but I considered the talk a success anyway, since I remembered not to use words like *fortnight*.

"I am an a cappella singer," I told the fox when I got home, "and I have been trapped in a jazz band."

After the presentation, a student walked me back to my cabin and asked about my pets.

I didn't grow up in a house with pets. Since leaving college I'd been too transient, and I'd been taking jobs like this one, which had me sleeping in a different bed so many nights of each month. And now that I was spending time with Fox, I couldn't imagine that I would ever be willing to own an animal.

"No pets," I said, shaking my head until I realized that she'd think I was abnormal and then I'd have to explain myself. "Not *now*," I added when we stopped at my cabin door.

"That's funny about not having a pet."

Fussing with the stubborn door lock kept me from making eye contact. "Really? Funny?"

"There were a few animal slides . . . ," she said, turning to walk to her cabin in the dark. "I was sure you were going to call the little fellow 'Foxie.'"

Foxie? As if he were a pet. As if hanging around a fox was tantamount to decorating a terrier in tartans or teaching a parrot to solicit crackers.

During the show, I'd treated the fox slides as though they depicted a typical wild animal passing by somewhere. I did not give any indication that I had a relationship with him. How did she know? How had she sat through a two-hour slideshow and picked out the *one* animal in the entire lineup who differed from the rest? There had been just two slides of Fox, the angles and proximity no different from those of other animals on the screen. But Fox, unlike the others, was modeling, decorating the screen while I discussed the dynamics between wolves, foxes, and coyotes. In the slides, Fox wore an enigmatic expression, looking a bit like the famous woman in the da Vinci painting. Students, I hoped, would see a demure wild animal while I would see a droll one. Just like the famous model, Fox was posing three-quarters to the artist in front of mountains, hills, and a river. But now it appeared that my pictures of him weren't mysterious at all. He had been called out—not as a wild animal or the *Mona Lisa*, but as a *pet*.

I reminded myself that it was only because I was not The Leonardo.

At breakfast, Jenna and I caught up with each other's lives and re-viewed logistics: hiking distances, bus schedules, the impending rain, whether normal people spent all that much time talking to foxes. But I did not tell her about my fox. Then the bus arrived to bring us into Yellow-stone Park for the day and we hadn't even finished our cereal.

"Talking to foxes," Jenna said, scribbling students' names on the sand-wich bags in the cooler, "is not something that normal people do much." I wasn't trying to emulate normal people, but I did like knowing what they were up to.

On the bus, I told her a little about the fox, the slides I took of him, and about the "Foxie" comment. She suggested I explain my relationship with Fox to the class. *Awful idea.* "Maybe no one else noticed," I said. "Maybe that one woman has a sixth sense."

"She doesn't."

I had barely enough social intelligence to understand that adults, least of all trained scientists, don't go around treating wild foxes as if they had personalities. I reminded Jenna about the author of *The Little Prince*, his boa constrictor drawing, and his conclusion that there are some things that people will never understand. Things like my relationship with a wild fox.

"But this is your *job*. Talking to people. Explaining things."

"Saint-Exupéry said that explaining things to people who were never going to understand was exhausting. So he just ignored people."

"Don't you think that's a lonely way to live?"

"He was *not* lonely. He had the little—"

"I *know* what you're thinking," she interrupted. "But *you*? Don't you already have enough make-believe friends?"

That night, back in my cabin, I turned the big armchair from the television set to the sliding glass doors. I understood that I could not keep my relationship with Fox a secret. One thing a private person cannot afford is secrets. People will leave you alone if they know you're not hiding anything. I also knew I had no idea how to explain my relationship with Fox.

I picked up a notepad and my chunky seven-dollar pen, let my legs dangle over the side of the chair, and asked myself how to explain the relationship. *Start at the beginning.* I tried to imagine when Fox and I first became more than just two itinerant animals crossing each other's paths. I wrote "April," then realized that there was no "Eureka!" moment in our relationship. There were no exclamation marks at all. Maybe the relationship had developed so smoothly that I never doubted that all was as it should be, or maybe it had developed rapidly enough to keep me perpetually confused. I crossed out "April" and wrote "March." I closed my eyes and listened for the river, heard the TV from the attached cabin and voices from its married occupants. Crossed out "March." Having never acquired a television or a spouse, I wondered how to illustrate my fox with enough clarity that no one would mistake him for a hat.

LITTLE BROWN BATS

The next day of field class, hot wind hit us like a blow-dryer. That evening, pungent humidity from the big river lured me out to the deck, while *Myotis lucifugus*—little brown bats— kept me standing near the sliding door. No one wants to get whacked by a bat.

Lucifugus means "avoiding the light of day," like Lucifer, El Diablo. Common in caves, the Little Devils also enjoyed sneaking into tall, dark lodges and ricocheting between ceiling beams. When they intruded into our classroom auditorium, I would swat them with fat whips of terry cloth towels. But you cannot swat bats out of your head so easily. They are haunted. I was convinced that ghosts of cave creatures were visiting those deck bats. Never mind that I've never actually seen a specter and hadn't been inside a cave for years. Irrationality is the hallmark of ghosts.

Back inside, I sat sideways across my cowboy-motif chair, drumming on my notebook with the tap end of the seven-dollar pen. Good pens were free; better pens were inexpensive. As a homeowner, I could have collected and stored scores of cheap, free pens. But I couldn't shake the idea that all my belongings needed to fit inside my car. So I carried one good Pilot pen. The notebook was blank, except for a few crossed-out words, but I wasn't looking at the pages. The river had reached high water, and it was surging through the willows as it ran past the patio.

I needed to be thinking about how my relationship with the fox began and why we rendezvoused every day at 4:15 p.m. We were meeting, after all, under odd and uncomfortable circumstances. Foxes are supposed to avoid people, free spirits are supposed to avoid schedules, and everyone except a person with the wit of a nit is supposed to avoid humanizing wild animals.

I wanted to believe that Fox and I were meeting every day because we had followed a logical and inevitable path. I decided that I could diagram that path and drew two stick figures in my notebook: one on the bottom left wearing a ball cap, the other on the bottom right with pointy ears. One line extended toward the center of the page from each figure. The two lines converged, and a single line continued up the page. I flanked the line with overlapping isosceles triangles that symbolized impassable mountains and left only a narrow corridor for the route on which Fox and I would have no choice but to meet. The line passed through stars, which represented key events. All journeys have key events. All I had to do was figure out what they were and label them.

Then I could bring the map to class and show everyone that my relationship with Fox had followed a natural course of events and that nothing happening between us was bending the immutable laws of science. "Here's what happened," I would say. "One thing led to another." Running my finger along the line and the stars hemmed in by mountains, I would wait for everyone to reply, "Yeah. Well. When you look at it that way"; shrug their shoulders; and agree that they too would have befriended a fox.

. . .

I WAS A PARK RANGER before I earned my doctorate in biology. In fact, I was pressing a Stetson on my head and cinching up that iconic pinecone-embossed belt before I finished my bachelor's degree. I'd studied botany and zoology in college. In Washington's Mount Rainier National Park, I patrolled the backcountry; my trail circuit included a region known as Three Lakes, where I stayed in a tiny cabin that smelled like wood and wax. A few feet shorter than my blue-roofed cottage, the Three Lakes Patrol Cabin and its outhouse perched on a knoll above First Lake, the largest of the three lakes. Giant, shaggy-barked evergreens surrounded and almost completely shaded the lake. I never called it First Lake. I treated all three lakes as a single body of water temporarily separated by a transient meadow and called it all Three Lakes no matter which shore I stood on.

Not many hikers trudged the six miles uphill to Three Lakes from the nearest road. Even fewer came by way of the Pacific Crest Trail, a long journey that required camping overnight. Every morning, I rose from a sleeping deck that ran flush with the cabin's window and scratched myself into a uniform—one badge on the shirt and another on the jacket. Wearing a .357 in a shoulder holster, I hiked down to the lake with coffee in one hand and a government-issued logbook in the other. Across my green cloth logbook, in fat black cursive, I had written a quote from Ishmael, the narrator of Herman Melville's *Moby-Dick*: "Meditation and water are wedded forever."

For Ishmael, an impecunious sailor hustling jobs in "Manhatto" in the 1800s, meditation meant exactly what it meant to me at the Three Lakes cabin in the twentieth century—pondering. If it had any other meaning—scholastic, formal, or religious—I wasn't any more aware of it than Ishmael would have been. Overall, our lot and luck didn't differ by much. We'd both found ways to keep wild animals and wild water nearby.

Melville could have dropped Ishmael along the Shriner Peak Trail and let him join me on the eight-mile hike up the exposed ridge to the fire lookout. After surveying wildlife and hammering PVC pipes into snow-banks, we would haul jerricans filled with meltwater back to the fire tower. In the evening, we would stand on the tower's railed balcony to admire our priceless view of Mount Rainier, and never mind the thousand miles or the 150 years that separated us, the same thought would cross our minds—an eight-mile hike: no better view in the northwest asked less of a person.

After a night at the lookout, we would follow Laughingwater Creek through old-growth forest, using Leatherman tools and pruning paint to repair graffiti that scalawags had carved into the thin, gray bark of silver firs. Laughingwater Creek traces the park's border around the rim of the Three Lakes basin, so we would have to check on boundary signs. Pausing periodically at the white metal signs with green embossed letters, one of us would slip the reverse end of a claw hammer under a double-headed nail, pulling just enough to prevent the sign from eating into the bark of a boundary tree. We wouldn't mind the workload; we were outdoors, away from civilization, and free from anxiety. An impecunious sailor in "Manhatto" in 1800 expressed anxiety by "deliberately stepping into the streets and methodically knocking people's hats off." To a backcountry ranger in the twentieth century, anxiety meant turning into mercury, a metal that evaporates in ambient temperatures, becoming invisible, odorless, and completely unassuming. Disappearing into the woods saved me from questions that caused anxiety: *Where are your parents? Why are you all alone? Doesn't anyone care about you?*

When Ishmael needs open air and physical labor, he quits a respectable job as a schoolteacher and joins a whaling crew. Except for the part about killing whales, the job is perfect. When it comes to locating whales to harpoon, Ishmael keeps "a light hold" on his obligations. On masthead duty, instead of watching for whales, he meditates and thinks through life's necessary philosophies. In fact, he never calls a whale on any of his watches. I wouldn't either. If I had to stand masthead, I'd close my eyes and wear mirrored sunglasses and a "save the whales" T-shirt. Like you. Or someone you know. Or someone you used to know.

Or someone you used to be.

"The whale-fishery," writes Ishmael, "furnishes an asylum for many romantic, melancholy, and absent-minded young men [who] . . . in their secret souls . . . would rather not see whales than otherwise . . . lad[s] with lean brow[s] and hollow eye[s]; given to unseasonable meditativeness . . . sunken-eyed young Platonist[s]. . . . Lulled into such an opium-like list-lessness of vacant, unconscious reverie is this absent-minded youth by the blending . . . of waves with thoughts, that at last he loses his identity; takes the mystic ocean at his feet for . . . that deep, blue, bottomless soul, per-vading mankind and nature. . . . In this enchanted mood, [his] spirit ebbs away to whence it came; becomes diffused through time and space."

Yes, sometimes I had to stop reading and call "man overboard" on Ishmael. At Three Lakes, I learned to keep my feet grounded when I went pondering. Otherwise, one moment I could be sitting on Three Lakes' shore listening for the pitter-patter of an elk poacher's gum-soled boots, and then, without any warning, I might find myself in "unconscious rev-erie" at Fourth Lake.

Like Ishmael, I cured anxiety and boredom with jobs in wild and beau-tiful places: North Cascades, Mount Rainier, Voyageurs, and Glacier Na-tional Parks. But when The Real World spiked out the bait—a checking account and health insurance—I bit hard. Still, my head swiveled back behind me as I left, filling up with regret and memories: red berries the size of toad eyes scattered on deep soft moss that bounced under my boots; cobalt-colored ponds so nearly frozen that when I dove in I felt a wave of closing capillaries from fingers to toes; pond-pocked meadows below fields of thigh-high blue lupine so beautiful I held my breath and whis-pered, "So this is what *breathtaking* means."

I memorized scenes because I didn't have photographs, and I ended up carrying them as talismans to calm me or chase away my worries. These images prowled around in my mind for years and, over time, transmogrified, merged, became chimeras. An image from a Glacier Park trail might collapse into a memory of North Cascades. In my mind's eye, I would be leaning against my cherished North Face Moraine, a red-and-navy internal-frame pack—one of the first designed for females—in some rivulet-scored mountain meadow, inhaling buck scent, listening to bumblebees, watching monkey-faced flowers the size of fox paws bob above curvy, subalpine deadwood. I used several tents and bivy sacks, but the red-and-navy Moraine went everywhere.

When I stumbled into cavernous problems that seemed insurmountable, I called out one of the chimeras, watching it in my mind's eye. If I got lucky, new ideas—creative, viable, and edifying—filled the space vacated by the deported worries. Usually, I wasn't that lucky, but the habit of pulling up these beautiful images kept them from disappearing. A lack of money caused most of my stress, and my health suffered: infected wisdom teeth, a nonmalignant tumor, no medical insurance. I thought that if I lived long enough, the images of the backcountry places where I lived and worked would benefit my life more than the lack of healthcare would detract from it.

At graduate school in the city, it seemed that every living thing wore a leash or a collar or sat in a cage. I felt like I did too. Worn down and landlocked, I had time for only the most scripted thoughts; my opportunities for pondering diminished, then disappeared. Instead of wilderness, a manmade environment surrounded me: asphalt and elevators and fake ponds pitted into manicured lawns where croft ducks on the lam ate caramel popcorn. The acrid smell of excess carbon monoxide, the sound of electrical buzzing, and the purple illumination of fluorescent lights filled the lecture halls. Classroom windows, out of reach and out of sight, lined up along the high ceilings to prevent distraction and discourage jumpers.

Now, six years after leaving university, having gone back to the wilderness, and back to the academy, and back to the wilderness again, I met a wild thing: a fox. The fox was alluring, almost magical. But the timing was inconvenient. I had recently begun to wonder whether I belonged in this isolated mountain valley. The academy offered more than a paycheck and health insurance; it offered companionship with people. A long time ago, I had arrived at the prudent and logical conclusion that when your own parents don't want you, no one else will. So I had been living a solitary life. Now that I was teaching field classes for the second summer, I had a sneaking suspicion that if I knocked persistently, and not too loudly, the doors to social acceptance just might open. But only if I left Fox and the mountain behind.

MOTHS FLEEING LITTLE BROWN BATS were sneaking through tiny rips in the patio's screen door and making their way into my cabin. I slid the glass door shut to protect the owner's shiny new upholstery. The River Cabin students were probably already asleep. I thought about past afternoons spent watching for a fox with a demanding schedule and not an iota of patience. On those days I had nothing to do but wait and watch and think.

I remembered the first step we took toward our friendship.

"Start here," commanded the map. I picked up my pen. Next to the solid blue star, I wrote, "Vole Forest."

VOLE FOREST

After dinner on the second evening of the class, I continued filling in the map. If the students were still interested and asking questions about Fox on their last day, I would have an illustrated story prepared.

Fox first crossed my path the previous October, during The Great Vole Debacle, a performance I planned, orchestrated, and directed—sometimes while glimpsing an errant fox in my audience. Months later, at the Debacle's finale, the errant fox was conducting; the voles and I played from the pit.

I had spent the summer teaching field classes for the University of Montana Western in Yellowstone National Park. The theme for the students was wildlife and wildflowers. For me, it was *Homo sapiens*. For three months, they surrounded me all day and most nights too. I observed the world like one of those fancy pet telescope goldfish, eyes popped open and treading water. All the women were wearing cropped pants, so I cut my green jeans at the knee and sewed on cuffs of orange and gold ribbon.

Terrible idea. But Patricia, one of the popular instructors, complimented my handmade crops, so I wore them almost every day.

When I finally figured out from all the smirking that Patricia's compliment was actually a *comment*, summer was almost over. I doubled down on my observations. Stopping in West Yellowstone on my way home, I bought brown cargo-crops that matched those Patricia had been wearing.

(The next summer I wore my brown cargo-crops; Patricia did not wear hers. "Do you know you have these exact same pants?" I asked when I got tired of waiting for a compliment. "No," she said, while I tried interpreting her stare, "they don't look familiar at all.")

I was relieved to return home to the country where I could wear what I wanted, because, as expected, there was no one keeping me company. Not anyone with hide or hair anyway. I did know one special black widow spider. I would not call her "company," but she'd been a reliable occupant for over a year now. She used to share my dark, windowless garage with eight other widows. They're not accustomed to the cold, and when the wind howled, seeping into the cracks around my roll-up garage door, they gathered up their billowing webs from the top edges of the doorsill and high-stepped to the sheltered interior, cozying up in inconvenient places—near the light switch, the car doors, the hanging tools. My college textbook said a widow's bite was "rarely fatal." But it can cause temporary blindness, which is something to worry about if you're living alone. So I carried an old sneaker into the garage in case I needed to whack any of them. And now only one remained. Unlike her wind-averse and widowed sisters, she built her web in the front of the garage, where it didn't threaten me.

When I got home from summer classes she was hanging upside down beneath clouds of silk she had spun in lieu of a cobweb. Despite her disheveled home, the widow had eaten well in my absence; three-inch-long grasshopper exoskeletons dangled under her silk drapes like Chinese lanterns. Though beautiful, the widow was not terribly dynamic company. Sometimes at night I would retreat to the garage to see what she was up to. Usually nothing. One night she trapped a moth in her web. Gripping it with long, lacquered legs and thrusting her fangs, she injected the moth with poison and stilled its fluttering. When the moth dissolved, she sucked up the slurry until nothing remained but an empty, winged case. While the silk-wrapped case spun around, we both stepped back and admired her crinkly new lantern.

The first morning home, I woke to the nearly forgotten annoyance of black-billed magpies thumping on my three-year-old steel roof and portico. Our summer classroom had tucked into a tame landscape where well-behaved birds pandered to us by singing or displaying dazzling plumage. The dominant avian fauna at my place were raptors, meat-eating birds whose ability to feed and fend for themselves meant they rarely needed, wanted, or noticed human attention: red-tailed, rough-legged, and Cooper's hawks; falcons, kestrels, bald eagles, ospreys, ravens, shrikes, magpies, and golden eagles. The latter two species were roof thumpers. That was all I knew about the golden eagles. They were nesting on the cliff when I built my cottage. I'd chased them up and down the rocky hills to learn more about them, but between constantly retying a broken binocular strap and keeping my bloodied knee clean, I hadn't learned anything about their sexes, ages, or social arrangements. The eagles ignored me. I suspected that was their plan all along, but it didn't stop one from landing on my roof now and then with a signature thud and what I imagined was a freshly killed eastern cottontail.

The magpies had no business thumping; none of their biological obligations required the use of my roof. And whereas I believed the majestic eagles were ignoring me, the magpies, I was sure, were thumping simply to annoy me. Either way, that first morning home, disgruntled by the drumming, I pulled on jeans and a fleece pullover and stumbled downstairs.

I splattered four egg whites on a hot cast-iron pan, saving the raw yolks and half shells in a blue melamine bowl. After shaking spiders from my mukluks, I grabbed the bowl and a coffee and headed out to Tonic, a twelve-foot-tall juniper tree across the draw. The sun filled a deep pass in the eastern mountains, facing me head-on and blinding me. Scrunching my face into a tight squint, I trudged ahead until a thicket of thigh-high plants blocked my way.

Three months earlier, when I'd left home to teach, short grasses were growing here: blue grama and fescues interrupted by a few airy sprigs of Indian ricegrass. *Short* did not simply describe their stature. Short grasses imbibed shortness; it was their personality. Whether neglected or coddled, a short grass could never grow tall enough to reach my thighs.

And now, where was my fox barley with the long fringe tails that I liked to stroke? Where was my Indian ricegrass, whose seed head I would ruffle with my fingertips as if it were the head of a small puppy? Gone. Thick-stemmed aliens had swallowed the path to Tonic and taken a large bite out of the front pasture; I was under siege. And not just by plants. Beneath the masses of tangled branches, now dripping with spilled coffee, two voles played bumper cars with my padded footwear.

No, not *moles*. Moles have a wrestler's forearms, claws like ivory rakes, and long, naked snouts. By contrast, voles look like russet potatoes. Not exactly, but then, no two potatoes look *exactly* alike. Fat, pin-eyed, seemingly both tailless and earless, the voles in my pasture were as similar to potatoes as any two potatoes could be to each other. Ranchers called them "red-backs," even though their longitudinal symmetry obscured any semblance of a back.

Moles had the better reputation; they ate unsolicited insects. Voles were bulb-suckers—daffodils, tulips, crocuses, and onion. They chewed the bark off expensive trees and the roots off well-tended shrubs. Worse yet, like Norway rats, voles harbored bubonic plague. They were tough little creatures, showing up in all my favorite wildlands, enduring subzero temperatures, hurricane-force winds, and single-digit relative humidity. I liked to remind myself that while voles were as homely and troublesome as any rodent, they were significantly smaller than Norway rats. They had earned, after all, if not praise, then at least this faint damnation.

A few years earlier, I'd trapped, bled, weighed, sexed, and measured hundreds of voles for the CDC. My field partner did the same, but many of the voles he handled died of fright or committed hari-kari. All the voles I handled survived. Now these little creatures were invading *my* property. Most gardeners would be running for their illegal stash of zinc phosphide bait. Not me. I wasn't interested in filling their intestines with lethal volumes of swamp gas. Unashamedly, I was attracted to all animals that tolerated me.

I carved depressions in the dirt under Tonic to cradle the yolk-filled eggshells. Then I searched for a place to sit among the ankle-high *Opuntia* cactuses. They'd been waiting for me to come home so they could stab their barbs into my innocent heinie. Tonic was the primary socializing and hoarding tree for the thumping magpies, all but two of which looked pretty much alike to me. I had assigned arbitrary genders and appropriate names to the two I did recognize, the main nesting pair for the past couple of years. Tennis Ball had a big, round belly; her mate, Torn Tail, crossed his wings behind his back like he was handcuffed.

TBall clamped her bill on an eggshell and decamped to Gin, the juniper adjacent to Tonic. She perched on the highest branch, tipping the shell upward as though it were a tankard. When she finished guzzling the syrupy yolk, she dropped the shell into the juniper leaves and wiped both sides of her bill on a branch. Spreading her wings and fanning her tail, she descended for more yolks. Three smaller birds, who had been stabbing the dirt with beaks like black daggers, rose as TBall lowered herself. It was as if they were levitating on a pillow of hot air that pushed under TBall's broad wings. After rising and sinking, the smaller magpies resumed scratching and pecking the soil. While searching out every edible morsel of yolk that had spilled from the shells TBall had carried off, they turned the clay soil into a loose mound of dirt as soft as talcum powder. Then they flew off, presumably to loot a birdfeeder somewhere in the valley.

Later that month I sat by Tonic, tucked my hands into soft-fringed sagebrush, and watched four hyperactive magpies pulverize hardtack soil during their frantic search for yolk droplets. When the foursome left, a pair of red-shafted flickers—ground-feeding birds often accused of being woodpeckers—took advantage of the loosened soil to dive in and suck ants.

Tennis Ball tolerated the trespass because flickers vacuumed up poison-spitting thatch ants that would otherwise be eating her food. The size of cooked rice grains, thatchers were not big eaters, but they conveyed a clever-enough carryout business to deprive the magpies of sizeable globs of yolk.

Having figured out that their niches overlapped, soil-stomping magpies and ant-sucking flickers were teaming up, reminding me of the John Muir saying: "When we try to pick out anything by itself, we find it hitched to everything else in the universe." Aphorisms like that set Muir up to be one of the twentieth century's most famous conservationists.

What about me? To whom was I closely hitched? No one.

I wasn't sad about that, only curious. I had been alone as far back as my memory could reach. I saw myself alone in the furthest future that I could imagine. Sometimes it seemed natural to me, as if my psyche fit into only this single way of living. I left home when I was fifteen. It wasn't, at first, a clean break. I'm sure you can imagine how it feels to live with people who don't like you. Unpleasant but tolerable. My father was violent. I could live with that because—you can ask my doctor—I am quite tough. But he treated me with disdain, and that was something that I could not live with. So I left. I moved to the Georgetown University campus for summer school, and in the fall, when I was sixteen, I started at the American University, the closest college to where I was living. The university accepted me in a rush, based on my academic portfolio, grades, and test scores and such, and I found work to support myself. Demographically it was strikingly different from what I was used to. I had moved from a middle-class neighborhood where it was safe for me to rummage in the thick, adjoining woods to a city where most people seemed to be rich or poor, and the campus guards strolled around the library telling us to beware of the foot fetishist and to stay out of the woods.

I liked meeting people from all over the world but hated the city, and when I wasn't running on the track, I bicycled on the Chesapeake and Ohio Canal's towpath. The land belonged to the National Park Service, and I started hanging out with a ranger, who told me stories about fighting wildland fires in the Rockies. I left college and drove 2,280 miles to Glacier Park, where I found jobs waitressing (although I was too young to legally serve alcohol) and volunteering for the National Park Service. This time the break wasn't just clean; it was immaculate. I never saw my father again. Decades passed before I saw my mother. The ranger and I kept in contact for a while and met again in San Francisco, where he'd been promoted, and we spent time hiking and touring around the Presidio. I was always terrible about building relationships, and now I've forgotten his name.

Just as I've always been alone, I've never felt lonely. But I did want to fit in somewhere and belong to something. I tried lashing myself to the land, but it wasn't reciprocating. Land, I discovered, does not behave like a pet, offering unconditional love just because you own it. I thought I was buying space and rocks and dirt and a creek, and instead I ended up with a community of animals who wanted me to work for my welcome. For a while, I'd been working on TBall. She wasn't the biggest animal here, but she was the most influential; she had loads of followers. I brought her egg yolks, and, in return, I imagined her perching on the deck and cooing while I read; pacing reverently beside me when I gardened; waddling politely behind me while I carried yolks to the tree; and refraining from roof-thumping forays.

Tennis Ball goose-stepped toward me. Two birds followed her, one on each flank. Three birds filled the next row, four in the back. All stiff-backed, they were dragging fat white bellies and propping up long necks and narrow heads. They looked so much like a rack of bowling pins that I didn't feel guilty about imagining I was aiming a big, shiny ball at them. They waddled unnervingly close. "Don't bite the hand that feeds you," I said, knowing that their little bird brains couldn't possibly realize that I wasn't actually feeding *them*. I had been delivering the yolks under Tonic for *whoever* to eat—the weasel in the woodpile, the skunk, the baby badgers. I ate eggs every morning but rarely ate yolks, since they had fallen out of favor with the medical community.

Stopping just beyond my arm's reach, the magpies raised their wings and stretched their necks impossibly forward. When their beaks popped open, they extruded skinny wet tongues. An unfinished adage had duped me: Don't bite the hand that feeds you . . . *or else?* Or else *what?*

I might have continued trying to appease the magpies, but every morning when I walked over to Tonic with egg yolks, voles ran over my feet. Those tall invading plants that attracted the voles had grown right up to my siding, flush to the front steps. At midday, for the price of a few moments at the front window, uninvited weeds parted to reveal a vole who was, if not entirely friendly, at least moving too slowly to escape the illusion of conviviality. All I needed to hitch those unpretentious rodents up to my metaphorical wagon was a mutually beneficial activity. Something like a gardening project.

While trapping rodents for that CDC research project, I discovered that voles harvested liatris seeds and stacked them outside their burrows. Liatris (*Liatris punctata*), sometimes called blazing star, was one of my favorite plants. It stood stiff and upright, a stalk of densely packed purple flowers, tall as a crocus. In these endless fields of dun-colored grasses, liatris produced just enough pigment to be visible, but not so much as to call attention to itself. And it endured deer and drought with less complaining than any other flowering plant. Liatris, I decided, could re-habilitate my north meadow. All I needed were lots of seeds. And now I knew who was going to collect them. Tolerating me, I realized, was not the voles' only endearing trait.

My role in this mutually advantageous gardening project was tending their patch of tall weeds. Vole Forest, as I would come to call the weed plot, provided voles with a safe harbor in a world rife with foxes and hawks. My plan would proceed as follows: in late summer, voles would gather liatris seeds from the adjacent open lands and stack them outside their weed-fortified burrows. I would wander around my property like a great provincial land baron, scooping seeds from burrow heads. By early next fall, my replanting project would be underway.

Before you denounce my lack of judgment, ask yourself if you haven't engaged in a lopsided relationship with an individual even more demand-ing and less likeable than a vole. Take your fifteen-second count.

❧

The broad glacier-carved valley was so dry and sparse it could not forgive meat eaters or grain growers a single misstep. If the valley tossed them a modicum of good fortune, the sirocco-like winds would blow it away. For the past hundred years, humans and magpies were ene-mies. They stole each other's food: chicken eggs, crop seeds, wild and domestic fruit. They mimicked each other's tactics: rabble-rousing, mob-bing, explosive fecundity.

Now the round-bellied matriarch was tasked with sharing her home range with a human. The matriarch, born the scion of eleven generations that had survived the enmity, was self-possessed. She was a calm bird anyway, calm in an ethereal sense, calm beyond what one would expect from the upheaval surrounding her.

Condemned to communal lives, most magpies did not possess the skills necessary for independence. Community members divided their tasks—not without violence—according to how each bird perceived its relative abilities and needs. Most birds considered their options and chose the best way to assuage their constant hunger and avoid unwanted responsibilities. The matriarch didn't have options. She was destined to travel a path with no junctions, crossroads, or choices. She inherited wisdom, amended it, passed it on.

She also inherited instinct, which wasn't always an advantage. Instinct is a genetically inherited pattern of behavior that, at one time and in a specific environment, increased the population's fitness. Sometimes the specific environment that fostered the beneficial behavior changed before the genome could catch up. For thousands of years, instinct compelled magpies to follow people. That instinct was an artifact of an ancient détente, long since invalidated. People who had lived peacefully with pied birds for thousands of years no longer existed. A new human culture dominated the landscape. Now that people and birds were competing for the same foods, friendly tolerance was impossible.

As millennia passed, magpie genes performed their magic tricks: poorly adapted genotypes diminished, and fitter genotypes flourished, such that descending generations employed better tactics to avoid humans. But in accordance with Charles Darwin's prediction, small amounts of behavioral variation persisted. The matriarch's nestlings were fledging, and the same urge that made them raise their arms when she poked them out of the nest for first flight would drive them to houses, to people, to buildings— for food. She could not reconcile the urge with the reality: people were not as reliable a shield against starvation as wings were against gravity.

Her torn-tailed mate was balancing on the portico's pediment when a girl carrying yolk-filled eggshells emerged from the house. When the girl set the egg yolks under the juniper, he flew toward her. Gawking fledglings joined him, flying in decreasing concentric circles around the girl until the matriarch darted toward her foolhardy family.

All her life, an innate quantum of wisdom overrode her genetic predisposition to tolerate people, and she remained wary of humans. "Don't trust," she croaked. "Don't trust the hand that baits you."

A

It's a safe assumption that any plant called *weed* goes through life with low expectations. The corollary is that husbanding a thirty-square-foot weed patch should be a cinch. Still, I could not identify a single species in the patch. If you don't know what they are, you can't know what they want. My professional plant guides, *Flora of the Pacific Northwest* and *Flora of the Great Plains*, both thick, faded cloth-bound books, did not deign to document weeds anywhere within their cumulative 2,132 pages. The owner of a saddle shop forty miles upriver in a 600-person hamlet sold me *Weeds of the West*, a compendium of rap sheets for every plant that had ever been cussed at by a farmer. It included mug shots.

Four Eurasian weeds dominated Vole Forest: kochia, yellow sweetclover, Russian thistle, and Russian tumble mustard. The kochias looked like miniature Christmas trees. Annuals, they regrew from seeds each year and wasted no time producing nondescript flowers on their stiff branches. If the weed patch were a forest (and it was if you were a vole), then kochias belonged to the midcanopy. By shading the forest floor and humidifying this high-altitude desert, kochias kept voles cool and dewy.

Yellow sweetclover, which appeared to be strangling itself with a confusion of wiry green arms, was the least attractive and most euphemistically named weed in the bunch. Thousands of minute flowers overwhelmed each plant. Tissue-thin petals responded to mist or dew by twisting themselves into unrecognizable clumps that no subsequent amount of sunshine could reverse. Gyrating upward, green clover stalks intertwined into messy mats. Shooting below ground, sweetclover's dense, warty taproots provided voles with a constant source of sugar.

Semiwoody Russian thistles, two feet high, armed themselves with stiff, sharp spikes. The spikes discouraged foxes and hawks from diving though the canopy to capture voles. In autumn, after their seeds ripened, the Russians snapped free of their roots and rolled away. They set their spawn in soil they had rototilled with their own spikes. Underneath the thistles' ground-scraping skirts, voles foraged and fornicated, stopping only to blow raspberries at hovering hawks.

Russian tumblers, both thistle and mustard, entered the United States in the 1880s, stowaways in sacks of seeds shipped from Russian farmers to relatives in North Dakota. They answered to the common name *tumbleweed*. Despite having originated on another continent, tumbleweeds liked to pose alongside saguaro and pass themselves off as quintessentially American. Do not let them fool you. Saguaros saw America's first nations come and go before the first tumbleweeds crashed into their stocky boles. Tumblers have now interloped into acreage the size of North and South Dakota combined. Rolling across the sets of iconic Hollywood Westerns, they have accumulated a substantial number of fans eager to believe that any dueling facade is real if tumbleweeds and dust blow between the shooters.

My Hungarian partridge, natty dressers in their maroon-and-gray tweed, would do well without tumbleweeds rolling into their autumn-colored *Ribes*. Described by Aldo Leopold in *A Sand County Almanac* as "red lanterns," *Ribes* is a genus of maple-leaved shrubs that includes common currant and blackberry. Standing less than two feet tall, my *Ribes* turned softly in the wind as if wondering who had eaten all their berries so early in the fall. (It was the skunks.) Partridge, Leopold tells us, want nothing more from autumn than a stroll under *Ribes'* red leaves.

I lived on the east front of the Rocky Mountains, far to the west of Leopold's sand counties. Out here, if partridge chose to bask under fall's red leaves, they would soon find themselves basking under nothing at all.

First, they would look up and become intoxicated with the beams of red, orange, and yellow light passing through the currant leaves. In a day or two, still light drunk, they would hear Mother Nature laughing. "Just kidding!" The partridge would scurry to the junipers while shriveled, rusty cadavers swirled about their ankles. Oftentimes, frost came so hard and fast that *Ribes* bypassed their multicolored illusion; green leaves turned black overnight. In the year of Vole Forest, autumn was long and warm. Tiny broad-leafed currants turned into Leopold's red lanterns, and a partridge could find itself a shrubby solarium with no trouble at all. Well, it could have if I hadn't let the tumblers proliferate so that the voles could proliferate so that I could harvest liatris and rehabilitate the land that bulldozers had torn up to make room for my cottage.

Hungarian partridge, like tumbleweeds, were immigrants. For this, they forfeited even an iota of protection under the Migratory Bird Treaty Act. The federal government reserves the term *migrants* for native birds migrating *within* North America and classifies Hungarians as *game*. Killing migrants is a crime; killing game is a sport. A clumsy paradigm justified the indignity by suggesting that foreign-born creatures, or those with foreign-born ancestors, maligned our ecosystem and upset the natural habitat.

I wasn't sure there was enough habitat for Hungarian *people* in Hungary, let alone partridges. And I had plenty of land. For the past several years, I had been maintaining a Hungarian partridge refugee camp on my property, protecting the immigrants from weeds, feral cats, and the whims of an ill-conceived paradigm. Now the endless weed patch known as Vole Forest was overtaking their currant bushes. But I had hitched my wagon to the voles. Goodbye, red-lantern autumn!

By early October, I was gathering seeds from over a dozen vole hatchways, enough to fill a brown paper lunch sack. I stored the mystery seeds in a manila envelope inside the garage. When June arrived, long days would initiate the growing season, and I could poke the seeds into warm damp dirt. Voles, I was pleased to discover, were surprisingly productive for animals who appeared to lack appendages.

❦

Abandoning their wet, writhing newborns in the nursing chamber, they marched past the voles and into the tunnel. Silent, solemn, and quick, the adults pushed through the thick vegetation at the entrance and joined with thousands of fellow emigrants fleeing parallel tunnels. Keeping their heads down, they merged into a single line and marched into the sun. Condemning all the summer's newborns to a slow and lonely death of starvation was not a decision easily made. The queens, however, did not have the sovereignty to think exclusively about their own colony; a greater command forced the abandonment. A species cannot survive if its leaders do not know when to say "die."

The queens selected a three-tooth sagebrush that was splitting at the base, and their minions swarmed, biting into its soft bole and spraying it with formic acid until the vessels collapsed and the shrub withered. The stem hole became the ants' new main chamber.

Thatch ant mounds the size of red-tailed hawk nests blistered the territory. They were indistinguishable from every other pile of detritus. Who would notice if an ant nest moved from one side of a blue-roofed house to its other side?

The aphids noticed. They clung to the soft, velvety branches of white sage, sucking its sap and excreting honeydew. Orange-headed thatch ants were addicted to that honeydew. With their sharp, deep mouths and formidable arsenal of venom, they fought off any creature threatening the aphids. In this way, aphids and ants, like magpies and flickers, had twined their lives together into one thicker, stronger cord.

The white sage noticed. When the ants left, red polka-dot ladybugs swarmed the white sage, devouring the aphids. Bigger, hungrier insects followed the ladybugs. By the next new moon, most of the sage had been squeezed through grasshopper offal and returned to dust.

The round-bellied magpie noticed. Mindful of her neighbors, the matriarch waited until the ants' evening dormancy before wallowing in the thatch mound and dusting off her mites. It mattered very much to one of her fledglings, who waited until after the ant emigration before dropping feetfirst into the abandoned ant nest. A cloud of fungal spores enveloped the fledging, blotting his black hood feathers until they turned gray. He was still gasping when a boney-legged Cooper's hawk grabbed him.

The ants had feared only one enemy: shade. As they had for thousands of years, for a part of each day, for eight months each year, the thirty thousand ants needed sunlight. In that sagebrush steppe country of short grass and cactus, it had not seemed like much to ask. But a blue-roofed house—the first permanent human-built structure in that township and range since the most recent ice age had abated—had sprung up in an instant. It sheltered a person who tended weeds that blocked the sun and brought forth a monster shade that devoured the ants. Weeds and people were impractical enemies. Weeds were too numerous and dynamic to battle, and houses—even cottages—were too large to attack. Thatch ants had not survived thousands of years by casting blame. They'd survived by recognizing their immediate enemy and choosing, correctly, whether to fight or flee. Because they could not fight the shadow, they fled.

In that sagebrush steppe country of short grass, cactus, and cottage, eight hours of sunlight was, in fact, too much to ask.

A month shy of the year's shortest day, the adult black widow disappeared. A couple of months later, I would find a beaded curtain of tiny brown-and-white juveniles along the far wall of the garage, each suspended spider looking like a carved wooden ball. I was without any black-and-red adult spiders until late the following spring, but I still had the voles. As long as the weeds grew unimpeded in front of the cottage, I never ate breakfast alone.

That same month, a vole flew over my pasture. It was riding in the talons of a tawny-hooded and pale-eyed hawk. Juvenile, rough-legged. Born on Arctic tundra and raised on voles, the juvenile hawk had arrived in November, discovering familiar climate and unfamiliar neighbors: yellow sweetclover, thistle, tumbleweed, kochia, and me. It landed on Gin, the juniper downslope of Tonic, and without waiting for the vole to die began picking it apart.

One day, the hawk hovered and dropped, feet first, into Vole Forest, tangling its toes in the thorny shrubs. After getting snagged several times, it pitched over into a patch of sweetclover. After that, it hunted mostly in the swale meadows across the dirt road, coming back to bounce on Gin's top branch when it needed a lookout post. I watched from inside, binoculars pressed against the window. Eventually the hawk would stare back, mesmerized by the large black binocular "eyes." Generally, after striking a rodent, the hawk would ignore me, flying off a quarter mile to the wooden "private property" signpost to eat its catch. But sometimes the rodent it was aiming for escaped and the hawk would hit the ground with a loud thud. Realizing there was nothing between its claws, the juvenile would turn its head and look right into my big binocular eyes. I felt sure that it was looking for comfort in its time of embarrassment.

The first time I saw Fox, I was playing binocular eyes with the juvenile and he was pawing around in the egg yolks under Tonic. I had stashed four yolks in the soil that morning, adding them to the one uneaten from the day. Before he headed into the swale at the edge of my property, Fox ate one yolk and left four behind. It was one too many for Tennis Ball. Calling for reinforcements, she circled the yolks. A battalion of magpies now devoured the yolks they had ignored that very morning. They ate like there would be no tomorrow, like this was their last day on earth. Which was exactly how the fox ate. And why not? Life was precarious for the unboxed animals; they faced an unknown future. The devil of a difference was that one wanted to be fat while facing that future; the other, the fox, wanted to be fleet.

Two weeks before spring equinox, the juvenile hawk was strutting through the resting alfalfa field, now serving as a paddock for someone's cattle. When I dialed down the spotting scope's magnification, black Angus cattle and Fox came into view. Trotting through the paddock with their heavy hooves, the Angus were flushing sleepy rodents from their underground cubbies. Fox and the hawk scurried behind them, bagging the drowsy rodents. It was as if the Angus were novice bird dogs, always flushing, never retrieving.

On March 15, a thirty-minute morning walk along an irrigation canal brought me to the cottonwood copse where the rough-legged juvenile slept. Thirty-foot-high cottonwoods shaded patches of foamy, dirt-encrusted snow. Rivulets seeping from the snow dampened a patchwork of duff. In the adjacent pasture, a deer carcass had attracted a motley crowd of scavengers, including the roof-thumping magpies. After swooping on me, TBall commenced flirting with a turkey vulture. The rough-legged juvenile was already soaring high above the trees. The clouds had written themselves into long lines composed of a random series of dots and dashes, covering the sky in a Morse code so evenly dispersed that anomalies like soaring hawks couldn't hide themselves from me. I watched the juvenile join more hawks, circle higher, disappear. Next year, it would return from the Arctic with indistinguishable adult plumage and enough world-weariness to avoid a little person waving big binoculars.

Too often in life, I was propelled forward not by what I chose, but by what did not choose me.

I walked home through a strong crosswind blowing down from snowy mountains that were five miles and two tiny houses upriver. A band of dried grass and forb stalks separated the gravel road from the paddock's barbed wire fence. I called out the plants as I passed: fescue, mustard, cheat, mullein, sunflower, Russian thistle, rabbitbrush, knapweed, sage-brush, wild rye, bluestem, wheatgrass, sow thistle.

As I approached a horse-mowed pasture, an odd pattern of vegetation broke my stride. Turning into the wind, I spread my arms, hovering like a kestrel. Seedlings lined every vole runway, waving their single pair of leaves like flags at a motocross race.

They were not liatris.

The voles had been foraging along the gravel road and bringing home piles of seeds from a heinous yellow weed: the not inappropriately named *sow thistle*. Imagine an armed dandelion with the flower shrunken to near invisibility and the stalk stretched to a menacing height. Translucent barbs covered the white stem and the spindly taproot.

Somewhere in Montana, voles were collecting liatris seeds to stock their pantries. Not here. I had hitched my wagon to less hungry and more clever voles than that. These voles had been collecting sow thistle seeds in order to grow a protective fence around their homes and highways. And since Vole Forest had been protecting the voles from predators all winter, vole holes now pockmarked three acres. Their runs covered the ground like netting. In the following months, I would pinch so many sow thistle seedlings out of the soil that my thumb and index finger tore into bloody fissures deep enough to hide an ant. Luckily, I hadn't added to the disaster by planting my bag of seeds, all of which ended up sealed in a glass jar and brought to the dump like common bagworms.

Mule deer paraded across the west pasture and onto my packed-snow driveway, a neat sled line of herbivores heading to herbs. Seven pairs fol-lowed the lead deer, all moving sprightlier now without rotten snow cav-ing beneath their hooves. I waited behind the cottage to say good morning. Cutting away before reaching me, they pranced uphill, joining scores of mule deer already polka-dotting the slopes with their bright white rumps. That's how I spent the ides of March: dismissed by deer, abandoned by hawks, double-crossed by rodents. Already, viridescent weed rosettes were poking through the dense, dry stalks of the deeply rooted Vole Forest. Maybe we are all hitched together in the universe. Maybe Muir's quote was not referring to rodents. Either way. I decided (some would say immodestly) that I am less tightly hitched to voles than I had once imagined.

AFTER ANOTHER DAY with the River Cabin class, I changed the Vole Forest label on my diagram to *voles*. The fox had been attracted to my property when he realized it was a vole sanctuary. It hadn't been Vole Forest that had attracted him. In fact, the forest had been keeping him at bay. I labeled two more stars: *egg yolks* and *dogs*.

.

TWO BLACK DOGS

The aborted liatris project left me with a weed sanctuary and a new appreciation of voles, which is to say: none at all. Other than shading a thatch ant nest and then reducing it to a concave mass of damp detritus, Vole Forest served no purpose. Meanwhile, underneath its canopy, voles proliferated to an unimaginable density. One day, a desperate dam grabbed hold of my leather boot toe. Wrinkling her hindquarters like an accordion, she squirted out two shiny babies. They looked like kidney beans in tomato sauce.

I thought about decimating Vole Forest. I thought about the voles who had kept me company for so long. Without the forest for protection, hawks, weasels, and rubber boas would slaughter most of them. Imagine blood dripping from a vole impaled in the talons of a red-tailed hawk as it flies over the pasture. Imagine a weasel slinking into a vole's tunnel and sinking its jagged canines into a vole's hairy hind end. Imagine a turgid vole bulging from either side of the tightening belt of a rubber boa. The more I imagined, the guiltier I felt.

Owning land is a big responsibility. Every step taken, path set, weed pulled, and tree planted fosters a hundred million or so consequences. A great land baron, Nature's tenant in chief, must justify her actions and their consequences. She cannot level a forest—not even a vole forest—simply out of spite. The voles had done their damage; razing the forest wouldn't change that.

❧

The fox lay on the top edge of the draw's shady side listening to a mess of knotty weeds rustling in the wind. Across the draw, in the bright sun, a spring runoff was seeping into cattails, down a culvert, and under a dirt road. The fox's bright orange mother, twice his size, was standing on the bald hill beyond the dirt road, watching him. He had played this game before. She had positioned herself just so: upwind, proximate, and elevated. She wanted to see without being seen, to hear without being scented. She would be looking for him to misstep, to expose himself needlessly, or to wander off chasing some useless creature. She was making sure that he completed the tasks necessary to stay alive, and when she caught him out, she would scream to force him back in line.

The fox sucked a sticky bit of mouse tail from the corner of his upper lip. Maybe his mother screamed because she enjoyed watching him—last year's smallest kit—jump up with hackles raised, toes splayed, and toenails clicking on the rocky ground. Swallowing the mouse bit, he ran his tongue along his upper lip. Keeping his back to her, he, last year's runt, curled his tail around himself as if in repose. *As if.*

Turning his head toward a vole run, he imagined light beams from her two blazing eyes converging over the cattails. He flattened further into the dirt, and the single beam, gleaming like sun off a water drop on a beetle's hard shell, slid right across his back. He uncurled into semi-attack position. She would see him posing between spring and voles, water and food; his upright ears tilted forward as if listening for prey. Raising his rump, he rocked back over his heels. He looked like any normal fox preparing to pounce. Like any one of her ordinary offspring.

When she failed to uncover any punishable offense, his mother, deprived of a reason to discipline him, retreated to the horse corrals to waylay mice on their trek to the feed bins. The imagined beam of light dissipated.

He had fooled her. He was not hunting; he was spying on someone, wasting time watching another animal that wasn't food or foe. At a cursory glance, it would seem to be a useless activity, and yet it was serendipitous, not to the vixen but to the one individual in our story who at that point believed in serendipity.

Maybe you have never experienced voles. But some creature has disrupted your domain: rabbit, mole, pack rat, Russian boar. Maybe a gopher has decided to feast on your young cherry tree. You try to steer the invisible menace away from the tree by lighting gas bombs. When that fails, you flood its tunnels. Next morning, you find more tunnels and realize the gopher is moving faster because damp clay facilitates digging. You fill the tunnels with disincentives: coffee grounds, mothballs, urine, a Macabee trap. *Terrible idea.*

For days afterward, you find mothballs pitched out of the burrow, and now your throat stings when you work. Using a spade, your thumb, and the two fingers of your right hand that the Macabee didn't crush, you tear open all the tunnels you can find. The gopher digs deeper. While you sleep, it railroads on, eating away roots and leaving piles of soft dirt and coffee grounds increasingly closer to the bole of the baby tree that depends on you for its care—the only cherry tree on that acre. After you (and a mammoth amount of your time and money) have chased the gopher around the tree for three weeks, you find the tree tilted over in the wind. You lift the seven-foot tree—no longer tethered by lateral roots—into the air and see that it terminates in a finely chiseled point. Your tree is dead; the gopher is not. The fat, healthy gopher is down in its nursing den giving birth to a bevy of bucktoothed uglies. Before you chop the cherry tree into the world's most expensive mulch, you bring out the strychnine.

Really?

Strychnine?

Because that, my friend, is a revenge killing, and I won't do it, no matter the animal. I have been there with that gopher. As you read this, I am probably still here with the uglies or their descendants.

Land stewardship, especially in harsh country, is hugely difficult, and more so if you are the kind of person who feels compelled to kill tiny rodents simply for spite. That's why I hesitated to level Vole Forest. I needed something more honorable than revenge to motivate me.

Advancing across my land, Vole Forest was sucking water and spreading shade. Sun-loving plants—round cactuses no bigger than golf-balls, thick-leaved yellow violets, circular mats of purple pea, and rare fuchsia bitterroot—were withering in the weeds. I especially loved the ball cactus. In another month, those that had escaped the hegemony of Vole Forest would sprout a crown of pink recurved petals. On days when I worried over a pile of applications for university jobs that I didn't want but should have been applying for anyway, I remembered I owned land in a high-altitude desert where tiny five-headed ball cactuses bloomed in the shadow of snow-capped mountains, and I stopped worrying.

And so, I found a reason to level Vole Forest—fighting on behalf of my sun-worshipping tenants.

W

The fox dug the fingernails of his forepaw into the dirt and pulled his head up and over until his chin crossed his wrist. The person from the house was spinning around, swinging long metal objects, and shouting at the air. Her long and flexible fingers were curling and stretching in too many places at once. Like a woodpecker drilling sap holes in smooth-barked willow, she jerked her hands rapidly, but without any discernable pattern. Even ant-sucking flickers drilled in only one direction. The fox swatted two grasshoppers coupling and pressed them into the dirt until he felt their wet innards. Her hands reminded him of a hurricane, his least favorite weather event. So much energy, so little purpose. But, maybe, if entrained, so many possibilities.

Lifting the ball of his paw off the now-still grasshopper pair, he impaled them with one fingernail. She waved arms, fingers, and implements; he munched on grasshoppers. Clanging and booming tools reminded him of a windstorm's harsh, unpredictable noise. Her grunts and puffs merged to a cacophony. Debris rained on him, and he shut his eyes tight. Pulling his tail across his nose, he waited for the cloud of dirt to settle. When he opened his eyes, she was gone.

A slight opening, quite possibly illusory, appeared in the knotted shrubs where she had spent the entire afternoon. Somewhere within the mess, voles were taunting him. The thorny weeds would blind, slash, or impale anyone foolish enough to try and jump through them. He wasn't in the mood for a hard landing. He sunk his head below his shoulders, poking his snout forward into a clearing barely wide enough to fit his shoulders. Deer could have eaten the entire thicket into a field in the time that had passed that very afternoon. They *could*, but they wouldn't. Deer never licked a slobber on that type of weed.

He was still considering the incommodious nature of deer when Hurricane Hands returned with more equipment and the battle between person and plant recommenced. He enjoyed the animation, all the twisting, pulling, and throwing; less so the banging, clanging, and shouting. When she finally retreated into the house, daylight was disappearing and the weedy thicket looked unchanged.

On more than one occasion, Tennis Ball, who always seemed irritated—the morning's yolks were late, or sparse, or poorly presented—abandoned a nest-patching work party a quarter mile uphill to return and berate me. Magpies weren't always so antagonistic. Thomas Nuttall, author of America's first field guide to birds, and for whom John Audubon named the West Coast magpie—*Pica nuttalli*—writes about watching children from America's first nations feeding and domesticating the birds. Nuttall was traveling along the Snake River in the 1800s. Shoshone country. He was a hundred miles from here when he observed native children with tamed magpies. The camaraderie between birds and boys surprised him. In Europe at that time, magpies were "proscribed and persecuted." If they saw people, they attacked. If they saw lots of people, they fled. Abundant anecdotal and experimental evidence tells us that magpies, along with their close relatives—crows, ravens, and jays—are among the animal kingdom's most intelligent members. Like people, if you persecute them, you can expect them to act persecuted.

Black and shiny as a mirage, Tennis Ball slipped onto Gin's farthest overhanging branch. I was cleaving weeds with my hunting saw. She raised her tail, squirting uric acid in my direction. Frankly, were it not for its bloodstained shaft and dull edges sticky with pieces of venison, my saw could have masqueraded as a pruning saw. Either way, you simply cannot work efficiently with gimpy tools and birds squawking. I needed a mattock. A week into the project, I had razed only a fraction of Vole Forest. Groveling in dirt left me with ant bites that swelled for hours. On windy afternoons, ticks stuck to me like I was wet tar. On calm afternoons, black flies covered me so fast I felt like a carcass. Crested wheatgrass, another invasive European weed, grasped the clay soil with a million fibrous roots that would not yield even to a good spade. I was working with a *broken spade*. I might as well have tried to dig the weeds from a cement block using a toothpick. I lowered my expectations. What had begun as a logging project would finish as a thinning project. Besides, I didn't own a mattock.

❦

The fox poked his head out from under his patio's juniper-branch awnings and inhaled. Roots from the big juniper reached deep into the ground, shaping his den into three main cubbies. Stretching his neck, he felt the warm pull of muscles. He stretched further and shivered. The morning air felt bad and looked worse. A fuzzy gray mound had replaced the blue-roofed house. Clouds would soon be sitting on his head.

Weather notwithstanding, an elk-scavenging project was waiting across the dry channel in the knee-high grasses below Round Hill. He circled the elk carcass, confirming that no one had trespassed overnight. Someone tugged on his tail. *Weasel pee!* In a flash, he was back in the den.

He crouched around the central root post, scanning the den's three main chambers. Light entered two of them from the tunneled doorways; the third, farther into the hill, remained dark. It was rock-free, cool, dry, and safe. And still, it was no place for a grown fox with four good legs to spend the day.

The tail tugger turned out to be a knee-high blade of opuntia, now waving a clump of his long white hairs. Light drizzle left the hair clinging like an old seed head on the unrepentant cactus. He laid his chin along the melting snow and hissed. Pulling his lips back and planting a leg on either side of the cactus, he hissed again. All winter, snow leveled the ground, filling holes and covering cactuses. Now the snow was melting and leaving behind slick mud and fur-thieving opuntia. They were just more weeds in his path. Sulking, however justifiable, was not part of the day's plan. An elk carcass was waiting.

Pulling on the mired elk femur with his teeth produced results that a less optimistic fox would have considered hopeless. Gnawing through the joint attaching the femur to the pelvic bone freed his trophy, and digging into the moist ground loosened it. Yanking with his teeth, he edged his long bone homeward.

Midmorning the following day, spying on Hurricane Hands. When he left for home, he found that the best way to avoid sun blindness required crossing a shallow basin that was filling up with deer. Fawns blemished with disorganized spots on their flanks pushed their faces under their mother's bellies. Cows wriggled, and the cowbirds picking ticks off their backs stretched their wings to regain balance. The deer stayed in the basin for the same reason they'd originally entered it: it dipped. They had simply slumped into it. Deer often slumped, a movement like falling, but slower and less dramatic. Nature was not infinitely flexible, and deer were no more likely to slump upward than to fall upward. Getting out from the shallow basin required exerting energy, which the deer clearly lacked or they would not have slumped into an uninspiring depression in the first place. Compounding the conundrum, the relatively small depression could accommodate only a few deer, and a long line of them waited to slump in. A deer jam. *Off plan!* The next best route wove around sandy hills. They were bare and smelled like cat pee. Undaunted but circumspect, he skipped between the mounds. A cat stepped out from under a pile of logs, swinging a wide head on a short, fat neck.

Detouring around the cat left him on open grassland with a shadow passing overhead. After moving upslope and disappearing, the shadow returned, blocking the sun in a series of passes. The shadow-caster was a dark eagle. It could grasp his entire head in one foot; a single eagle leg was wider than his neck. Common at carcass feeds, dark eagles specialized in disemboweling deer, often in gratuitously creative ways. And they were moody. Some eagles would happily rip your throat if you got too near their carcass. Others would do so less happily. Some eagles didn't care if there was a carcass nearby; if they felt like ripping up a fox, they ripped. Every eagle had its own personality. Trying to analyze them could get complicated. And why bother? Every eagle had its own mood—all of them bad.

Bluebirds ruffling up a juniper tree above the meadow were favoring the branch tips while they chattered. The birds' behavior was a good sign that the eagle whose shadow kept passing overhead was not hunting. Not yet. Running and interpreting birdcalls simultaneously, he reached the den in good time. It was quiet and undisturbed, except for fresh bird poop on top of the main boulder. A task for another day or another fox.

Stretching out on his belly, he sunbathed in the den meadow below a crumbling cliff. Above that cliff, another meadow and another crumbling cliff. Mountain lions—shorthaired cats as big as elk—prowled both cliffs. Most foxes kept their noses to the wind to sniff out lions. He knew better. The safest way to sunbathe was to let wind blow your back hairs up against the grain. And listen. If rocks trickled down the cliff in synchrony with the wind, all was well. When rocks trickled in the still air, it was time to dash into an abandoned badger hole.

The next day, deer droppings coated the lone switchback on the shady route to Hurricane Hands and the blue-roofed house. A procession of female deer filed down the trail, each one sliding on fresh pellets that were simultaneously ejecting from the preceding animal's anus. Deer were grass eaters, a characteristic that freed them from the responsibility of overanalyzing their surroundings. One doe skidded onto the gravelly bank. Another who had skidded earlier was rolling up from her backside. No wonder so many deer were limping. And the rain was only just starting.

The long-trunked sagebrush that provided cover from the rain was close to the house. But it was a noisy spot, near the round-bellied magpie's nest. Stuck on brood duty, waiting for her long-tailed mate to bring food, she was squawking loudly. Between the sagebrush and the house, deer were chomping up and spitting out waxy leaves from a pungent shrub. Of course, an abandoned badger hole offered him a quieter refuge, but clouds and rain had shrunk the world so much already, there was no need to make it even smaller by hunkering inside a dark hole. Besides, the sagebrush offered a view of Hurricane Hands staring out the window.

After the rain stopped, after every drop had fallen from the sagebrush, after the sun pushed off the clouds, Hurricane Hands was still inside. No animal worked a shorter shift. When he had waited long enough for her to come outside, and because he tolerated boredom poorly, he went looking for a place to expend some saved-up energy.

That evening, on the way home, he stepped over piles of mushed-up shrub. No doubt the same deer that had regurgitated the sticky leaves that morning had returned to eat and spit up more leaves. The deer would eat from the same plant tomorrow, and the next day, and every day until autumn. And every day after spitting the leaves out, they would turn their long jaws this way and that and look at each other in astonishment, as if to ask, *Who knew they tasted so bad?*

Waking to the sound of rain waves pummeling a steel roof is unnerving. Unless, like me, you are jaded from living with packs of roof-thumping magpies. And the storm looked worse than it sounded. I pressed my nose and open palms up against the window: oobleck.

Dr. Seuss illustrated his book *Bartholomew and the Oobleck* using only one color. He probably intended the book as an exploration of man's relationship to weather, but who can control well-meaning pirates after his or her writing sails into unknown waters? The moral of Seuss's black, white, and green book is *Settle down and don't fuss with Nature*. In the story, a king who is bored with snow and rain and other humdrum weather events commands his magician to conjure up a novel form of precipitation. To remind the king that she controls the sky, Nature responds to his whining by dropping oobleck, a thick, sticky substance that neither melts nor evaporates. Realizing that boredom is better than this new stuff, the king recants his demands.

Today I looked out into amorphous gray oobleck with unabated dismay. When I ranged in Mount Rainier's wilderness, a similar thick mist often blocked the sun, homogenizing sky and ground, but it never dampened my mood. When mist hugged my thighs, I found refuge from the aerial morass by squatting on my heels and searching for tubular maroon flowers hiding under the heart-shaped leaves of wild ginger. Nearby, I would find a spotted banana slug, pull off my polypropylene glove, and depress its rubbery trunk with an index finger. I might have a week without seeing another person, but contact with a slug was all I needed to keep from feeling alone. On rainy days in the lowlands, I hiked under canopies of old growth. On rainy days in the high country, I edged along under white rock overhangs. Of course, if you did not have claustrophobia, you could just as well have stayed inside your tiny, dry cabin and lit the Coleman.

I have never liked being indoors without a view of blue sky during the day. When you hear the word *claustrophobia*, you probably think about closets, elevators, and public bathroom stalls. I avoid elevators, don't have a walk-in closet, and often jump out of bathroom stalls before I've zipped up my jeans, but I feel especially confined by heavy, low clouds. They unsettle me. Psychologists might label claustrophobia as an "irrational fear" of confined places, but my avoidance does not seem irrational so much as instinctive.

Still, if you were no longer a backcountry ranger but a part-time college professor teaching two ecology classes while at the same time under contract to Chelsea House Publishers to write a middle-grade forestry textbook, you needed to stay inside. Never mind the claustrophobia.

Eventually, the grayness chased me downstairs to a room with fewer windows. Oobleck, omnipresent at 7:00 a.m., seemed immortal by 7:00 p.m. Windows were looking back at me. I counted six hours of work completed in a twelve-hour shift. Trying to run out the weather by moving between rooms, looking out windows, and staring into the abyss for a glimmer of sun- or moonlight took as much time as grading papers. Before quitting, I returned to the Rainbow Room to discuss clumped and scattered patterns of prey distribution with my online ecology students.

The Rainbow Room, with its inset bathroom, spanned the entire upstairs, thirty feet end to end. Like the Shriner Peak fire lookout tower where I used to work, it was small and surrounded by windows. The contractor had warned me I'd need to wear sunglasses inside. He was right. Because I had the cottage built into a hillside, the Rainbow Room's backside was level with the ground. Two glass doors led outside, the front to a deck and the other to the back field. Six double windows, two single windows, and two doors left little room for artwork. Still, I had squeezed in photos of Mount Rainier, Crater Lake, Yellowstone, and Arches National Parks. A photo of Glacier Park hung from the ceiling. It prevented the smoke detector's red light from disturbing my sleep. Three enormous Georgia O'Keeffe prints—all abstract flowers—hung on the wall behind my desk.

Bookshelves, photos, and a door-mirror with a rainbow-colored frame filled the remaining wall space. The mirror, which I passed every time I used the bathroom, was decoration; I didn't do much about hair or makeup. Anyway, I liked my looks—except for the pink puffy tissue ballooning between my upper front teeth. Which I hated. People generally didn't say anything about the enlarged frenum, and anyway, my high cheekbones always got most of the attention. Yes, they are very high—you can tell I'm smiling when you're standing behind me. But dentists always asked why my parents had never taken care of the frenum. "This is always taken care of in childhood," said my current dentist (and the two dentists before him). He'd never seen an adult with a frenum growing to the bottom of the front teeth. Well, neither had I. And I'm pretty sure I'd spent more time looking than he did. The frenum announced that I was not a coddled child. Was I sad about that? Well, the frenum tore and bled if I smiled too big or too fast. Ditto for laughing. And it seemed to be always bleeding. So I guess that's your answer.

Honeycomb blinds, each one a different color—violet, blue, green, yellow, orange, red, and navy—covered each window in the Rainbow Room. Through late spring and summer, rainbows looped around me every few days. Double rainbows were common. Sometimes, clouds spat out fat, truncated rainbows called "raindogs." I learned about raindogs from reading Mark Twain's *Roughing It*. He'd learned about them from sailors while exploring the Sandwich Islands in 1866. Twain was so impressed with rainbows and raindogs that he suggested changing the islands' name from Sandwich Islands, bestowed by Captain Cook, to Rainbow Islands. Of course, the islands didn't need a name when Twain visited (or when Captain Cook visited, for that matter). King Kamehameha I, the first person in recorded history to unify the islands, had already named them Hawaii decades before Cook's intrusion. If you can overlook the arrogance, then Twain's suggestion is a powerful statement about the charisma of rainbows. Yes, rainbows are rare and ephemeral, but I was judging nature by what it did best, not by what it did ordinarily. I hope it judges me the same someday.

In *Moby-Dick*, Ishmael believes that "heaven" shows her favor for the sperm whales by sending rainbows through their spouts. His shipmates don't believe whales are mammals, let alone worthy of heaven's blessing. Does anyone ridicule him? No. Either a paradigm has shifted, or nobody messes with a guy whose best friend is a 300-pound cannibal.

✹

Mating season was long over when the fox encountered an older male, one of his mother's consorts, sheltering in the cottonwood copse. He stopped a tail's length away, tilting his head up to look into the old fox's eyes. "Qwah."

The old fox, hoping to enjoy a lazy afternoon free from the vixen and other perturbations, let out an exhausted yowl, then backed behind a cottonwood and lay down between clumps of tight-skinned mushrooms.

Looking over the old fox's shoulders, Fox spied sandhill cranes, all fanned out and hunting for frogs. With their long beaks plunged into the marshy field, they looked like three-legged birds. They would be a great diversion if only they would pull their heads up. The old fox, tilting his muzzle sideways into the soft, damp dirt, was siphoning a suspicious-looking mushroom. It would either kill him or occupy the remainder of his afternoon. Either way, pestering three-legged birds whose knees rose above his head now moved to the top of the agenda.

He slipped under the cranes' legs as if they were snowberry branches arching under the weight of mealy white berries. They leapt, kicking at him in midair. He circled and scuttled while they reached toward him with long sharp toenails, croaking out loud and redundant threats. When they pushed him into the alfalfa field, he played at dodging the shadows of the rolling irrigation pipes.

Two black dogs, taller and wider than coyotes, romped out of a distant barn. They were coming for him. He ran downhill along the irrigation canal, jumping over some cottonwood logs and through a cloud of elk scent. When he reached the river, ice shelves were bobbing along the banks. *Off plan!* He scampered along the pliable stalks of the still-leafless willow shrubs. Then he turned to climb back uphill.

The dogs followed. *Uphill? As if.* The dogs were collar bound, overweight, and weak from confinement. And those were just their physical handicaps. When the hill leveled out for a brief reprieve, the dogs slowed. The next hill came too soon, and the dogs started yelping. Their barks did not seem aimed at him so much as complaints against life in general.

Up ahead, ice formed a thin crust over a snow-filled draw. Flying across the icy crust, he felt like a long-winged hawk. The two heavy brutes behind him crashed through the ice. After he'd wallowed in snow the consistency of dry sand, the dogs reappeared, exhausted and panting. No doubt the sharp-edged ice had left their shins cut and bruised.

By the time he reached the blue-roofed house, the sun had sunk. He was on familiar ground. But not the dogs. As they ran through the pasture in front of the house, new odors and obstacles left them insecure and confused. This was their mental handicap.

Dogs almost never bark out here. I was up and out at the sound. Two shepherd-sized dogs were chasing a fox straight across my front field. Faster than anyone could have processed a single thought, I grabbed a mop and charged after them. The field was cactus-strewn, slippery, and rotten with old snow. Had it been a rabbit or a deer, I would have let it be. But my reaction to a fox I didn't yet know was visceral, probably atavistic, and completely beyond my control. I returned home distraught and unsuccessful. A fox could not possibly know if I was chasing him or the dogs. Now he was running—under a cloud-trapped moon—from ten legs and three crazed animals. The higher the moon rose, trying to escape the clouds, the more stubbornly the clouds clung to it.

Coincidentally, the only neighbor whose phone number I had written down was a dog-owner. "I know who you are," I stammered when Marco identified himself, "I dialed your number. Your dogs are running down a fox. A *fox*." I shouted a string of exaggerated statements, using words like *heinous* and *iniquitous* while chastising Marco's inability to control his dogs. Or maybe they were someone else's dogs.

Reciting nonexistent fox-protection laws as fast as I could fabricate them, I prevented Marco from replying in full sentences.

The receiver hummed Italian-accented words and phrases: *ex-wife*, *city*, *one dog*, and *sorry, sorry, sorry*.

Switching to hypothetical examples, I explained that veterinarians treat dogs with broken legs and punctured paws. "Injured foxes die. Alone. Cold. In pain."

"Fox, yes? Runs more fast than dog. White. Very fast."

"The law protects *wild* animals," I lied. "You cannot let pets run down wildlife." No matter, it sounded like his ex-wife had absconded to the city with their only dog.

The fox was sitting at the edge of my steps when the call ended. I flipped the porch light on, and he squinted so tightly his cheeks reached his eyebrows. I apologized for scaring him when I only meant to chase the dogs. He spoke to me for the first time. "Qwah," he said. I could tell right away that he hadn't any vocal chords.

After slipping into a puffy down coat, I guarded my tiny visitor while he sniffed around the front pasture, presumably checking for voles. But I knew he was learning my odor, too, and convincing himself that I wasn't living with cats or dogs. I followed him up the ridge for about three hundred feet before he disappeared. Dogs were still barking intermittently. Foxhounds aren't fast or clever, but they're patient and persistent. Their strategy is to work their fox until it's worn out. Decades of selective breeding have endowed them with the mantra *Time is on our side*. Meanwhile, the moon remained trapped, and I walked home in near darkness.

🜂

Like any sensible short-lived animal, the fox kept a fine tally of his time. Another day had passed with too many hard landings and too few voles. The rough-legged hawks were gone, and he'd been hunting in the alfalfa field without the juvenile to help him hustle cattle. But a curious encounter with a dog-chasing girl had given him an idea, and he now had a plan.

Jumping from the dirt road onto the hillside, he landed between a juniper and a thorny shrub and headed toward his den. He could easily arrive home without resting or tiring, even as he gamboled up the steep slope with his nose in the air. Instead, shuffling into a clearing, he leapt onto a flattop boulder so that he and Hurricane Hands, who was following behind, could see each other. She wasn't much taller than a deer and kept disappearing into the shrubs and the darkness. He waited until she was only a few strides away before turning back uphill, downshifting into prowling mode, and picking up a trail that elk used for marching side by side. The girl, who smelled of goose feathers, traveled faster on the wider trail, but no one can match a fox in the nighttime. When he sensed that she was lagging, he stopped to dig up a buried mouse, pausing as he stroked the dirt until the girl caught up with him. She kept pace for a while, but then her footfalls stumbled, and she grasped at—or fell into—the sticky rabbitbrush, and he had to run ahead so she could wend her way back home. Letting his new partner succumb to exhaustion was definitely off plan. He would have to train her slowly.

Working the full moon to his advantage, he slowed when clouds covered it, ran when the moon busted loose. All while his mantra played: *Time is on no one's side.* After jumping on a boulder to avoid brushing against a sticky-leafed currant bush, he worked his way around one last nuisance of the day, mounds of sleeping deer. They were dumb animals, but not dumb enough to live alone.

RAIN FOX

Goblin light, missing rainbows, and a mysterious knock on the front door: it had been an odd day. "Who's there?" I asked the venison stew. While wiping carrot-stained fingers on my blue jeans, I reasoned out the only logical response: nobody. Nobody was there because getting "there" required finding my driveway. Narrow and brush-lined, it was nearly invisible from the road. Even if anyone could actually find it, the 135-meter-long gravel drive prevented stealth entries.

But it had not been a day constrained by logic. At first light, a single cloud covered the entire sky, settling midway down snow-striped mountains and taunting me. For all its boldness, the cloud remained thin. If gravity abandoned me for a split second and I spun through the sky with raised arms and open hands, I could pierce it with my fingers. By midday, the cloud swirled around my ankles, swallowing me. In the evening, a light rain blew past, dispersing the cloud and revealing sawtooth mountains. I watched for rainbows, but none came. Instead, a goblin light sank into the damp evening, a light so dingy that even wet grass didn't shine.

There was no second knock. I had stew to stir on the first floor and a radio that only received on the second floor. If I had known the news would be important, I would have been eating jerky instead of cooking stew.

Why wouldn't a visitor have used the doorbell?

You really think I had a doorbell?

Any normal evening, I kept the blinds up and lights off until natural light could no longer prevent me from tripping over books or barbells. The habit had nothing to do with conservation or stinginess. My monthly electric bill matched the price of a deer tag, a bit less than dial-up internet service. I could well afford to leave plenty of lights on. But I needed dusk's primitive light to soften and pause a day's work. Tonight's light was harsh and creepy, so I blocked it out by jerking down the blinds and turning on the wobbly torchère.

Wiggling one hand into the pliable aluminum blinds covering the front door's inset window, I separated two slats with my thumb and index finger and peered outside. Nobody. Nobody close enough to have knocked anyway. But beyond my vacated portico, well within a stone's throw, someone was sitting upright and looking at me: a little wet fox. I opened the door. "Hello," I said, extending my neck as a turtle from the shell of my cottage. The fox lowered his head and twisted his neck around so that he was facing down driveway. I followed his gaze: nothing. My Bushnell spy camera, which I had set up to see who was eating my echinacea, didn't turn on until after dark.

If he had been a person instead of a fox, I would have interpreted his behavior as a tactic for diverting attention from the real knocker (him) to a nonexistent knocker insinuated to have fled down the drive. *He's trying to put one over on me*, I would think to myself. He's pretending that both of us share this grievous inconvenience perpetrated by some thoughtless evening knocker. But the fellow outside was not a person. Despite folklore and myths, scientists did not include foxes in the ranks of tacticians or impostors. Those personalities required forethought, planning, intention, and umpteen other traits not known to have ever been visited upon wild foxes. My doctoral training had taught me that much.

The fox continued alternating between staring at me and staring down the driveway.

I checked for intruders by walking down the drive and calling "Hello?" as loudly as you would expect someone to call if she did not want anyone to reply. Circling through the back meadow, I found one doe-eyed doe and two lying fawns. Possibly, the double knock I had heard had come from one of them kicking the wooden door, although neither of them looked spunky enough to have sashayed around the cottage. Skunks denning in the front pasture could have pushed a rock against the door. I often heard them stumbling across the doorstep on their meanders. Usually they kept busy stalking wasps, uprooting perennials, and striking vulgar poses in front of my spy cam. But they rarely did any of that before midnight.

I went upstairs to listen to the radio, and, before long, a warning odor and sticky smoke followed me. It was mildly unpleasant but less compelling than the news, so I ignored it. The smoke alarm blew too late to save the stew. Dinner transitioned to a pear perching on a white ceramic plate encircled with slices of deep red venison sausage. Three squares of gold-wrapped chocolate lined up diagonally behind the pear and complemented its smooth green skin. I sunk into the pinstriped rose sofa, balancing my dinner on an oblong tray of weathered wood. Except for the fully lowered blinds, it was a good dinner by any accounting. The blinds, thick honeycomb fabric, were soft green. The walls and both doors were rose adobe. The palette matched the bloom and leaves of *Geum triflorum*, a wildflower commonly called "prairie smoke." I'd copied the color scheme from the sunroom in Lake Yellowstone Hotel. Sometimes I thought about houses where sofas faced televisions and wondered what it would be like to eat without looking out at calm colors, mountains, or clouds. Sometimes I simply wondered what it would be like to own a television.

On the radio, bells were tolling behind deep and somber incantations in a foreign language. Latin, I think. Interviewees in various combinations of age and gender and accent recalled the benefactions of the recently deceased holy man—a man I knew almost nothing about. Everyone agreed it was a sad day and that millions would miss him. The bells kept tolling while more somber voices added items to a growing list of the deceased's blessed deeds.

Usually, when someone died, I wanted to know the cause of death. *Will I die the same way?* Tonight, I wanted to compare my good deeds with those of the deceased. *Will people mourn me in the same way?* The accomplishment of which I was most proud was having survived, in the literal sense of *not dying*. I carried with me one quotation from my father, not only because of *what* he said, but because he rarely said anything to me at all: "I didn't want to have children, I don't want to know if you ever have children, and I'm not interested in what happens to you." After a pause, he added, "The good news is, if you make anything of your life, at least you won't have to worry about thanking me." He said this to me when I was twelve, and those statements, which represented his entire attitude toward me, overwhelmed my emotional state and all my relationships and everything I had ever done since. I always suspected he said it to be cruel, and I interpreted it as a warning that while I was living in the house with him, he hoped I would disappear.

I became very good at disappearing. When I was still an undergrad, my father tracked me down and told me to sign for a college loan. He took the money and disappeared. I paid off the loan.

I became better at disappearing. Besides surviving, that had been my greatest achievement, but it doesn't qualify as a good deed. Of course, the mourned man—I hadn't known his name before now—was older and had a forty-year head start. Still, if bells rang for me today, they would be terse. Saving a skinny fox from fat dogs was one good deed. Another deed was . . . well . . . there had been *two* fat dogs.

I opened the door without exposing more than my arm in the doorway. The fox, soaked like a wet gray dishrag, hadn't moved. But it wasn't raining. It had rained earlier, but raindrops had fallen so sparsely that only pudgy animals should be wet. Anyone small and fast could have dodged the drops. I thought about the possibility of those big dogs dunking him in a ditch. *What ditch?* More likely they had run him down to the river. A pursued fox will run to a watercourse and even swim across. But today's river was so swollen he could not have swum more than a short distance in the shallows before returning.

He thrust his face at me. A normal fox would have run away when the door opened. His boldness suggested that I was in his territory, instead of the other way around.

I closed the door and stood there for a while, sliding the blind up and down a few times before locking it in its fully open position. I peered outside and pondered the scene, then concluded the obvious: there sat, just beyond my doorstep, rain soaked and shivering, a few hours after the death of Pope John Paul II, a fox.

DANCING FLY

A little cottage, a lot of windows, a fluid fox. Avoiding him was a mathematical impossibility. Surely there's an algorithm that proves it. 2-story cottage. 1 room per story + 1 bathroom. Windows facing 4 directions. Visibility: ∞. Avoiding the fox = an event with a probability of 0.001. Sum of the cottage: a lookout with nothing to look for; a belfry without bells. An equilibration for my claustrophobia.

Besides the claustrophobia, I do not sit well. Longer than the fox's eighteen minutes, but shorter than the normal amount expected of a person. I figured out the normal amount by attending elementary, primary, and secondary school until I was fifteen years old. The American student sits long enough to rival the most sessile organism ever to evolve on planet Earth. Yes, excessive sitting was a form of physical torture for me. But it wasn't mental torture, so despite the physical discomfort, many of us (myself included) earned As anyway.

Teaching internet-based classes allowed me to lecture while standing outside. If I was working inside, a wide window ledge served as a desk. After finishing classwork, I fixed fences, collected rocks, cleared culverts, mulched shrubs, shoveled snow, poured gravel, pruned plants, and counted birds. If I wasn't working outside, I was looking outside.

No reasonable person should find it odd, then, that a few days after the death of Pope John Paul II, I once again saw a fox that I was *not* looking for, no matter how pitiful and needy he had appeared when he came to the doorstep. I continued seeing him every day: he strolled up and down my driveway, sunned on my boulders, hunted in my meadow, and absconded with my voles, the supply of which was now infinite thanks to the liatris debacle and the indefatigable reproductive prowess of animals who appear to lack sex organs.

❦

Standing on the stone wall, the fox rooted his rear feet, elongated his neck, and peered around to the front of the house. Hurricane Hands was swinging a dangerously hefty tool so erratically she seemed to have lost all control. Either that or the tool was trying to escape. He pushed a rock twice the size of his head down from the wall, keeping his eyes on Hurricane. Without moving, he listened to the rock clacking down the stone wall, rustling through dry grass, and thudding as it bounced on the hard clay. All that noise and not a flinch of recognition from Hurricane. He—clever fox—was invisible and on plan.

Time could be set aside in the coming days to watch Hurricane. An important task was waiting, and he did not abide truancy. An older fox had moved on without denning. This left an abandoned territory that he would fill. In dry upland foothills, open territories came and went so fast they seemed imaginary.

Pissing occasionally to mark the new territory, he trotted down the gravel path behind the house, listening to the rhythm of his footsteps. The beat was so boring that anyone less keen would have fallen asleep. But keen observers appreciate boring rhythms; they amplify syncopations. Soon enough, an odd beat intruded, the faint sound of rough dragging. A thick black beetle had expanded its long legs and was pulling itself upward to mount a single stone. After a moment of silent stillness, a beetle's head cracked under a forepaw's toughened edge. Running in a crazed circle, then zigzagging to change direction, the headless insect circled back. It was a miniature Hurricane Hands without a head.

Even a whiff of repugnant she-skunk odor didn't justify changing direction. Today he was moving so fast that she would be just another weed in the path. A hillock up ahead was a promising cache site, a distinct landmark above the water table where he could bury excess prey for a rainy day. Encircling it took a few strides. Topping it required only three leaps.

Loosely packed cobbles filled the hillock. The construction mimicked a badger's kickback pile—a badger the size of a bear, anyway. *A badger the size of a bear?*

Weasel pee! He'd be stomped into the ground. He slumped on the summit. Hurricane Hands was outside attacking the pea shrubs with a long metal tool.

Could those flexible fingers and that tool bludgeon a bear-sized badger as flat as a gopher on blacktop? Yes! *On plan!* He jumped down, pissing to the outside of the hillock and incorporating it into his territory.

At the highest edge of his territory, he turned and headed downhill. Under a raised leg, over spread toes, another stream of pee shot toward the Alfalfa Flat den. His older siblings had disappeared; this year's hatch would follow. He, the runt, had claimed the highland. A cozy of foxes incapable of imagining his feat would soon be fighting over a gift he'd left: a half-chewed mouse with Styrofoam in its belly.

Leaving the hillock, he continued his mission. When he finished *les pipis sauvages*, urine encircled a grand new territory. There was nothing to do but swagger from one boulder to another, brushing his bright fox tail along each acquisition. Stopping to sniff the largest boulder, he discovered a surface so rough its minute grooves held tiny specks of water. They would moisten his skin when he returned later to massage his belly.

He stood on the highest boulder waving a white-tipped tail in a wide arc, informing incoming ruffians that a new captain was ready to scuffle. But there was not a ruffian in sight.

The rock was dark, like a fox's nose, and smooth, dry, and warm enough to sunbathe on. He splayed his legs over its sides, the biggest toe on each foot clinging to it. A vole was sniffing at the boulder's base—poor creature. The fox noted that the vole could not look up unless someone rolled it over. Voles, observed the heron-necked fox, were missing their necks.

Back at the hillock, the vole—almost impaled but not quite punctured—was now twitching against the fox's lips. Biting down with his back teeth, the fox severed the creature's backbone without breaking any hide. Buried two paws deep, the neckless vole became the first jewel in what would become a large trove of hidden treasures.

I sat on the wooden steps, my toes playing with soft-fringed sagebrush. A fly was clinging to my fresh knee scab, sucking blood with its filthy little mouth. Blowing on it steadily, I sent it airborne. But it only took a few reconnaissance laps before it struck back at the scab. I blew, it buzzed, and the taunting continued. I became less interested in dislodging the fly than in watching it. Time fell away, and I magnified my focus on the ugly creature sitting on its haunches, rubbing its "hands," and strobing its head.

He was less than two meters away when I saw him. He was crouching down and swaying like a serpent, each curve of his tubular body seeming to push him closer to the fly on my knee. I wondered if he could see me at all while he stared so precisely at the housefly. Stopping within a length of my arm, he rolled his eyes up to meet mine. The tip of a mouse tail clung to his upper left lip.

"Fox," I whispered. He tilted his nose down toward my knee, exposing a sleek muzzle and leaving us eye to eye. And then I saw nothing but a fly and two amber eyes. "Foxsssssss," I hissed, extending the final *s* until I needed to inhale. "Foxsssssss." And then there was no fly no sound no smell no movement. Just two amber eyes. Something snapped, and I caught his image and trapped it in my mind. After that, whenever I wanted, I could close my eyes and see Fox's face just as clearly as if I were still staring at him. I was grateful for the image whenever it appeared. His eyes were beautiful and wet and astonishingly convex.

From a distance, he had looked to me like just another small animal, a hundred pounds lighter and not even knee-high. But our eyes aligned almost perfectly so that when we were facing each other head-on, our size difference disappeared. I'm not sure I expected anyone to have such kind eyes, but certainly not him. How did I know he had such kind eyes? I hadn't ever looked into anyone's eyes that closely before, so it must have been intuitive. He couldn't have known I was smiling, but he probably sensed the welcoming pace of my breathing: slow and steady.

When I saw his front right foot move the tiniest bit, I knew I needed to replace the fly with something to keep his attention. Slipping a hand into a pocket, I felt something cool and round, like a large marble or a small ball. It had to be a rock. Except for brass rifle casings, which I recycled, only natural things made their way into my pockets: pinecones, feathers, seedpods, snail shells, sagebrush leaves, juniper cones, unopened rosebuds. Until the day a coworker showed me otherwise, I would have told you that these objects just fell inside my pockets. Curtis and I had been counting fuel loads for the National Park Service and traveling cross-country. We were heading to a pond for a break when he stopped ahead and leaned on a boulder. "Man! There you go again. Stuffing things in your pocket."

"No," I said, turning not just my head but my entire body for emphasis. "I don't."

"You just *did*."

I pulled a soft, ruddy Rocky Mountain maple leaf out of my pocket. I could not have been more surprised if it had been a human eyeball.

"I'm watching you. I see what goes on. And you're like . . ." Curtis rolled his eyes and tilted his head skyward.

I PULLED THE COOL ROCK out of my pocket. It was a geode, mostly round, with a dark pink rim around its crystal face. After placing it on the steps, I reached into the back pocket of my field vest for a trinket to hold his attention and pulled out a mass of cottony fireweed seeds, bright indigo feathers, a wire cutter, and another geode. The vest and all nine pockets—zippered, buttoned, velcroed, and flapped—seesawed with the shifting weight. "Stone," I said, plunking the other geode, a walnut-sized rock, on the steps.

"It's really a geode. Like it?" I held it up in front of my face, telling him where I'd collected it, who I was with, and what I was doing when I found it. I banged the geode against the steps a couple of times, and Fox, who now was sitting upright, pulled his ears back, stared, and kept his mouth closed. I think he knew his sharp teeth would alarm me. I was excited for his company, and happier than I had been in a long time, but only briefly. I couldn't shake the feeling that someone would see us, that communicating with a fox was a taboo. My fearfulness of the wrongness of the act soon overwhelmed the happiness it brought me.

I tried tidying up the indigo feathers by stroking them, but they only twisted into unattractive clumps. "Not too nice," I apologized. But I thought they were pretty enough. Fox's sparkling eyes reminded me that they were, after all, *feathers*. Extracting another one from my pocket seam, I asked him if he knew anything about the recent bluebird carnage. "I found these feathers on the boulder you've been sitting on."

That boulder was a multicolored collage—pink, white, and black. Potassium feldspar and a little garnet provided the pink blush. The white pieces were mostly calcium feldspar. A variety of minerals contributed the black specks. Three-point-something billion years old, nearly as old as Earth itself, the large rock perched on the high point of my back field, reminding me that our planet has been beautiful from its beginning. A glacier moving north through this valley dropped it here about fifteen thousand years ago. I didn't mind if the fox snatched a few of my bluebirds, but I preferred that he didn't eat them on my precious Precambrian boulder.

He pushed his face closer to me, dipping his nose downward and staring with round, open eyes. Even if you have never seen a fox, you would have recognized on the fox sitting before me a face so innocent that you would have concluded that he had never stalked a bluebird, let alone dismembered one.

"Yes, Fox, kestrels eat bluebirds too." I rolled my eyes. "*My* mistake."

A clump of dried root looked like a pale, tiny carrot. Its genus name, *Lewissii*, honored Meriwether Lewis from the US Corps of Discovery, the Lewis and Clark Expedition. On July 1, 1806, near what is now the Montana-Idaho border, Lewis collected a bitterroot which sprung to life after months of dry storage at the Academy of Natural Sciences in Philadelphia. *Rediviva*, its species name, is Latin for "rejuvenating." Bitterroot, as we commonly call it, blossoms into a quarter-sized fuchsia cup. Stemless, the blossoms sit on the ground. I placed the root on the wooden steps. Pulling a manila envelope the size of a large postage stamp out of a vest pocket, I emptied whale-shaped seeds next to the bitterroot.

"Probably columbine seeds. Liberated from the stash of a bushy-tailed wood rat. Mount Rainier. Three Lakes cabin. I raided the rat's midden when my spare mantle socks disappeared." Mantle socks, which would fit nicely on a housecat's foot, slipped over a gas pipe inside my propane lantern. Without two good socks, my Coleman would not light. "Anyway, I let the rat keep the socks." I sighed and shook my head. "Tooth holes everywhere." I shaped my index and middle finger into gnawing teeth and motioned. Fox put his nose right up to the shiny black seeds. I told him that I had swiped the seeds to discourage further pilfering, but it was a lie. Like the bushy-tailed wood rat, I too treasured shiny trinkets.

When a relationship begins, dialogue is easier when the parties are not facing each other. Concentrating on my trinkets, I forgot about Fox. Sniffing all the trinkets, he forgot about me. That's the trick of show-and-tell: it opens as a soliloquy and sneaks into conversation. No wonder teachers use it in kindergarten. It alleviates self-consciousness and teaches shy kids to talk.

I rattled two beautiful brass shells from a .30-06 in my cupped hands. The fox jerked upright. "I don't know where these are from." (Of course I knew.) Rolling between my two fingers, the brass cases glimmered in the sun. "Ohhhh . . . maybe that mule deer. Up on the East Front near Dupuyer. Can't say for sure." He came closer. He could look through the window and see the mule deer's rack hanging on my wall, but, like any guest who wants to be invited back, he pretended not to notice.

I've always liked guns. The old-fashioned kind with wood stocks and grips. When I was little, my grandfather put me in the back seat of his T-Bird with his handgun, drove me around, and told me to look out for cops. He was probably kidding. But I loved the game and the excitement of doing something important. We never got stopped. My grandfather wasn't violent toward me, so I never developed a fear of guns or an association of guns with violence.

When the fox turned his head as if to leave, I pulled out another trinket. We jockeyed back and forth before settling on one and a half (human) arm lengths between us. At that point, if I scooted two inches closer, he would move back two inches; if I scooted two inches back, he would move forward two inches. Our movements could not have been more precise if we were Doctor Dolittle's two-headed pushmi-pullyu.

He nosed through the loot piece by piece, keeping one front leg raised and his back arched. The quick-getaway pose. Several months on, I mimicked that very stance when I found myself stuck behind talkers at the grocery. The two people who cornered me ignored my off-putting forward-shoulder crunch, but my tensed midsection and slightly raised leg facilitated a fast escape.

Later that week, I worked on student essays using the violet window's sill as a desk. By "worked on," I mean looked up euphemisms for *plagiarize* in the unabridged edition of *The Random House Dictionary of the English Language*. I had purchased the ten-pound book two decades earlier, along with a ten-cent cup of coffee, in Kalispell, Montana. In lieu of *plagiarize*, Random House suggested "-napping," to which I could append *word*, *idea*, or *fact*. Or perhaps, and derived from the Latin root "to snare," the kinder word: *appropriation*. Above the dictionary, out the window, with his nose hell-bent for hunting, the fox trotted steadily across Pillbox Hat Hill: too close to ignore, too far away to appreciate from inside. The wordnapping student would wait.

Fox zigzagged up and down and turned gentle corners, gradually advancing in my direction. When he reached my spring seep, a rusty rear flank flashed a balding patch.

Mange.

When I first bought my land and paced across it, clutching my deed, lunular heads of ripe blue grama struggled above the dun and gunny to greet me. I fell in love. At that very instant I assumed responsibility for the land and everyone on it. No one would die of mange while I stood the masthead.

"Sarcoptic mange," I read on the internet site, pausing to consider the word *sarcophagus*, "is caused by a mite, and generally kills a fox in a slow tortuous manner." The website, sponsored by the National Fox Welfare Society of Great Britain (NFWS), featured medical information, offers of help, and before-and-after photos of foxes successfully treated with synthetic medicine or (if you were in a pinch) garlic. If your fox was too fussy for garlic, NFWS would send the medicine free of charge.

Maybe they figured free medicine would make amends for three hundred years of foxhunting. The modern event, involving horses, a long-distance chase, and packs of dogs tearing a fox apart, began with a British teenager's hound-breeding program in 1750. By 1910, the hunt was so entrenched that foxes became scarce and Britons had to import more from continental Europe.

Foxhunting was more or less outlawed in England in 2004, but the "sport" (which seemed to me like the ritual brutalization of foxes) was no less popular for having been banned. The year I was trying to save one single mangy fox, hounds killed over twenty thousand foxes in England. That number doesn't include live kits fed to hounds by owners anxious to keep their dogs' appetites whetted. I found some information on the internet that shocked me. Veterinarians who managed to examine carcasses reported that the foxes "died in agony" from multiple and serious wounds. A nonprofit called Hounds Off displayed a photo of an eviscerated fox wrapped in its own entrails.

If my friends Doug and Chun hadn't recommended Julian Fellowes's *Downton Abbey*, I probably wouldn't understand the hunt at all. I bought the entire series on DVD from PBS. Season six opens in 1925 with footmen and butlers serving drinks—champagne, I think—to mounted riders wearing black top hats and red blazers. The horsemen mingle with a pack of energetic hounds that are preparing to murder a fox. How sophisticated they all look. Way back then, homosexuals stayed in the closet, unmarried couples who shared hotel rooms paid off blackmailers, and girls who fell pregnant out of wedlock gave birth abroad. Cars and landlines were rare. Skirts were midcalf. Less than a hundred years later, the mores of *Downton Abbey* are quaint memories. Except for the foxhunting.

It's one word—foxhunting—because it is no more like hunting than a titmouse is like a mouse. Horsemen do not harvest the meat or the hide. It can't possibly be an economically efficient means of eradicating problem animals. Foxhunting is a ceremony during which grown men and women mount high white horses and shout, "Tally ho!" while racing over hill and dale following as many as sixty baying hounds that are chasing after a relatively tiny fox. And all this while wearing red wool blazers and black knee-high boots made for rattlesnake country. What could look more ridiculous?

Doing all that without the fox, that's what.

Shakespeare's Othello tells us that a "glorious" war consists of "pride and pomp, and circumstance." Without the fox, the foxhunter's pomp would be missing its circumstance.

I can't imagine a worse reason for killing a fox.

THE FOX PADDED CAUTIOUSLY up a faint trace of flattened spring grass. A bowl with a shimmering mix of garlic and raw eggs was waiting for him. After one long sniff, he stepped back. Straddling the medicine with his front legs, he slid his nose all the way around the bowl's lip. He did not dip his tongue into those eggs, not even after I diluted it with another yolk. "Who raised you, Fox?"

"I know. Me too."

He took a few more steps back.

"But here's the thing: Super-healthy stuff tastes bad. That's the deal. Everyone knows it."

Think about it. Bad-tasting food promotes health; good-tasting food—fatty, salty, and sweet—diminishes it. Why else would anyone eat gross stuff? It didn't get any worse than kale when it came to taste, so I went inside and took a piece from the fridge to demonstrate. I told Fox about eating repulsive food because it was salubrious, bit off a piece, and chewed. When my mouth unpuckered, I said *salubrious* again because I didn't get to say it too often. I'd said it to students on a trail in the Tetons and they'd laughed somewhat nervously, like they felt sorry for me.

I waved a rank kale leaf in Fox's face. An odor escaped and screamed out kale's deficiencies: not salty, not sweet, and not rich. Who would eat it willingly? Not any fox. We sat and stared at each other until I saw, behind him, the waxing gibbous moon rising above the mountains. I ignored him to watch the moon crest the peak and float upward in a pale chartreuse sky streaked with violet clouds. Anyone, anywhere, would have stopped breathing for the sight, but Fox had suspicious greenery to keep an eye on, so he missed the moon buoy above a blue mountain ridge.

"This is supposed to be healthy enough to make up for the bad taste." I sampled another bite of kale. It was truly awful. Moderately healthy would not justify eating it. *Extremely* healthy would not even do. I collected all the kale from the fridge and, while Fox turned away, scattered it around the lilacs to repel rabbits. How healthy would kale have to be to make up for its taste?

It would have to make me immortal.

I don't believe that it will, and so I haven't bought it since then. Fox apparently felt the same way about egg whites. He would not eat them with or without garlic. When served whole eggs, he separated whites and yolks using his tongue like a spoon. Licking the whites round and round the bowl, he created a golf-ball-sized blob. The egg-white-saliva ball stuck to the dish rim, glistening and quaking, while Fox slurped up the garlic-and-yolk mixture.

From then on, I placed a bowl with garlicky raw yolks under Tonic and smashed the shells into my clay soil to add structure and improve drainage. TBall used to pull the yolk-filled shells up with her beak while in flight. Now the shells were gone and she was struggling to grasp the bowl's slippery rim with her toes. Her wings flew up and forward for balance while her claws scratched wildly. Still, she failed. Standing next to the bowl and stretching her neck over the rim left her beak within a centimeter of the gooey yolks. A smaller bowl or more yolks would have solved the problem. *Her* problem, not mine. She had been using the shells like grocery bags to carry the yolks to her unfledged nestlings. If you have heard the cry of a hungry young magpie, you too would try anything legal and effective to shut them up. I ignored the cries. Maybe I enjoyed watching TBall's anguish. But she had set the tone of our relationship because she was nesting here when I moved in. So it was her fault that I didn't like her, my fault that I was overly sensitive to being treated with disdain.

And P.S.: There isn't anything that's both legal and effective.

If Fox worsened despite the garlic, he would find himself in the Havahart trap stored in my outbuilding and would get a ride to the vet. If I couldn't locate any willing veterinarians, my US senator could expect a visit from me. The federal government had introduced mange to Montana; mitigating its effects was therefore their responsibility. Especially since the introduction was not accidental. They did it throughout the early- and mid-1900s to kill coyotes and wolves they believed were eating settlers' livestock. Here's how it worked: Land managers collected sheep and cattle carcasses and infected them with mange-carrying mites—*Sarcoptes scabiei*. They left the infected carcasses near dens. Foxes, wolves, and coyotes fed on the infected carcasses. Mites jumped off the carcasses and onto the living animals. Wrapping their six dirty legs around as many hairs on as many wolves, foxes, and coyotes as they could reach, mites injected *Sarcoptes* bacteria into the predators' bloodstreams.

Judas animals, those purposely infected by land managers and then released, also spread mange. The Judas technique was popular enough that Montana passed a law in 1905 mandating the use of such infected animals to control predators. The state veterinarian obliged by introducing *Sarcoptes* bacteria into six wolves and six coyotes and releasing the twelve Judas animals to infect their cohorts and comrades.

While searching for information about mange, I came across a sermon on the topic of senseless cruelty that referenced a 1948 *Life* magazine story about farmers torturing foxes. The story recounted a method of killing foxes that involved large groups of men, women, and children flushing foxes out of cover and onto fields where they could be surrounded and slowly beaten to death. I saw some of the photos myself. The weapons, about the width of broom handles, couldn't possibly inflict a fatal blow. One photo showed a mob of smiling people holding sticks and advancing on a single injured fox, while another depicted a child beating a fox; still another was captioned *hunter holding a fox before clubbing it to death*. After reading the minister's story, I concluded that the foxes were slaughtered in a way that maximized pain, anguish, and humiliation.

I believe that on the day of that fox massacre, someone—probably a young boy—stayed behind because he had read *The Little Prince*, and because stories matter. They do to me.

I was working seasonally in Glacier National Park, and a book exchange with a river guide left me with *The Little Prince*, a paperback that I took along when I went ski-camping. Alone in an empty campground in Lassen National Park, I came to adore the prince and didn't remember much about the fox. *This is how life goes*, I thought. *You just start from where you are and you go on, just like the little prince did. You don't look back and ask yourself dumb questions.* I loved him because he was young and old at the same time and because he had no significant backstory. Nothing behind him to blame and everything ahead. What I wanted ahead was to work with animals, a decision based on all the wildlife I was working and living with at Glacier National Park. Before I left the campground that week, I completed an application for a zoology degree at the University of Montana; I told them I wanted to write about animals.

E very Wednesday at 2:00 p.m., the saloonkeeper's wife takes a
two-hour break and becomes Winchester, Montana's sole librarian.
Today, as on most Wednesdays, a boy waits on the saloon's green velvet
love seat and turns his kaleidoscope. Outside, hundreds of pregnant ewes
flow past the saloon on their way to low-elevation lambing yards. Looking through the sharp, waxy leaves of the saloon's only potted plant, the
boy recognizes his brother, one of the sheepherders on horseback. He
doesn't want to smudge the glass, but he raises his hand as close to the
window as he dares without touching it. Iron-rich dust swirls skyward
and settles into rusty streaks on the sheep's nappy backs.

When the road clears, the boy slings his leather satchel over his shoulder and follows the librarian out the heavy oak door. "Boots!" she says,
pointing out a pile of horse droppings. She doesn't bother to turn around
to see him nodding, but she hears his uneven pace as he carefully dodges
puddles of urine and sheep droppings. Unlike the dark log saloon, the library is white clapboard with red frames around its single window and
door. Flower beds with a rock border circle it. The front of the library
reminds him of math class, a perfect square facade topped by an equilat-
eral triangle.

At the library, card tables covered with knickknacks greet him: pot-
holders, tea cozies, baby bibs, all knitted by members of The Grange and
sold to raise funds for buying books and heating the building. He goes
straight to the basket of new books and finds one whose cover shows a
towheaded boy standing alone on a planet. The planet is floating in a
navy-blue sky, the color of a Montana dawn. Copies have been circulating
in New York City for almost five years, but in this Montana sheepherders'
town, library committees hesitate to acquire books written by oddly
named, foreign-born authors. Before handing over his library card, the
boy sharpens the library pencil, signs his name in cursive, and blows away

the lead flakes. On the way home, he stops to pick a stalk of wild rye and then folds it three times and slides it between the pages for a bookmark.

Fantastic drawings decorate the book. Some of the characters are common as pudding: snakes and sheep, businessmen and kings. Rude thorny roses. The boy's father runs cattle and sheep, flies a single-engine plane, and maintains his own airfield. His mother ties red and yellow roses up and over their doorway arch. Inevitably, the roses fall out of the arch. "Untrainable," his father mutters every time one smacks him in the head. "If my heeler was as badly disciplined as your damn roses, I'd shoot it."

When the day arrives to massacre foxes, the boy follows ranchers and baying dogs to the killing fields until a cattle guard set into a line of post and pole stops him. The guard, a deep hole covered with steel pipes laid just a bull hoof's width apart, does a fine job of stopping cattle; they can't balance their hooves on slippery steel pipe. People cross using slow and methodical steps. The cattle guard assures that each rancher who joins the fold that day has made a careful and considered choice.

The boy hears foxes screaming, smells their blood, imagines their wounds, and thinks about the fox in his new book. He's only seen live foxes from a distance, but now he's curious about them. If he sat still in the farrow field, would a friendly fox approach him? This year, the boy doesn't cross the guard. He wonders if he is all alone on his own planet like the boy on the cover of *The Little Prince*, a planet so small there is room enough for only him and his retired blue heeler. Sometimes he feels like the schoolmaster, or the woman sitting at the dinner table, or the man bringing hay for the horses live on entirely different planets from him. "How can this happen," he says to himself, "that people who live in our own time and place act foreign, while a pilot from a country whose language I will never speak, on a continent I will never visit, is the one person in the entire world who knows how to draw me a sheep?"

What links the boy at his dinner table to the imagined foreigner who knows how to draw just the right sheep? Spirit. That's the essential thing that we see, according to the prince's fox, "only with our heart." Blood, law, commerce, or physical proximity link us to family, neighbors, in-laws, and colleagues. But connections of the heart transcend time and space. Saint-Ex knew this. If Antoine's mother, the Viscountess Marie de Fonscolombe, were to queue up acceptable friends for her son, Léon Werth wouldn't even have made the long list. Yet Antoine de Saint-Exupéry, the graduate of an elite Swiss boarding school, would come to describe Léon, twenty years older and a public-school dropout, as "the best friend I have in this world." Léon was famous for his acerbic-witted columns and critiques of art and society, and he was a bohemian, an anarchist, and a Jew. When Hitler's troops invaded Paris in 1940, Léon escaped on foot to the Jura Mountains. Saint-Ex, a Catholic, feted and already famous, was living safely in Manhattan, New York, at the time. Knowing that his best friend was cold, hungry, and destitute in the Juras, Saint-Ex returned to Europe to fight the Nazis. That decision ended with the fatal crash over the Mediterranean. I think that the fictional friendships between the prince and the pilot, and maybe even the prince and the fox, are based on this real relationship between Léon and Antoine.

DANCING FOX

Four Rocky Mountain juniper trees arranged themselves in my east meadow as corners on a rhombus, almost a square. In the center, water that had not seen sunlight for a hundred years was flowing from an artesian spring. After seeping downhill through a cattail meadow, the stream funneled through a culvert, eventually joining the Yellowstone River, flowing north, then northeast, merging with the Missouri, then the Mississippi, and finally discharging into the Gulf of Mexico.

Each of the four junipers was about fifteen feet tall and skinny enough for a porcupine to wrap around the bole and clasp its hands together. Members of the Cypress family, the junipers were conifers that didn't look like the other cone-bearing trees around here. Unlike the pine, spruce, and fir trees in the Pine family, each juniper identified as a single sex, displaying either male or female cones but not both. Gin, a female, and Tonic, a male, marked the rhombus's corners closest to my cottage. One of the unnamed junipers on the far end of the rhombus was female, the other, a male. The junipers were about three hundred years old. If no one blocked their sun, they would happily live another seven hundred years.

Like typical females, Gin was bluer than the males. Her flexible branches, spreading loosely in wide, elegant arcs, bounced gracefully under the weight of a single bluebird. Like humans, Gin produced eggs. The eggs stayed inside cones, where they were fertilized by sperm and developed into seeds. The cones, bright blue and pea-sized, had scales that were fleshy and fused, so that they looked like berries. If you looked at them through a magnifying glass, you'd notice they had seams like a soccer ball and bracts pinching upward like volcanoes on Asteroid B-612.

Tonic's branches packed tightly together, and he held them erect even when assailed by an army of blackbirds. His fragile cones, splaying from the tips of braided leaflets, released pollen grains skyward, where they would sometimes form great aggregates that people mistook for wildfire smoke. Pollen is meant to convey sperm to eggs, but it often goes astray. After landing on mountain lakes and swirling into unique patterns, mats of golden-colored grain turn cobalt water into spectacular liquid marble. One time a cloud of dehiscing cones flew into the windshield of my parked hatchback. Dipping an index finger into the dust-like layer, I drew one big arrow pointing to the nearest female juniper and wished their cohorts better luck.

For several weeks in the late afternoon, birds of many different species were landing in one of the four junipers, while leaving the other three almost unoccupied. They selected different trees each day, but without any predictable pattern. What intrigued me wasn't the process of choosing, but the act of sharing. Instead of segregating themselves, birds of different species were roosting together. Imagine humans eating at a picnic table alongside bonobos and orangutans. We're supposed to prefer the company of our own species. I wondered why birds didn't. We humans are serious about the species category. Heck, we're serious about the *genus* category. We guard our *Homo* designation as jealously as thatch ants guard aphids, hesitating to include Neanderthals in our genus despite knowing that humans and Neanderthals mated and produced fertile offspring. But maybe lineage is not significant to birds.

Now, with a good view of the junipers, I was wearing binoculars, squatting on top of a lichen-encrusted boulder, and clutching a particleboard clipboard that smelled like wet wool. I wanted to count the birds as accurately as possible and convince myself that I wasn't just imagining interspecies camaraderie. Yesterday, eighteen birds from four species rested in the far female, while no more than four birds perched in any of the other trees. Gripping the lime-colored lichen with my soft-soled mukluks, I steadied myself and focused the binoculars. Already a flock of bluebirds was perching on Gin, settling down as much as possible for naturally jittery birds. Bird scientists do not actually classify them as "jittery," but rather as members of the Passerine order. An order is a category of birds between class and . . . well, you remember the grade school mnemonic: King Philip Calls Out For Great Sex, or if you are like my students who roll their eyes and complain that they attended Catholic schools: kingdom, phylum, class, order, family, genus, species. Order is a category more general than family and more specific than class. Passerines tend to favor perching and singing. The exceptions, at least on my property, were magpies and ravens, oddballs who favored hovering and screaming.

Ravens didn't nest here but flew over frequently and congregated in large numbers whenever golden eagles tore open a deer. Carcass frenzies encouraged a level of selfishness incongruous with camaraderie, even within species, let alone between magpies and ravens. If T Ball and Torn Tail wanted friends, they would have to look elsewhere. But not to the other passerines. Magpies are meat eaters; the littler passerines are vegetarians. They ate seeds and insects on my property, but in town they scurried underneath outdoor café tables, collecting breadcrumbs. In parks, the songbirds jumped on picnic tables and nicked scraps.

You might expect to find eagles and hawks chumming with magpies. But they belong to a different order—Falconiformes—and eat only meat. Quiet epicureans, I've noticed, don't socialize with loud omnivores. TBall and Torn Tail were destined to be lonely misfits.

I wasn't tracking all passerines; the category was too diverse to be useful. Instead, I tallied birds under columns titled "BB" and "others." *BB* stood for "breadcrumb buskers." BBs migrated here in a staggered fashion, individual sentinels preceding small flocks in a simple, well-organized pattern of species: bluebirds, robins, waxwings, juncos, warblers, meadowlarks, assorted blackbirds, and sundry sparrows. The bluebirds, the first wave in the spring invasion, had been comforting themselves in the eaves of the cottage's overhang since March. Now that May had ended, all BBs had made landfall.

Like the down-valley ground squirrels emerging from nine months of hibernation, migrating BBs were easy prey for hawks: unprepared to defend themselves, adrift in new habitat, disoriented. Think of the staggered immigration waves as breakfast, lunch, and dinner. Between each wave, hawks had time to digest and renew their appetites. During migration, hawks perched in cottonwood branches, slurping wet intestines and snapping delicate bones. Sometimes I stood under the trees catching pretty BB feathers while the hawks ate.

Had they all arrived at once, BBs would have overwhelmed my auditory nerves, which had become hypersensitive from overwintering with taciturn mule deer. The bright colors that singing birds splashed on my fields were acceptable in March, unnecessary in May, and unwelcome by June, when wildflowers provided the same service without any noise or agitation. Tightening up ice-stretched fences requires concentration if you want to keep your eyes and the fence's alignment intact. Every May, I fixed fences while red-winged blackbirds played maracas nonstop. Every May, I dodged anxious and brightly colored generic BBs exploding around my face like streamer poppers and confetti canons.

I would have liked to thank the loud robin for waking me this morning by trying to sing "cheerio" over and over. But the noise made me flinch like wet fingers on a candle flame. Instead, I got up and closed the window. Silence was my necessary comfort. I listened to CDs only while lifting weights or cleaning. Commotion unsettled me. If I could change one thing about myself, it would be that—to be more accepting of unexpected noise, sounds that I couldn't switch on and off like a transistor.

I picked up the clipboard, swung the binoculars around my back, and recorded six Brewer's blackbirds (*Euphagus cyanocephalus*) arriving in a military lineup precise enough to shame the still-quivering bluebirds. Perching on a whorl midway up the tree, the brown females and yellow-eyed males sidestepped toward the shaded inner canopy. Gin's unclaimed topmost branch, bald and bent from bouncing hawks, looked like a long-fingered hand undulating gently with its palm opened skyward. A meadowlark singing a repetitive eight-note chorus eventually claimed the top roost. No one kept time with the meadowlark, not the orderly cyanotic blackbirds, not the two flickers whipping their tails while they balanced precariously in the wind, not the tanager stepping ever closer to the robin while keeping his head turned decidedly away.

I did not record the bluebirds' shame, the blackbirds' pride, or the tanager's inclination to gossip. Cells on the graph paper accommodated numbers, not words. I reduced each creature to a concise check mark on a chart. If you looked at birds any other way, if you failed to objectify them and instead saw twittering blue sparks infusing a juniper until it quivered like a propane pilot light, well then, you would be imagining things that were not happening: bluebirds and robins gossiping when they were only eating berries from the same shrub; bitchy blackbirds shitting on meadowlarks when they were only suffering from nearsightedness. The purpose of my collations was to prevent my mind from playing tricks on me. Everyone's mind plays tricks; otherwise, magicians would not make a living. Nature will fool you if you let her. She's a master magician.

Fortunately, I had studied the scientific method and understood how to keep my intuition at bay.

In *Wind, Sand and Stars*, Saint-Ex writes about a series of storms that grounded him at a Saharan air base. After hearing "All clear for takeoff," he heads outside with the other pilots and engineers and checks the sky. Everyone agrees that takeoff is propitious, even for Saint-Ex's tiny single-engine plane. Before stepping into his flying gear, Saint-Ex ventures into the desert, notices a dragonfly, understands that a windstorm has blown it to the air base, and realizes that a gale is coming. He contradicts his superiors and predicts that the sagging windsock will stiffen within three minutes. He's right. His intuition about a dragonfly stops his crew from taking off in a perilous sandstorm. "Like one of those primitive men to whom the future is revealed in such faint rustlings," Saint-Ex felt the desert's anger in the barely beating wings of a dying dragonfly. It filled him with "barbaric joy."

I could have intuited what these BBs were up to: sharing the same shrubs because they didn't design their communities around artificial barriers. Instead, I was quantifying the birds as if they were gusts blowing through an anemometer. In another week, Fox would set me on the path away from this foolishness. I would find a book to read to him. "Those of us who understand life," *The Little Prince*'s narrator tells us, "couldn't care less about numbers!"

Around 4:30 p.m., Fox trotted down the driveway and disappeared on the other side of the cottage. I guessed he was pacing out of sight near the front steps. I was struggling to identify the species of one slender bird at the top of Gin and was enjoying the sunrays heating my arms through my cotton jacket. I let him wait while I continued tallying birds before they figured out that my property was rife with raptors and found friendlier accommodations elsewhere. When he came back into view a while later, I twisted around on my boulder and watched him slipping his snout into a sagebrush to investigate a twittering robin. Plant debris rained all over him. He corkscrewed, shaking himself off. Both rear flanks were still balding.

The following evening, around five o'clock, I paced around the steps where we'd had our show-and-tell arena, waving my arms so that Fox would see me and trot on down. If I got lucky, he would approach within two meters and watch me knock rocks, wave feathers, and tell stories. I wanted to tame him so he would appear when summoned, or at least at my convenience, at 6:00 p.m., so I could check on his mange. In the 1940s, Adolph Murie, one of North America's leading wildlife experts, was studying wolves in Alaska when he trained a fox to follow his whistle by feeding it "tidbits." Saint-Ex's little prince tames a fox to dance to the sound of his footsteps "as if it were music." Today at 6:00 p.m., he ignored me.

Dr. Dmitri Konstantinovich Belyaev, the Russian geneticist whose work convinced me that foxes identify specific human sounds, spent fifty years taming his subjects. He succeeded in raising foxes who wagged their tails when people approached and who followed a trainer's gaze and point. His research began in 1952, the year Stalin banned—on punishment of death—this type of genetic research in the Soviet Union. Belyaev, you might say, was dying to understand the genetic nature of tameness. As is common in domesticated animals, some of Belyaev's foxes were white with black spots. These tame foxes entered my life while I was researching a lecture on the genetic basis of inheritance for freshmen biology students. I thought about Belyaev's foxes a lot because black-and-white foxes with blue eyes are one of the most pleasant things you can think about while preparing lectures about evolution for college freshmen.

Belyaev, who I am sorry to say died of cancer in 1985, tamed his foxes using artificial selection, the way breeders produced passenger pigeons and most of our common livestock. Charles Darwin described the method in his 1859 treatise, *On the Origin of Species*. Selection, whether artificial or natural, depends upon variation. Breeders need to have choices from which to select their desired traits. Belyaev noted that most foxes either feared or disliked us. He initiated his experiment with the outliers, foxes who were nether timid nor antagonistic around people.

As a population, we treat wild foxes the way they treat us: with animus or apprehension. Belyaev didn't, of course. And neither did I. That's why, at first glance, I thought I had a shot at taming Fox.

Starting with stock from Russian fur farms, Belyaev selected the tamest foxes and bred them with each other: tame by tame. From the resulting pool of offspring, he again selected the most approachable and bred those with each other, tame by tame, and so on for many generations. Over time, the percentage of docile foxes in Belyaev's experimental population increased.

These trained foxes did not only behave oddly; their morphology changed as well. Tails curled and ears flopped. And they wore spotted coats. In the wild, red foxes appear silver, blue-black, blond, tawny, blaze orange, or gray—but not spotted. Regardless of their main coat color, they all wave white tail tassels and wear tall black boots. Belyaev did not purposely breed spotted foxes; the change in coat color was an unintended consequence. He selected the foxes that carried the gene for domestication, and the gene for spotting went along for the ride. Belyaev's belief that friendliness had a genetic basis explained why so many foxes who had lived around me were unfriendly, and why Fox, who was mostly blond and red and gray, was going to be nearly impossible to tame.

The next day, between 5:30 and 6:00 p.m., Fox hunted on the far side of Pillbox Hat Hill, while I waved periodically to attract his attention. A popcorn-shaped cloud was blushing pink as it chugged alone through the gray sky. Its edges were so well defined that the cloud looked like a solid object. When it stopped blushing, it was 8:00 p.m. and everywhere was too gray to spy a small and poorly trained fox.

On the fourth day of trying to train Fox, I was sitting at the kitchen booth shortly after 4:00 p.m. with phone, electric, and propane bills waiting for my attention. Two gray-flannel deer ears popped up, rubbing against and smudging the kitchen window. Attached to the ears was a relatively small buck, quite conventional but for his bedroom eyes.

I joined him outside, almost tripping over Fox before I noticed him sidelined at the edge of the driveway, nose pointing at the deer. While the buck was too tired to let a little furry animal bother him, Fox was not equivalently inclined.

Fox raised one front foot, looking like a Brittany spaniel on point. I recognized his *May Day!* signal, but I stayed my ground, crossing my arms over my chest. Chasing slobbery dogs in the moonlight was a job with a bit of an edge. Bouncing bucks seemed like a demotion. Especially that buck.

"You see that he's an herbivore, Fox. No fangs. No claws. He's *walking*. Barely moving." I knew Fox did not like deer, which was a shame because they seemed attracted to him. In the past, I'd noticed that when deer sat down near him, he would stand up and move. Inevitably the deer would approach his new resting spot, and again Fox would get up and relocate. This time, Fox would not relocate.

I feigned disinterest. Fox stomped his leg and shuddered. No doubt he was afraid of the buck. Also, he was testing me, figuring out just how far he could push me to do his bidding. I let the buck alone so Fox could develop some experience with deer and build up his self-esteem. But he, Fox, continued to shiver. Stretching his neck high and tight, while his little body was still vibrating, he stared me down with squinting eyes. I was in Fox's sights. His irritation was increasing. I would have to bounce the buck.

I clapped and told the buck to get moving. The buck posed, mimicking an unpainted lawn ornament. I continued clapping. The buck turned to face me as slowly as if the air were made of Play-Doh. Counting his breaths as his nostrils expanded and his stomach heaved, I tried outpacing him with my own loud breaths. After listening to me exhaling in sync with him for some minutes, the buck realized I was calling his play and blinked. By then I had loitered long enough. The fox disappeared before I turned back to the front steps. He would not abide breathing contests between animals whose metabolisms matched that of a slug on a hairy leaf.

Day five. After dinner. 5:30 p.m. I couldn't spend every moment waiting for Fox. Across Yellowstone River, rain brooms were sweeping the ridge and stirring up dark fluffy clouds. They jumped like dust bunnies before resettling into the crevices of the foothills. Lightning scowled into the night. I needed to prepare my property in case of wildfire. A great land baron promotes his property's natural fire regime: slow and seldom. That's what this land of bunchgrass, creeks, rocky slopes, and scattered trees expected. But a rebellion was underfoot. Newer grasses introduced from Europe and Asia, like the thistle from Siberia that made up Vole Forest, were promoting their own fire regime: fast and frequent. The renegade grasses spread across the ground in solid sheets and dried during the hot, windy season, whereas native grasses grew in clumps and surrounded themselves with fire-resistant dirt and gravel. And they usually stayed moist until after the lightning season ended.

Bromus tectorum, a sheet grass called "cheat," died early in the season, a welcome invitation for wildfires. Cattle, deer, and elk don't eat dried cheat, so it just sat around, bronze and ugly and too sharp to touch with bare hands. Its worst habit was growing on steep slopes, something very few plants could do. Fires move fastest upslope, and I needed to keep my slopes rocky and semibarren. If you don't understand why fire races up hills, stand on flat land and pretend you're a flame. Look around. Extend your arms. How close are you to fuels you can ignite? (Answer: They're on the ground.) If the grass is ankle-high, then you can heat—and potentially ignite—the area between your feet and your ankles. Now stand on a hill, facing the slope, and extend your arms. The fuel has come up to meet you. You're close to an area that reaches from your feet all the way to your midsection, more if the slope is steeper.

You can't fight the war on wildfire without soldiers. Someone needed to push the cheat grasses back, chase them off the hills, and wrestle water away from them. Liatris could climb hills but bloomed too late to compete; the cheats finished setting seed before liatris germinated. And in any case, the vole debacle had left me wary of attempting to grow liatris on my property. Salsify was an early bloomer. A flat-faced daisy spruced up with spiky petal tips, salsify produces seed heads the size and shape of baseballs. The countless individual seeds in the head each terminate in a long shaft attached to a rotor with feathery blades. If you blow on a salsify head, each seed lifts and flies away sequentially, like a fleet of helicopters. It's a great distraction, but not a great soldier. Hermit-like, salsify arranges itself sparsely. Cheat and other flammable grasses can easily move into the open spaces surrounding each salsify.

Cutleaf daisies grow in mats dense enough to crowd out invading cheats. Their nickel-sized faces are ringed with petals cut straight and fine like fringe on a rodeo shirt. Daisies belong to a family that botanists called Composite, a reference to the composition of two distinct flowers that make up that round daisy head—ray flowers and disk flowers. You probably realize which is which. Each elongated white petal in the mane belongs to its own ray flower and therefore has its own ovary, and eventually its own seed. The yellow face is comprised of hundreds of disk flowers pressed so tightly together that there isn't any room for petals. You will have to take my word for it because you cannot see the individual disk flowers with your naked eye. Of course, you will need to bend awfully close to the ground to see the flowers at all. Bobbing on ankle-high stems, these daisies would wilt in the shade if they tried to invade a field of calf-high cheat.

Butterweed spreads its soft gray leaves outward from wide clumps. Its frail stems bend under the weight of orange daisy-faced flowers. Nothing special. Unless you notice its misarranged petals, though they are not unkempt enough to elicit pity. Butterweeds are charmingly disarrayed, as if a small child had pulled out every petal and then hurriedly replaced them. Big gaps separate some petals, while others squeeze tightly together. All the plants commonly called butterweed are *Senecios*, a genus that encompasses a million species. Or might as well do so, because the odds of me figuring out which species was growing here was the same. The species name didn't matter. It spread sheet-like and bloomed early. Tall enough to shade cheat and cure in autumn, senecio was my best defense and offense against hazardous grasses. All I needed to do was dig it up and transfer it to strategic locations.

Day six. Lunchtime. The big blaze vixen cruising along my property's east edge where gravel met grass didn't let her tail's shadow fall on my meadow. *Has Fox piss-marked a territory around the cottage?* I hoped so. I'd never felt comfortable around the blaze vixen. Her presence always forced me closer to the front door. I knew she would never attack without good reason, but when it came to defining a "good reason," I'd bet she'd go wide.

Fox arrived at 4:15 p.m. and wasted no time curling up and licking the forget-me-not stem. I took the timing as an aberration. He yawned, extending a pink tongue decorated with a perfectly intact blue petal imbedded in saliva.

Beginning on the seventh day, and regardless of the weather, Fox came by at 4:15 p.m. It was inconvenient. Shouldn't my convenience have superseded his? How did convenience even apply to a fox? He was out all day anyway, doing *whatever*. I had a *job*. If he waited until 6:00 p.m., I'd have free time and the magpies would be gone. Instead, trying to read and listening to Tennis Ball squawking nearly continuously, I waited for him. *Terrible idea.* To prevent her screams from being perfectly continuous, TBall carefully allowed between one and four silent seconds between squawks. When intrusive sounds follow a pattern, I can anticipate their arrival and assimilate them into background noise. But Tennis Ball cried out at random intervals. *Mathematically* random. They could strike at any time. Like malaria.

Maybe social interaction is your forte, and the last time you resorted to show-and-tell to ease your interaction with strangers, you were carrying a Superman lunch box. Maybe meetings, conferences, and soirees do not exhaust you, and your patience is as infinite as the demands of politeness. But if you shy from social interaction and tense up, leaving one leg slightly raised while people are trying to converse with you at the grocery store, then entertaining a guest day after day leaves you dusted. If your guest is an impatient fox who walks away when the wares you're displaying get boring, you need to rev up your repertoire. This is especially tedious if you are pathologically private. I hesitated to talk to the fox not because we were different species, or because he was mute, but because I didn't talk about myself with anyone. In fact, like the narrator of *The Little Prince*, I hardly talked about anything with anyone. The necessity of entertaining a visitor at 4:15 p.m. each afternoon left me no choice but to read. And so.

You have no recourse to balk at how an educated person might begin planning every day around a schedule that included nothing more important than reading with a fox. I have had to do worse in my short life than wait for the sound of a fox's footsteps so I could dance like a fly on a scab.

PANTHER CREEK FAWN

On the first night of the River Cabins class, while dodging little brown bats, I had drawn a map to show that my relationship with Fox had followed a natural route, that it was perfectly logical—inescapable, really—and that nothing happening between us was bending the immutable laws of science. At the end of that first night, my mapped route had only one landmark: Vole Forest. Now, four days later, before heading off on another field day in Yellowstone Park, I labeled several additional locations: black fly, show-and-tell, mange. And there were still two days left of class.

When our bus passed Floating Island Lake, I knew there weren't many distractions ahead, so I stopped lecturing and opened the floor. Someone from the back asked why I'd swapped the backcountry for graduate school. You would think I'd have a pat answer prepared, as often as people asked. Instead, I had a story. "The Panther Creek fawn," I said, flipping on the microphone.

The story takes place at Mount Rainier National Park and begins with my boss, Bob, and me heading down Cayuse Pass in our pickup, wrapping up a deer incident that had tied us up all week. Bob said, "It's never going to get any more exciting than this." He meant my job, ranging in the wilderness. His assessment followed a busy month: a few medical emergencies, a body recovery, a small wildfire. He was suggesting that I leave this job—the best job ever—before the worst possible thing happened: before I kicked steps down Sunrise Glacier with my Gore-Tex mittens wrapped around a stretcher pole, looked down on the splinted victim grimacing under an oxygen mask, and asked, *Is this all there is?* I knew that if boredom gripped me, it would never let go, and all the memories I had banked would depreciate. If I didn't get out with valuable memories, I'd have nothing. My measly salary would not sustain me into the future.

If I left the backcountry too soon, blame Panther Creek.

The call came over the airways from park dispatch. An eyewitness reported unleashed dogs running down deer at the unofficial Panther Creek site. Visitors used the site mostly for activities that involved things that they could easily carry downhill but were not valuable enough to worry about carrying back up. Things like beer bottles. Sometimes wine. Dogs, of course, could transport themselves back uphill. But regulations prohibited dogs, leashed or otherwise. "Unofficial" meant the park service did not maintain the site and discouraged anyone from using it.

In the Panther Creek pullout, with pinecones the size of walnuts crunching under my boots, I pushed aside a curtain of fir branches and found the site's social trail. Social trails start like game trails, with a few individuals stomping down dirt, breaking branches, carving a path that's just barely passable into an otherwise impenetrable forest. Park rangers did not build terraces or install water bars on the social trails, which meant the soil washed away, especially in steep areas. I always tried to cover the trails with branches to keep the visitors off and prevent erosion.

We avoided the social trail and bushwhacked. Bob said the chief scientist had come from Seattle to tour the park, "who knows for how long." It was not a question; by "who" he meant "nobody."

After several minutes, I said, "Well? Is he coming to our district?"

After several more minutes, Bob said, "He won't be going anywhere important." And so it went.

Descending the slope, I concentrated on keeping myself perpendicular to the ground. Stand with your feet together. Your heels are a vertex where two lines meet: one line runs up your back from your heel to your head (the spine line); the second line (the trail line) extends forward from your heels and runs along the floor or trail you are facing. When you stand on level ground, the trail line and the spine line naturally form a ninety-degree angle. Now imagine yourself standing on a hill. Whether you're heading up or down, you'll want to lean. But, if you don't want to fall, you'll work at keeping the trail line and the spine line at a ninety-degree angle. When a hiker carrying a heavy backpack is plodding uphill along a steep trail, he leans forward into the hill. As he tires, he leans further, shrinking the angle formed by spine and trail lines into an acute angle. Weight comes off his heels, toes slip backward, and his nose dives forward. His palms, after breaking his fall, skid downhill until they are roughed with trail rash.

When hiking downhill, people let the steepness worry them into a backward lean. The angle created by the spine and trail lines expands to an obtuse angle. That forces their heels to slide out from under them, dropping their butts and backpacks into the dirt and leaving them flailing like flipped turtles.

Neither Bob nor I was what would become known a decade later as "multitaskers." My personality precluded concentrating on more than one serious project at a time. When *multitasking* buzzed into the lexicon, I associated it with a level of nervousness more characteristic of red pine squirrels than park rangers. Did you know that red squirrels can race headfirst down a spruce trunk, count their cone stashes, track a potential mate, check on juveniles, cut spruce cone stalks, scold juveniles, and ditch mates, all while simultaneously chattering an alarm call? Did you know that red squirrels don't live very long?

Maple branches smacked my cheeks hard enough to score my skin. The trees had been fighting off encroachment from bigger mammals than me for thousands of years, and I couldn't match the speed or agility with which they fought back when I brushed their branches away. Pines huddled together, blocking the sun, dimming my view. The trail was steep, and the prior winter's torrential rains had sluiced all the fallen leaves. The absence of duff left ancient and angry roots completely exposed. Firs and cedars stuck their mossy, high-arched toes across the unmaintained path, catching my two-pound leather Pivettas and tripping me up as if they were J. R. R. Tolkien's mischievous Ents.

When we arrived, empty beer bottles were poking through a band of gray cobbles in an outwash along Panther Creek. We walked on top of downed trees to reach a logjam in the middle of the creek, where a fawn bleated for help. Her hind end was torn. None of her bones looked broken. We carried her to shore. "Yeah, so there's this animal policy," Bob said. I placed my hand over the fawn's warm ribcage and felt shallow, irregular breaths while he continued. "We can't do anything with this fawn until the chief scientist goes home."

"We could carry her up. Or ask a vet to come down."

"Not happening. No interference with the wilderness experience." That's what I heard Bob say, but when he winked one of his almond-shaped eyes, I knew what he meant was that overachieving managers from Silk Stocking Lane should not be making policy about things they knew nothing about. Things like animals and woods and Wilderness.

That capital *W* is not a typo. The United States Congress designated Mount Rainier a Wilderness in 1988. It was a special designation, setting the park apart from places like Glacier and Yellowstone National Parks, where any rube could tromp through woods all day, get spit on by a grizzly bear, and still not claim to be in Wilderness.

Like Paradise Meadows and Grove of the Patriarchs, Wilderness defined Mount Rainier. It affected our management policies and discouraged activities that disrespected nature. The Wilderness Act prohibited contraptions that were noisy, visually intrusive, or ostentatiously mechanical, as well as new roads, nonemergency trail and site markers, and permanent storage caches. I loved the word *wilderness* and the simple bits of the Act that I understood. I did not understand about the deer.

Bob reminded me that park visitors believed their entrance fee entitled them to a show. And the show included watching animals suffer. Worse, we were selling the rights to witness an animal's degradation, her painful death in front of camera-clicking, bulb-flashing, satisfied strangers. Too many people felt they could improve their self-image or make themselves appear more erudite or scientific or masculine if they were cavalier about observing another individual's brutal death.

"Is that a line item on their entrance ticket: degrading wildlife?"

Bob watched the fawn and winked again—to shake a wind tear from his eye.

We had worked in the Service long enough to have watched plenty of wild animals suffer and die because of a policy that deemed their death "natural." Now it was happening for the first time in an area where I could influence, in a small way, the outcome.

A senseless standard—a paradigm—was weighing us down. A paradigm is a nebulous and sticky substance. Like Dr. Seuss's oobleck, you can't figure out where it came from or how to rid yourself of it. As far as practice and policy, except for vehicle accidents, neither of us knew of any case where a park service employee had euthanized an injured wild animal, let alone called on a veterinarian to treat one. Bob and I agreed to rescue the fawn as soon as the chief scientist returned to Seattle. I covered

Panther Creek's unofficial trail with leaves and brush to keep hikers away while the injured fawn waited for help.

The next two mornings, I bushwhacked back down to Panther Creek with blankets for the fawn. Never mind maple whips, a heavy backpack, and running downhill; people my age didn't worry about things like that. Without any expectation that she would eat or drink, I filled my aluminum Sierra cup in the creek and set it next to her. Unfurling my damp fingers in front of her muzzle, I offered up translucent yew berries. She lay with her wound exposed and jaw reclined on an ankle, looking at me with eyes pleading for help. I believe that injured fawns have pleaded with people for help for thousands of years. Above her, a great hemlock tree curled its two central branches upward, so that they looked like wings on a green sea eagle. The tree's top bent toward Panther Creek, nodding as if scanning for trout. Exposed roots clung like talons ready for liftoff. I did what humans have done for the same thousands. "Don't worry, babe," I said, patting her shoulder with the back of my hand. "I am going to help you."

"WHAT THE HELL is that ammonia smell?" Bob roared. I slipped behind him into the garage. Turning sideways, we shimmied between two fire engines, following the ammonia cloud to the back. Crumpled up in a corner was a white towel soaked with deer urine.

"Oh, that's a blanket from the fawn," I said. Bob showed no intention of unhooking his arms from across his chest. Or blinking. I continued to parse out information. "Um . . . she can't stand up . . . she was cold . . ."

"Who does this sort of thing." It was not a question; by "who" he meant me.

I continued stuttering my explanation. "Well . . . she pees on the blankets . . . and then I have to bring them back here and get new ones . . . from the emergency rig." I shrugged my shoulders. "I don't own any blankets."

"Christ."

Overpowered by the ammonia smell, we retreated, while Bob yelled out, "Tomorrow!" Tomorrow, Bob assured me, our "friend" from Silk Stocking Lane would leave before breakfast. Tomorrow we could rescue the fawn.

"Six in the morning. Sharp."

"Fine."

"Five even better."

"See ya."

We drove in the dark. Bushwhacked without talking. Glacier glasses with leather side panels protected my eyes from whipping brambles, and my hands grasped thin alder branches as we slid toward the river with nothing but sound and its absence to guide us.

It was later that same day, driving over Cayuse Pass, when Bob said, "It's not ever going to get more exciting than this." I asked him what he was thinking would be more exciting if I were to move on. "Graduate school," Bob said. "A PhD, like what's-his-name. Bug guy."

Bug guy? The volunteer? The park service *paid* me for patrolling the backcountry.

Bob knew I was poor. The day I moved into my government dormitory, I left the Volvo on the ranger station's circular drive instead of using my assigned perpendicular parking space.

"And it doesn't even have a reverse gear!" he said. Then, "Welcome to the crew."

"I have the other four," I replied, "and good to meet you."

I was in college and thumbing a ride the day I bought the Volvo. A gray-haired man gave me a lift and a two-part lecture: *hitchhiking is dangerous* and *used cars are cheap.* I ignored the first part, but *I* could buy *a car?* He might as well have announced that moon monkeys had landed. My weekend job minding two little girls included a salary plus room and board, and I had a second job clerking. We picked up the cash from under my mattress and he dropped me at the dealership. I drove back to my basement apartment, proudly stopping at every red light, stalling fearfully at every green. To this day, I have never heard so many drivers honking at me. The stick shift hadn't come with instructions. The girls' father, a federal judge, taught me how to handle the manual transmission, and I've owned one ever since. Instead of hiding my cash under the mattress, I started jamming it between the leather-trimmed fabric seats. But I never stopped hitchhiking. I kept the car too long, and it broke down too often.

After a long career in the backcountry, including the premier job of backcountry ranger in Zion National Park, Bob had advanced into a more stable supervisory position. More importantly, *he* was stable. He had a girlfriend, and eventually a wife and child. Throughout my years at Mount Rainier, he was the oldest man with whom I had any regular contact. I was twenty-eight. We hadn't yet celebrated his fortieth birthday. I suspected his idea about graduate school held water.

But would a graduate program accept me? One of the younger guys on my crew brought me information about an important standardized test, the Graduate Record Exam or GRE. We read through the practice tests and figured out how to sign me up. I scored in the top ninety-eighth percentile for general verbal skills, analytical skills, and biological subject matter. Some school would accept me.

But I could not envision living in a city. And I could not imagine being a scientist. I always reached toward, and then moved toward, things I could envision but not touch. Anything I could touch would be too close, and anything I couldn't see would be too far. I always pictured myself alone on a subalpine ridge in some wilderness.

Bob felt that my hair ("you look like a backcountry ranger") was my biggest obstacle; I didn't own a comb. I agreed, and we proceeded to speculate about scientists in the manner that the chronically ill ponder the life of a doctor or the incarcerated imagine lawyers.

"Don't worry about *being* a scientist, for crissakes," said Bob. "Just get the degree and figure out what the hell those people are up to." That was all the advice I had ever received about graduate school.

And really, together with the comb Bob gave me as a going-away present, it was all the advice I needed.

Ever since I was a pissant ranger at Glacier National Park, I had been wondering what scientists were up to. One time, a scientist from park headquarters—a guy with a PhD—asked me to help gather samples for an aquatic study. I hadn't yet earned my bachelor's degree in Zoology and was honored to accept the responsibility, along with two glass bottles, an eyedropper, and written instructions.

After hiking to a backcountry cabin sheltered by a stand of aspen trees, I ran down to Cut Bank Creek, scooped water into a glass bottle, and added a drop of whatever from the eyedropper. Holding the bottle of creek water up to the sun, I shook it gently and watched mosquito-sized red shrimp flipping and rolling in their tiny glass chamber. Inside the cabin, I placed the bottle reverently on the bed stand. When the sheepherder stove was hot and crackling and water was heating, I checked on my tiny charges. *Oh . . . my . . . God.* All the mosquito-sized red shrimps had sunk. I had killed them all.

I slept poorly. At first light, I hiked twenty-five hundred feet up Pitamakan Pass. Then down twenty-five hundred feet. Seventeen miles. Breathtaking scenery, and I didn't see another person; people found the high concentration of grizzly bears off-putting. At the Two Medicine Ranger Station, I caught a ride to my regular post, the East Glacier Ranger Station, and shuttled to headquarters the next day.

Guess what? The scientist knew the shrimp would die. The little bottle with the eyedropper contained a poison. He wanted to count them. *I've killed animals so a guy with a doctorate in biology can count them?* To clarify: I killed animals so a guy with a doctorate in fisheries biology could supervise while another guy with a master's degree in fisheries biology could do the actual counting (while an undergraduate student recorded). There I stood—filthy and sweaty and sore. And there he sat—suited and comfortable and cool. You know how that goes. Everyone assumes the dirt-smudged person, the standing person, the one with uncombed hair, is the more ignorant of the two. *Shit on like a shrimp.* Yup, I might just like knowing what they were up to.

I might like to know why the Panther Creek fawn had to die. Oh, I forgot: *Death is natural! Nature is cruel!* Is that what the ranchers told themselves during the Helena fox massacre? The reverend who preached about the massacre juxtaposed the murder of the foxes with a description of the crucifixion of Jesus of Nazareth, the Christian God. The juxtaposition, according to the reverend, illustrated a mystery: *Why does senseless cruelty exist in a world with a loving God?*

By the time I ranged in Mount Rainier, people had stopped interpreting cruelty as a senseless act. We did not watch wildlife suffer because we were poor, ignorant sheep farmers. We watched them suffer because we were rich and college educated and white-collar. The animals' pain covered us with the dirt we desired so that we could pretend to know the cruelty of the world. We watched wildlife suffer and die and turned our short jaws this way and that. "Nature is cruel," we said, and then we pretended that bearing the burden of this knowledge toughened up our flaccid souls.

Meanwhile, on the bus with the River Cabins class, I tied myself in knots trying to justify what had spiraled into an unacceptable animal story. I stood on the bus with my back to the "Do Not Stand While Bus Is Moving" sign, facing students who were wondering what kind of person was leading them along bear-infested trails. What kind of person, professor, naturalist, did not understand that it was unnatural to minister to an injured fawn? They wondered if I was one of those people—*those* people—who bragged about not being able to kill spiders.

The bus swung into a curb wide enough to drop its outside tires on the soft shoulder. I was telling the students that every time the Panther Creek fawn had gazed up at me, she was pleading for compassion. The last time I saw her, she was lying dead with open eyes and I felt a gut-hollowing sadness. The bus hit a gigantic pothole, and I had trouble holding on with only one hand free. "I kill spiders," I said just before the momentum forced me to turn and, like the sign above the driver's head said to do, "face front."

LAST DAY AT RIVER CABINS

One strip of civilization—a garish stripe of Kentucky bluegrass, freshly shaved and watered—separated my cabin from the chaotic willow thicket at the edge of Yellowstone River. I stood at the riverbank cradling a ceramic mug with puce glaze as iridescent as a pee-filled dint in a buffalo pie. The university-sponsored adult education course had consumed its last breakfast. Very soon I would no longer have to hear the wall-muffled voices and crackling static from my married neighbors and their television or worry about whether they would mistake Fox for a hat—like Saint-Ex's boa constrictor.

Yellowstone River was brown as cocoa. Rafts of plant debris rode rollercoaster waves on water that in two months would become so flat and translucent it could be roiled from bank to bank with the dip of a mallard's toe. I rattled around on river cobbles, fat fleece socks inside my sandals just heavy enough so that the cold air felt cool. In less than an hour, students would gather for our final class hike. I inhaled, shook my shoulders against the steamy sensation under my arms, inhaled again. In my outdoor classroom, refusing to budge, was the elephant that had dogged us all week: a fox with traits that only humans should have.

My students did not believe that humans and wild animals shared personality traits. Several months earlier, one of my undergraduates from Florida State had helped me understand why. I was lecturing about *Homo floresiensis*—Flores Man—named after the Indonesian Island of Flores, where archeologists discovered their fossils in 2003. I presented the students with a drawing from *National Geographic*: *Homo sapiens* and *H. floresiensis* standing side by side. The juxtaposition was heuristic: although *sapiens* and *floresiensis* were both living in Southeast Asia thirteen thousand years ago, no one knew if they had ever stood next to each other. In the drawing, the human wore an animal skin over her breasts and pubic area; Flores Man, also represented by a female, stood naked. I asked the students to explain the clothing disparity. "Temperature," said my best student. "Flores Man didn't need clothes because they lived in a tropical climate." I explained that humans experiencing the same climate wore clothes. Most surprising of all, considering that Flores Man lived twenty thousand years *after* Neanderthals—another sister species—was the supposition that they couldn't create tools. "With such a tiny brain," one student wrote, "Flores Man probably didn't design clothes." Although the three-feet-tall *floresiensis* species had smaller brains than humans, they weren't morons. Tools found at the excavation site indicated that Flores Man produced wares and textiles.

Some students guessed that Flores Man was apelike and covered with a thick mat of hair and therefore did not need clothes. Wrong again. Biologists believe that members of the genus *Homo* lost their body hair about seventy thousand years ago. The speciation of body lice provides the evidence. Animals that are hairy from head to toe have one type of louse, head to toe. Because we hominins have a vast expanse of naked skin separating our hairy patches and preventing lice from interbreeding, we have two types of louse: pubic and head. Our pubic and head louse species are about seventy thousand years old; we had to have lost all our body hair by then; otherwise, there would be just one species.

The undergraduate who enlightened me explained that the artist's bias had informed the drawing. Her supposition was that the artist had subconsciously drawn upon (pun intended) the Adam and Eve story and assumed that only humans could feel shame about their nakedness. The female Flores Man was naked, she said, not because she was hot, hairy, and dumb, but because she was incapable of feeling shame. Shame was a trait reserved for humans: that's the Adam and Eve story. If the student was correct, then how do we ascribe a human personality trait to a fox when we cannot even ascribe a trait such as modesty to another hominin?

All week long, I had recounted as little as possible as seldom as possible about the fox. I withheld or edited anything too personal or subject to misinterpretation: Fox's eyes behind Dancing Fly; my acquiescence on the inconvenient 4:15 meeting time; my nightly predinner drives home from River Cabins to check up on him. I told the students about egg yolks and magpies; voles and liatris; mange and the duties of a provincial land baron.

So that much was good. But I had slipped up and used the words "the fox and I" one too many times. I needed to make them forget that, and I had a plan. Not a real plan, but an ethereal plea just shy of a hope that if I waxed eloquently about natural history, I could distract them from questioning my relationship with Fox. *Who could spot an elephant in a million acres of wilderness?* By now, the rising sun had topped the ridge crest and illuminated my empty mug. I headed inside to stock my backpack.

"WHEN YOU SAY '*we*,' do you mean it's like you're a *couple* now?" We were not five minutes into our hike, heading up the Beattie Ridge along a dormant Forest Service road. I stopped and turned to the group, but the questioner remained anonymous. Anyway, it was rhetorical, so I didn't answer.

"You and the fox," another student clarified.

The balding gravel road paralleled a dry creek reach through croplands. Cottonwoods that had died when the water stopped flowing were now providing just enough skeletal shade to allow young sumacs to flourish and flaunt their glossy maple-shaped leaves. All around us, plants were immigrating and emigrating. Plants that had migrated from colder, drier places were trying to stay. Those that found the newcomers repugnant, or themselves on the wrong side of the headgate, were trying to escape to harsher climates at higher altitude. Each plant population illustrated a story that was sure to distract everyone from thinking about Fox and me.

"This tall thistle—knapweed—immigrated from Siberia, and it's thriving in balmy Montana, along with its Siberian neighbors: lilacs, caragana, and Russian olive. All of them are happy to have relocated from a land with eleven months of winter to one with only nine months." Tall perennial knapweed stalks rose prominently in every direction. "Scarlet globe has lived here for thousands of years." I squatted and cupped a barely visible inflorescence floating in effuse curly leaves. "Right now, it's trying to get out. Escape the crowds, shade, and herbicides."

A tin-cloth hat with a man underneath moved beside me. Tin Cloth, who had been guiding me along throughout the week, whispered, "They will keep asking about your fox. Let's see what we can do." Tin Cloth was my translator. He translated references about television shows and pop culture into something that I might understand, explaining, for example, that various "desperate" women whose lives filled much of the background chatter during group meals were fictional "housewives." He translated YouTube's enigmatic spelling and tried explaining (unsuccessfully) its equally enigmatic amenities. Tin Cloth understood my search image well enough to realize that without a specific accessory like a hat, a person, even one whom I spoke to every day, became just another anonymous face. As Tin Cloth and I picked up pace to keep ahead of the main group, he slipped me a piece of petrified wood. "You'll need this," he said.

At our next stop, I wedged my fingernails under my bootlaces to extract a wild licorice seed. It was cinnamon brown, burred, and large as a peanut shell. "This seed is analogous to sperm, right?" They nodded their heads yes. Wrong answer. Trick question. Prior to about 1800, it would have been the right answer. In those days, Western scientists believed that sperm contained fully formed individuals called *homunculi*. A famous engraving from 1694 shows a baby squatting down in a sperm cell, ducking his oversize head and clutching his knees to his chest. Of course, there are not little people huddled up inside sperm cells, and that's why they are not analogous to seeds. "A seed is a baby in a box with its lunch," I said, repeating something they had probably heard when they were freshman.

Pointing to an eastern cottontail huddling under a sagebrush, I asked them to imagine that it was pregnant. "If we could remove the rabbit's uterus—a baby in a box—and plant it in the ground, it would be very much like a seed. If the baby rabbit in the planted uterus were to develop underground, it would need a protective covering, something harder than the tissue of a uterus—something like a seed coat—and enough food stored with it to make up for the severed umbilical cord. Essentially, plants enjoy surrogacy because seeds, which support the growth of baby plants until they germinate, are basically surrogate mothers."

Tin Cloth looked up from a bird book, tilting his head back and over to one side. I figured he was gesturing *Good show! Good job!* I was humming to myself when someone said, "He didn't have mange then?"

Another student preempted me. "No, he didn't. The fox did not have mange," she said, shaking her downcast head from side to side.

A series of parallel rock walls ahead would take everyone's mind off the fox. Each wall was about thirty feet wide and rose a hundred feet above the sagebrush. The walls were over twenty feet apart. Orange cinnabar sand was spilling into the spaces between each set of walls. These vertical walls had been horizontal at one time. Each was once a layer of sediment underneath a shallow sea, which over time consolidated into sedimentary rock. Millions of years ago, the earth shook violently enough to tip these sedimentary layers on edge; horizontal layers became vertical, and floors became walls. The walls, which geologists call *hogbacks*, consisted of different types of sedimentary rock: sandstone, shale, mudstones. Each type responded to weathering forces in its own manner. Above those walls a single stroke from a worn-out varnish brush had painted the only clouds in the sky.

"Yes. That's right," I said, "he did not have mange. When was this happening—the creation of these sedimentary rock walls?" Wearing oversize sunglasses, the students buzzed around me like wasps on the sting.

It would be another three years before I saw a fox dying from mange. Looking downy-feathered, like a nestling robin, it raked itself with rear claws as if to remove its own skin. If Fox—my fox—was severely mangy, I would not have mentioned it to near-strangers who were paying for my company, especially not on a day with only a single stroke of cloud in the sky. I would have found it less distressing to say, "On the way here I passed an auto accident and saw an eviscerated guy whose eyeball was hanging into his crushed mouth while a turkey vulture yanked out a long piece of his gut." Apparently, none of them had ever seen a mangy fox either, or they would not have asked as casually as if it were chicken pox.

"So, back to our tableau. The creation of these walls?"—I saw a hand go up to ask about the fox and me—"Relative to dinosaurs?" I continued, ignoring the hand. I had never discussed dinosaurs on this trail and had nothing prepared to say about them. Someone rescued me by picking up the dinosaur thread. It was Sixth Sense, the woman who had referred to him as "Foxie" after my opening-night slideshow. She had been zigzagging through our herdlet all morning at a peripatetic pace, disappearing over a cliff to examine something, then skipping along fast and popping up behind Tin Cloth.

From my right Tin Cloth whispered, "*Tab* low not tab *blow*."

Sixth Sense was right. Cambrian and Cretaceous Seas both preceded dinosaurs. Everyone had seen Steven Spielberg's movie and knew that dinosaurs had run amok in the Jurassic. Someone else knew that dinosaurs had lumbered about for a million years before they attained dominance, which meant that they first appeared in the Triassic period. Inappropriately, the sedimentary shelves before us predated dinosaurs by three hundred million years. Colorful hat brims turned this way and that as confused students looked about for enlightenment.

"You were going to get treatment for him?" And then the dominoes fell. I could not make out individual questions, but I think I answered all of them when I replied, "Yes. Treatment. A veterinarian."

Remember that metaphorical gorge I wrote about in the first chapter? The one that separates humans from other animals and prevents us from attributing human traits to non-human animals? The students figured out that if "fox and I" rendezvoused every day, one of us had crossed that chasm.

The questioning stopped while we bridged a creek barely wider than the culvert steering it under the road. The trail switchbacked from there, and we began winding into the mountain. Anticipating a renewal of interest in Fox, I continued, "But I wouldn't say I had a plan. I do not know any veterinarians who treat wild foxes."

When you cannot change an adversary's mind, erase it. Hypnotize your foe with marble-sized water droplets shooting from a geyser's white cone, or show her a green river busting through a deep red canyon; let a waterfall mist him while he looks three hundred feet over its edge to the foam rising through a rainbow. I looked around: there was just a cloud. A single cloud painted on our blue canvas sky with one sweep of a worn-out brush. There's not much you can do with clouds; if you're smart, you won't even mention them.

I waved Tin Cloth's petrified wood, dropping it into the first hand that uncurled under it. "In the age called the New Dawn—the Eocene—this 'rock' was a breathing tree. Maybe redwood or cypress. It stood here," I pointed out a ledge overhang, improvising. "In its shade, on this ledge, the tiger-like Mesonyx crouched. The most charismatic megafauna of the time." No one contradicted me or corrected my most certainly incorrect pronunciation, so I kept talking.

"Mesonyx looked like a serpentine-tailed wolf. Until you saw its tracks and realized Mesonyx was hoofed."

Only a few days earlier, the sight of bison, elk, or antelope sent the class running into meadows with cameras and binoculars swinging. After watching hundreds of bison and elk in the park, and herds of antelope cruising past our cabins every night, the students had altered their search image, as predators often do. Now they were looking out for bears, cougars, and wolves. If I wanted to get them excited about a wild, hoofed animal it had better be dead, ground, and served over pasta.

"Mesonyx was a predator, but a really odd one: a *hoofed carnivore*. All hoofed carnivores are now extinct. Think about it." I paused. They thought about me and the fox.

"So, you're pretty sure the fox didn't have mange."

I did not hear an upward inflection, so I assumed it was not a question. Crossing my arms over my chest, tucking my chin, and hunching my shoulders together, I wove my way through the student cluster.

Tin Cloth suggested that the fox's mange was incipient and that my garlic and eggs had cured him.

It was true that Fox ate a lot of garlic with his egg yolks. Still, my science background nagged me, prodding for proof. I didn't own a digital camera. Kodak film for my single-lens reflex camera required a 120-mile round trip, over one mountain pass. By the time I made that trip and bought the amount of film one might deem reasonable for a person with serious financial limitations, his balding splotches were gone. I could not reject Tin Cloth's hypothesis; likewise, I also could not be sure that

I had not imagined the mange because the fox seemed so slight, so shaky, so needy.

"Maybe," I said.

As we climbed steadily upward, I found reasons to pause: admiring the wilted leaves of flowerless evening primrose, listening to a screaming red-tail hawk, passing around a delicate white snail shell.

Someone suggested that I'd bolstered Fox's immune system by protecting him from dogs and unnecessary stress. I heard ideas about support systems and social networks, and "well, there *was* the garlic." I smiled, thanked everyone, and retained a bit of doubt. I didn't know anything about support systems.

I slowed when the panting behind me got too loud, stopped when it disappeared altogether. We paused for magpies, which the East Coast students found interesting until I admitted, "No, they do not sing. And, also, they do not soar." We broke for flycatchers and towhees. The olive-sided flycatchers were singing, "Quick, three beers!" (according to Cornell University's online bird guide). The green-tailed towhees sounded to me like the *Popcorn's ready!* bell on a microwave oven. Everyone knew I was joking about the microwave. It was obvious I had never owned one.

Our road continued wrapping itself upward around the mountain. We followed, students hugging the mountain, me favoring the outer exposed edge. They whispered to each other; I was sure they were collaborating on a plan to ambush me with questions about Fox. I had plans too. I was a fisherman, after all. I carved a hole in the ice and dropped bait: questions instead of salmon eggs. The first one to rise to the challenge explained that *Homo sapiens* were among the smallest Pleistocene or Ice Age mammals; they were more like prey than predators. I continued setting the hooks—intriguing questions—and the students, finally animated about something besides Fox, responded. Keeping all the lines taut, I said, "Yes, humans—basically cavemen—spent their time running and hiding from big predators. The super predators decreased in size about five thousand years ago. Why?" I asked. "What was happening five thousand years ago to cause that?"

"But you read to that fox, kept him around, so you could check on his mange. But now that he doesn't have mange?"

"Oh. That is a good point. That is." (It really was.) The fisherman became the fish. Pinned on the outside edge along a sheer drop, I could not defend myself. Not while standing on a precipice so narrow that no one could fit behind me to cover my back—not tiny Jenna, not even skinny Tin Cloth if he removed his brimmed hat. I stood alone, guilty of abetting a fox who was not to a single hair mangy. My crime was imagining he had traits only humans should have. I pointed up at a birdless pine branch, and, in a voice loud enough to distract everyone, I said, "Quick, three bears."

Addressing the question about the 5,000-year-old predator-shrinking event seemed inappropriately complicated. No one had attempted to answer that question, and ecologists were still weighing two possibilities: an increase in *Homo sapiens* hunters or a warming climate that favored small body size.

Neither honesty nor evasion would see the fox story to a satisfactory ending. I thought back to another time I'd tried being honest and open with my thoughts—that time hadn't worked out so well either. One year earlier, in the Grand Tetons, I was heading down trail with three female students. The trio had traveled together from Pennsylvania, two professional women and one single mother with a romance problem: her resident son disliked her soon-to-be-resident boyfriend. She was an advice vacuum the older women were anxious to fill.

Hobbled by a pack one-third my body weight, a pebble in my boot, and a runny nose, I stumbled down the gravel trail behind them. Both older women favored dumping the boyfriend because "Men are a dime a dozen, and children" (by which they meant sons) "are priceless." An inarticulate flaw marred the boyfriend, one perceived only by the son. In the boy-friend's defense, someone mentioned that a highly intuitive twenty-two-year-old child should be leaving the nest. *Leave the nest?* That inad-vertent metaphor propelled me into the discussion. What I lacked in knowledge about boyfriends and children I could make up for with my knowledge of nesting behavior.

"I know what you should do."

They did not hear me the first three times.

"Wait. Look. We haven't seen any mountain hollyhocks in bloom yet today." I entwined a cluster of pink blooms between my fingers and pulled them gently forward, causing the trio to pause. They turned slightly toward me.

"I know what you should do," I said for the fourth time, stepping down trail while they turned away and continued walking. "Once upon a time—two years ago—a pair of bald eagles nested in a spruce snag on the banks of the Snake River. Three of their chicks fledged as usual around the end of August, but one would not. It stayed in the nest and cried."

Their tightly braided group was loosening just enough for me to feel less obviously excluded.

"The adult birds tried a bunch of strategies to get that last chick air-borne. First, they ignored it. They stopped feeding it. Then they tempted it, flying past with fish in their talons, hoping the starved chick would leap from its nest to grab the fish. Nope. While perched on a lower snag, Mama tried calling it down. This chick, nearly the size of its parents, would not leave that nest. It would jump to the edge, peer down to the river seventy feet below, look back into the wide cozy nest, and hunker back down."

"Yes?" responded the oldest woman without stopping to look back. "And?"

Even while staring at the backs of their heads, I could see their eyes rolling.

"The nest was seventy *feet* high. And yet, for horizontal distances you use metrics," the other woman interrupted. I read her accusation as a question. All week I had been directing them to stay twenty-five meters away from elk and a hundred meters away from bears.

"Target distances, I guess. I shoot."

After they muttered, "Of course you do," I continued the true and witnessed story of how two adult eagles, under pressure to get their last chick fledged before autumn's snow, began taking their nest apart. The acrophobic chick remained inside, gripping twigs and exhausting itself with distress calls. Nest deconstruction would eventually leave a structure so insubstantial that the chick would tumble out, raise its wings instinctively, and realize the miracle of flight. Or effect a crash landing and never recover. "Either way, we end up with two adults liberated from their chick." Emboldened by the younger woman's smile, I added, "If the chick won't leave the nest, the nest must leave the chick."

"Anthropomorphism," said the matron, imitating a whisper while her glance indicated that I was meant to hear. She was implying that I was scientifically incorrect and emotionally immature. Unsure whether she was going to extend that insult or leave it truncated, I stopped, turned my palms upward, and waited.

The younger woman admitted that the eagle story amused her and quickly added that she would never expel her son from the nest because . . . well, she had to think about it.

"Because," interrupted her companion, "humans are *not* . . ." She paused to glare at me with eyes like a double-barreled shotgun before spitting out the final word, "*Animals*."

There we stood, each of us working from an infinitesimal sample size and a gargantuan bias.

I don't know whether that eagle chick survived. I could guess a definitive maybe.

Still climbing, the River Cabin class and I entered a forested area along a stretch of logging so long retired it looked more like a two-track than a graded lane. Short-leafed Douglas firs and slightly longer-leafed pines waved us on. I waited for a group of downhill hikers to catch up with me before entering the shady abyss. When I paused, they faced me with their backs to the slope. If I had been taller than the students, or if they'd stood farther away, I would have seen bright green hillsides streaked with yellow bands of arrowleaf balsamroot, but their bodies blocked my view of the Northern Rockies' most spectacular hillside display. I was a pygmy owl being mobbed by gnatcatchers.

Eventually we could no longer see sky for forest. Shade-loving clematis vines with pale purple sepals twined into cherry and serviceberry shrubs. Waxy spikes of yellow lilies pierced sheets of melting snow. Tin Cloth reminded us about the chocolate brownies in our lunch sacks, so we climbed out of the forest and onto a hill with a single tree, whitebark (*Pinus albicaulis*). Purple pollen cones, one-inch long and heavily waxed, encircled the tips of the cantilevered tree. We scattered to find rock seats facing Yellowstone River, hundreds of feet below us. Some of our classmates, glassing the dirty snowfields across the river, hoped they would turn out to be mountain sheep. They would not.

All week long we mistook boulders for bison, and bison for boulders. I told them that lonely boulders disguised themselves as bison to attract attention. I said that so they would not stop looking closely at boulders. I also said that bison disguise themselves as boulders because they want privacy. I said that because I thought it might be true.

I reminded everyone about the cow buffalo I once knew who comforted a drowning comrade while coyotes circled, nightfall approached, and my backpack thermometer read thirty degrees below zero. When her comrade sank and the pond froze over and trapped the body inside and none of the above conditions abated, still that cow buffalo stayed, pawing at the thin icy crust covering her sunken friend. No one had answered the question from the first night of class. So, I asked again. "How would you classify that type of behavior?" I asked. "Would you call it sympathy, respect, or loyalty?"

A few months after the class ended, I published that cow's story, "Buffalo's Last Stand," in the magazine of the American Mensa society. I interpreted her behavior as loyalty. In the 1800s, Dr. William Hornaday, the father of wildlife biology, observed similar behavior in bison cows. In *Extermination of the American Bison*, published in 1889, Hornaday wrote that the cows' habit of standing with fallen comrades exemplified "stupidity." I revered Hornaday. I've underlined passages and scribbled in the margins of my copy of his book. He can have his belief about the bison. I am keeping mine. That is why they're called *beliefs*, after all.

A student interjected to enlighten us about bison behavior. "When a bison raises its tail, it's getting ready to . . ." She paused, waving on her classmates until they intoned, "Charge or discharge!" After hearing that old joke from every park interpreter we encountered, everyone still found it hilarious. They swallowed the idea that a buffalo could eat, shit, mate, and die. But the notion that a free-living non-human animal expressed sympathy was unpalatable. Sometimes things we do not like to eat are good for us. I asked if any of them ate kale. They stared at Tin Cloth for a translation. He shrugged and tented his bird book over his face.

🔻

D r. William Hornaday, a man for whom temperature should have been of the utmost importance, waited until noon before checking his thermometer. Wearing long cotton underwear tucked into wet leather boots, he was running out of food, camping without a tent, and only halfway through a task that seemed endless. Traveling on horseback with a mule train for supplies, he'd allowed himself the company of a small party of workers, one of whom, Private C. S. West, was already missing and presumed dead. Bivouacking in treeless sagebrush and butte country east of Ingomar, Montana, Hornaday was boning and skinning the half-frozen carcass of a 2,000-pound buffalo. Brush-choked ravines bisected the flatlands, while snow-filled sloughs booby-trapped it. Wind scoured the rest. Even in a gentler season, this was imposing country. Mule-sucking mud covered the lowest elevations; steep-sided buttes, nearly vertical, commanded the highest.

But after all, it was "at all hazards," as Hornaday writes in his journal, that he had pledged to collect the skin and skeleton of America's last wild bison. When the thirty-eight-year-old chief taxidermist for the Smithsonian Institution finally checked his thermometer on that fall day in 1886, it read six degrees below zero.

Beyond a physical climate that appeared life-threatening, there was the incessant reminder of political turmoil. Hornaday was collecting bison—commonly called buffalo—on lands of ambiguous ownership. US government claims, almost certainly ambitious, overlapped with those of native tribes. Custer's fall was ten years behind him, Chief Joseph's surrender only nine. It was the year of the Dawes Act—tribal lands were becoming private holdings—and just four years earlier, federal soldiers had massacred hundreds of Sioux at Wounded Knee.

In a sheltered niche at the base of what would come to be renamed Smithsonian Butte, Hornaday leaned over and secured wind-whipped pages of his journal with both forearms. For more than twenty-four months he had traveled through the most isolated areas of Texas, Dakota, Wyoming, and Montana to observe, measure, and record America's last bison. He measured and counted ubiquitous bison wallows, pits denuded down to bare mineral soil, most of them hundreds of years old. After watching bulls wallowing in mud until their "degradation is complete," Hornaday wrote that they emerged "not fit to be seen, even by their best friends."

Moby-Dick, published a couple of decades before Hornaday entered graduate school, must have influenced him for the same reason the public denigrated it: excessive encyclopedic reporting of whaling and zoology. Melville's eye is sharp, and he warns readers about the imminent extinction of the American bison.

> Comparing the humped herds of whales with the humped herds of buffalo, which, not forty years ago, overspread by tens of thousands the prairies of Illinois and Missouri, and shook their iron manes and scowled with their thunder-clotted brows upon the sites of populous river-capitals, where now the polite broker sells you land at a dollar an inch; in such a comparison an irresistible argument would seem furnished, to show that the hunted whale cannot now escape speedy extinction.
>
> (*Moby-Dick*, Chapter 105, "Does the Whale's Magnitude Diminish?—Will He Perish?")

While the humped herds of bison were perishing on the plains, the horned herds of elk—or *antlered* herds, as Hornaday would call them in his journal—fared better. The US government was aggressively protecting cattlemen in the 1880s by eradicating mountain lions and wolves and enforcing open-range laws. Elk benefitted from these practices; bison did not. Because elk readily ensconced themselves in thick forests and did not congregate in huge herds, they were harder to shoot.

Hornaday also studied the breeding behavior of these two species of ruminants, which differed dramatically. Bison bred seemingly indiscriminately within herds of thousands, while elk bred very selectively within harems that averaged between fifteen and twenty cows. Bison had more opportunities to breed than elk; their mating season was months longer. And while in bison society, most mature animals took part in the mating process, in elk society, females selected their partners, and not all males ended up with a mate. How did females choose?

Hornaday assumed that they picked the meanest, biggest, toughest bull as determined by jousting matches.

A hundred and twenty years hence, in the 1990s, DNA technology would allow scientists to run paternity tests on elk calves. These tests failed to support Hornaday's conjecture. In fact, the bulls who won the jousting matches did not win all the females. Cows gave birth to calves whose sires had lost the matches, and who had small, crooked, or misshapen horns.

On his way to Calf Creek camp, Hornaday stumbled upon a small group of bison cows and shot the lead. Blood spurted from the cow's nostrils, and the herd pressed their noses to her flesh, refusing to leave even as Hornaday fired several more shots. Congregating around the endangered animal was behavior he had witnessed many times. He wondered why bison cows, unlike other reasonable animals, did not flee to safety. "Phenomenal stupidity," he wrote in his journal, concluding that bison stand in the face of danger because they are inescapably "complacent." The "stupid brutes," he opined, were complicit in their own extinction. Hornaday's unfortunate conclusion might have been different had he heeded this piece of advice from *Moby-Dick*:

> Had these leviathans been but a flock of simple sheep, pursued over the pasture by three fierce wolves, they could not possibly have evinced such excessive dismay. But this occasional timidity is characteristic of almost all herding creatures. Though banding together in tens of thousands, the lion-maned buffaloes of the West have fled before a solitary horseman. Witness, too, all human beings, how when herded together in the sheepfold of a theatre's pit, they will, at the slightest alarm of fire, rush helter-skelter for the outlets, crowding, trampling, jamming, and remorselessly dashing each other to death. Best, therefore, withhold any amazement

at the strangely gallied whales before us, for there is no folly of the beasts of the earth which is not infinitely outdone by the madness of men.

(*Moby-Dick*, Chapter 87,
"The Grand Armada")

Below Smithsonian Butte, elk bulls battling for mates were locking horns. Returning to camp, Hornaday shot a harem cow, pulled the backstraps from her spinal cord, and wrapped them in waxed cotton to roast for dinner. After splitting both rear quarters over his mule's flanks, Hornaday abandoned the rest to the circling coyotes. Meanwhile, as the jousting bulls snorted and pissed on their front legs, cows escaped into the shadows, their hoof beats silenced by the sound of crashing antlers. Each cow was searching for her perfect partner, and despite years of research, no scientist has ever been able to discover the criteria that females use when choosing mates. Maybe it's because each cow chose, for herself alone, the one bull that would most displease her mother.

MY FOX STORY needed a satisfactory ending. I didn't have one. But I knew how it *should* end.

"Little wild animals do not enjoy long stable lives," I said, implying that Fox could be dead when I got home. In fact, the lifespan of a wild red fox is three to five years. "The average fox dies early." Meeting Sixth Sense's gaze, I flashed a droll smile. That was our joke: events cannot be both "average" and "early." She raised her eyebrows and rolled a tight little fist into her nose to mask her expression.

Earlier in the week, we'd spotted a doe antelope nursing two tiny fawns. While we were admiring her long eyelashes and the twins' Mohawk hairdos, two coyotes arrived. They boxed her in, one coyote on each side, a steep hill behind her, and a busy road in front. Good strategy for the coyotes. An antelope can sprint sixty miles per hour but not while running uphill. And she wouldn't cross a road lined with bumper-to-bumper buses. After stashing the twins in a clump of wild rye, she charged the coyote to her west, kicking it as she passed. The east-side coyote ran toward the twins. She reversed, and the west-side coyote ran for the twins. Back and forth it went. After several attempts to immobilize the coyotes, she came up limping, unable to defend her babies. The coyotes ate the two fawns while we watched, snapped, and recorded.

One student: "Cool. It's like Godzilla eats Bambi."

Another: "Good thing my daughter isn't here. She won't kill a fly. Traps spiders and releases them outside." *Yes, everyone's daughter is like that.* No one's daughter finds spider squashing edifying or entertaining. But that does not mean *anyone's* daughter empathizes with spiders. Meanwhile, someone who wasn't anyone's daughter watched crowds enjoying the spectacle: a coyote shredding an antelope fawn, a wilderness experience that does not dirty your couch.

Me: "Wow, we are like Roman spectators watching Christians get torn apart by lions."

Jenna (whispering): "I really wish you would mutter that sort of thing."

Yes, death would be an acceptable ending for the fox story. For another possible ending, I suggested that he would be off looking for a mate. No one asked when foxes mated. (February.)

"He's gonna find a mate, being a runt and all?"

"Yes, because he has especially nice digs."

Sixth Sense glanced up and squinted at me not a split second after I regretted admitting I had visited his den.

Another student asked what I would do on the off chance that he was hanging around when I got home. Everyone concluded that the only legitimate business I had with him would be if he was a research subject. "You can collect his droppings, right?"

I could.

"You can get DNA and stuff."

Yes.

I could, in other words, objectify him, reduce him to data points. And why not? I valued their opinions; these were no ordinary students. This was a continuing education class, filled with doctors, engineers, teachers, counselors, administrators, and artists. They were mature professionals, and every one of them successful in the common meaning of the term. For a moment, surrounded by members of my own species who seemed engaged—maybe even concerned—and who were themselves interesting (somewhat), I considered discarding the belief that Fox had any kind of personality. I considered just fitting in. With people.

I insisted that the fox would be gone when I got home. He would be hunting down a mate or a territory, or would be otherwise engaged in the vagaries we associate with wild animals. I was lying. I'd been checking in on him when I drove home every night before dinner, staying long enough to water plants and pull a weed or two. Besides, he already had a territory, mating season was eight months away, and he was significantly less peripatetic than I was.

According to the tradition of the River Cabins class, we returned from our hike without lecture or leader. But not without a rudder. Jenna swept trail. Everyone else hiked in pairs or packs. I hiked down alone because, unlike the students, I didn't need to have people around me. I stopped when Jenna caught up with me. We listened to gravel rolling under Vibram soles and watched colorful backpacks bobbing below us. "They think I am feeding him." I reached for my water bottle but kept my eyes focused on the buck antelope pacing toward the cabins; students would soon be passing nearby. "Maybe they think I am *imagining* his fidelity, and that he comes by every day coincidentally and not to see me."

"People believe what they understand. That's all." Swinging a plastic bag of mint chocolate wafers my way, she added, "You know that."

"Not really." I poked the chocolate wrapper into a pocket of my cotton coat. "I don't understand gravity, but I accept its existence."

When a clump of students reached the cabins, they congregated around one of the owner's obsequious pet dogs. Students conversed with "man's best friend" as though the old mutt were a child. By the time we caught up to them, they were sharing anecdotes about its habits and personality, which segued into their own dog, cat, and pet iguana stories. At dinner each night, everyone discussed each other's pets' psyches, and by the time vanilla ice cream pooled around our apple dessert cake, I knew exactly what outfit everyone's "best friend" would be wearing for next month's Independence Day parades. We hesitated to call out as anthropomorphic those feelings or attitudes expressed by animals that allowed us to leash them. If I'd kept Fox tethered like a horse, hawk, or pet skunk, I would have been allowed to assign a personality to him. Animals that we control mimic us. The more we look at them, the more we see ourselves looking back. Like a mirror.

Jenna and I reached the cabins just as "man's best friend" shit on the lawn right in front of us. Fox did not shit in front of me. Do you think I would be strolling about discussing *The Little Prince* with someone who shit in front of me? A diagnostic trait of *Homo sapiens* is that we do *not* shit in front of our friends. Boxed animals, the ones we own—either as pets or commercial property—do not abide that decorum.

Another diagnostic trait of *Homo sapiens* is that we love mirrors.

IF THE OWNER of River Cabins thought it odd that I asked permission to collect a large rock from her property, she did not say. I lifted a half dozen rocks, each about eighteen inches across and relatively flat on top. While carrying the trophy to my car, I noticed Sixth Sense staring. I dropped the rock. She was sitting on a wooden bench near the car, her short black hair shining around a wide grin on a tanned face.

"Your car's been gone every night before dinner."

Only because it was not a question, I did not answer.

"And you live only thirty minutes away."

Watching pink and white streaks crossing the cobalt sky like a variant of the locally common opaque opal known as hyalite, I said, "Yes."

"Well, I'm glad Fff . . . um, *your* fox is um . . . let's see now. It . . . he? He doesn't have a name then? But it's okay? Your fox?"

I would not blaspheme an ice-cream opal sky by going inside before the colors faded. Tense, trapped between her and the evening sky, I reached into my pocket. Plunking a walnut-sized stone on the bench, I said, "Geode. Do you like it? From a butte I climbed in Northern Montana."

A REPTILE DYSFUNCTION

The fox pressed a calloused pad on top of his dark, grainy boulder, glanced up at the sun, and stepped away. Alongside the cool boulder, voles were rustling through their runs. But he wasn't hungry, so he wasn't hunting. While waiting for the boulder to heat up, he would toy with an energetic patch of butterflies. They would not be as entertaining as three-legged cranes, but he didn't need entertainment; he needed a warm rock.

Yellow wings poked straight up from the center of the butterfly patch. Because they had crammed too closely together, most of the butterflies couldn't lower their wings. Butterflies along the outer edge, each flapping one wing, kept the group pulsating in a mesmerizing rhythm. One of them broke from the edge, fluttering above the others and taunting him out of his reverie. The fox would not swat it. Not this time. But the insect continued rising, sinking, and fluttering around his face. With a single swat, one paw could smash the creature back into the pile. One set of claws could rake through the butterfly bunch and drag them slowly over pebbles until they were wet and rumpled and still. He knew better. Beneath their light, yellow bodies, a pile of droppings would be glistening and sticky. He was too old to whimper home with sticky paws that smelled like the rear end of a short-haired animal.

Finally, he was hugging the sun-warmed rock. Elongating his back and spreading his legs wide until they dangled around the boulder, he made himself as large as possible, surveyed his surroundings, and confirmed that his was the highest and finest resting rock in the meadow. From this distance, the bendy river looked wide and still. Overhead geese were honking, and he hoped they weren't heading to the little island that he liked to watch. He didn't mind geese for their company, but they made huge messes and he didn't like sharing everything, as little as he had.

Flopping over the edge of the boulder, his tail landed in an uncomfortable position because a stiff balsamroot stalk refused to bend. As if the weight of a fox tail were inconsequential. To remind the flower that it was just another weed in his path, he used the flower's stiff bristles to scrape hound's-tongue seeds off his hocks. Then, turning broadside to the sun, he left the weed paling in his shadow.

He fell asleep listening to crickets and watching a wave of dark pink clouds pouring from a mountain pass like blood seeping from a wounded marmot. It was dark when an unwelcome sound roused him. He stood on his boulder, unable to quiet his shaking body. A quixotic smell was drifting toward him. Something big and unknown and frightening was upon him. There was no time to plan. He went numb.

🌲

Back home, plunged so suddenly into the solitude of my isolated cottage, I moved around the Rainbow Room with small, hesitant steps, as if I might tumble off a cliff without a human body or building or bus to block my fall. Except for short predinner breaks, I had been surrounded by people from 6:00 a.m. until 10:00 p.m. for an entire week. I hadn't been able to stand undressed in my own cabin without closing the drapes. To convince myself that isolation had at least one tangible benefit, I left my clothes on the front steps and walked around the outside of the house in my mukluks. When I completed the circle, I still hadn't entirely shaken off the images of the thirty-some people all eating at the same big dinner table.

I had come home overexposed to the sights, sounds, and smells of a human-dominated world, and now I needed to concentrate on hearing wing beats and smelling deer musk. I wanted to stare at clouds again without worrying about seeming impolite. So I recalibrated my senses, readjusting my signal-to-noise ratio by pushing some stimuli into the background and pulling others forward.

While I was inside and unpacking, I recalled—almost fondly—voices and faces from the River Cabins class. By the time I finished unpacking in the early afternoon, their images were dimming. I avoided driving to town that first day home because some of our class would still be around. I knew from experience that if I bumped into any of the students—except Sixth Sense—I wouldn't recognize them. But I remembered things about them. This had been a special class. Unlike my hundreds of undergraduates, the continuing education folks at River Cabins had been older than me, and professionals. People with credit cards and actual hairdos, and not just clothes but *outfits*. Their opinions mattered to me. Their camaraderie was tempting.

In the evening, I waited for Fox but he didn't show. Every evening when I had driven home before eating dinner with the class, I had seen Fox, except for the last visit, when I found only paw prints. They ran across the muddy spot under the bay windows where the absence of bedding plants had inspired a profusion of bedding mice. Mouse tracks—four evenly spaced round toes and a tail line whisking between the right and left feet—ran from under the bay windows to a pile of coffee grounds shaded by a blue spruce. The pile of coffee grounds mixed with eggshells that I'd discarded with each morning's cowboy coffee had been attracting calcium-starved mice. Splotches of fuzzy fox prints superimposed themselves over the mouse tracks. I squatted low and stared, more convinced than ever that Fox was one very clever individual. He was running a trapline for mice and baiting it with my coffee scraps.

The day after I returned home, mice were still visiting the coffee bait. Their fresh tracks decorated a translucent sheet of ice. Fox's prints, spreading and thinning as the ice melted, were not fresh, and he didn't show at 4:15. Distraught, I went to the back meadow, turned on the water without engaging the pressure pump, and wrapped my hand around a hose with no nozzle. Staring at the cascading water relaxed me. "Meditation and water," says Ishmael, "are wedded forever." My plants didn't need this much water, but it wouldn't hurt them too much. Between sunshine and gravity, water can't sit long enough on an east-facing slope to drown anything. And, like Ishmael, I needed the water therapy.

All the plants on this back slope grew wild. I controlled them, like any provincial land baron controls his subjects, by wielding water like a scepter and a sword. Favorite plants—ground-hugging rings of fuchsia locoweed, beaded sprays of Indian ricegrass, plumes of fringed sagebrush, curls of blue grama—received water and grew faster. I ignored skeleton weed, hound's-tongue, and alyssum, and as a result, they were moving out. Well, not alyssum; it would not leave simply because you ignored it. If ever a plant had no shame, it was alyssum. If I wanted it out, I would have to drag it by its rough racemes.

Orange rind curled around a lupine bush where it was supposedly serving as an appetite suppressant for skunks. (No one likes a fat skunk.) A rubber boa slipping under the rind stopped to flash a come-hither look— wet red tongue, gunmetal skin, invisible scales. Unlike foxes, rubber boas are difficult to misplace. I could go inside, use the bathroom, grade a student's paper, go back outside, and relocate the boa within seconds. Knowing where voles lived, I enjoyed trying to anticipate the boa's moves. But sometimes—suffering from some kind of reptile dysfunction—the snake would raise its slender limp forebody and stare in the direction of a freshly dug vole hole before veering off in the wrong direction.

I abandoned the boa as 4:15 approached. Aiming my spotting scope above Fox's den, I searched for flying scavengers that might reveal a carcass. I quit, without success, when the evening light rendered the scope useless. Fox's little body would disappear quickly out here. In the spring, two turkey vultures had picked a skunk carcass clean in a single morning. When they finished, there wasn't enough organic material left for a fly's aperitif.

Three days after returning, I headed out on recon, searching for a track or a scat from a fox or something that had recently eaten one. A mouse's tail waving from under the siding near the garage door disappeared when I stomped. A mouse's head, and then an entire mouse, quickly replaced the tail. After running under the hose bib, the mouse slipped into the siding. I found more bad news at my oldest lilac, where a Roman-nosed rabbit poked its head out from under the world's most expensive mulch— the remains of my former cherry tree. Pulling its nostrils down tight, the rabbit glared and chucked a wad of soil at me.

"Fox, where are you? We are under siege," I said, forgetting we were no longer on the same team. Forgetting that I was carrying a rippled, red Folgers coffee can and lid so I could collect his scat and use him for research. *You can collect his DNA*, they had said. They probably thought I would use it for paternity tests. But I had forgotten my backpack shovel.

I was side-hilling up a steep slope, when a shiny brown mammal with white feet darted past. I lost my balance and dropped to one hand. When I turned to look uphill, the weasel, now paused, set his black eyes on me for a moment before darting away. It had surprised me because my default hiking gaze focused one meter above the ground—bear height—a habit from living and working in bear country, where I'd bumped into them often at Mount Rainier and Glacier National Parks. If you cannot spot a bear within thirty meters, neither your running ability nor the sidearm in your shoulder holster will save you from injury. Yes, I stubbed my toes and tripped a lot, but I never had a confrontation with a bear that didn't end in a mutually agreed-upon resolution.

The weasel, an ermine, ran down a hole at the base of a slate-colored boulder. Hoping it would emerge, I sat down, sliding off my backpack and rummaging for the camera. As far as I could see in any direction, I was alone—even when I spied through binoculars. So it was odd to hear someone say, "Here at last is someone who has a real profession."

My conscience was mocking me. Fox and I had met the man with the real profession in *The Little Prince*: a deskbound, self-identified scholar, who hasn't discovered anything because he is "too important to go wandering about."

I didn't *want* to be too important to go wandering about; I *needed* to be too important. Well, important enough to have health insurance anyway. Stepping off the bus in Lamar Valley earlier in the week, I had appeared so peaked that a student had told me to find a doctor. I did not tell the student that what I really needed was a *surgeon*, and that I could not afford one; that my affliction was not fatal, and that I was still guiding backcountry tourists, teaching field classes, lifting weights, and jogging. Yes, I was exhausted and still sleeping too much. But never mind the four-pound tumor. It wasn't malignant.

Any job that seemed an appropriate match for my PhD in biology, and that offered steady pay and health insurance, would require casting aside the life of a terrestrial Ishmael. I would need to give up living in a wild, isolated area where I felt emotionally comfortable. I would be exchanging my known world for the chance to live and work around people in an environment that might always be fraught and in which I might never fit in. Wouldn't it be swell, when I could afford surgery, to write someone's name on the line next to *Person to Contact in Case of Emergency*? I might have been chugging down the wrong track, but I couldn't see any other track to follow. My conscience usually did a good job highlighting problems, but it disappeared before providing solutions.

"Here at last is someone who has a real profession!" the voice in my head repeated.

I was pouring myself warm tea and Tang from a stainless steel thermos when Ishmael propped a boot on the boulder and leaned forward, resting his forearm on his thigh. His monkey jacket was gaping open where a button was missing. "I abominate all honorable respectable toils," he said, knocking off my baseball cap. It was a phrase from *Moby-Dick*. In the book, Ishmael has a real profession—schoolmaster. He quits. Pursues his purpose. Rides the *Pequod* and communes with whales.

"But here's the peculiarity of 'respectable toil,'" I replied to him. "It's just a tithe, isn't it? In exchange for membership in society?"

Ishmael responded that he didn't want membership in society, and therefore he didn't need to pay his dues. I reminded him that he'd ended up with only one friend, Queequeg, a pagan cannibal and shipmate. Ishmael had written in his journal that Queequeg was his "only heir." I considered whether the cannibal was any more verbal than a fox.

I watched as the wind, already guilty of removing my cap, blew it down the steep ravine into the thorny arms of a wild pink rose. Ishmael quoted *Moby-Dick* again. Something about Heaven's gate opening just as wide for schoolmasters as for slaves.

I reminded Ishmael that he was an atheist. And that I was knocking on *society's* gate, not Heaven's.

A swarm of biting thatch ants put an end to my daydreaming and I ran downhill. In the evening my calves swelled up with ant bites and my back hurt from bending over an indolent boa constrictor while shouting,

"Left! Left! Hard left!" as I rooted for it to shove its blunt nose down a mouse hole.

I WAS SETTING up the scope when the sun swords appeared.

The thick puffy cloud stack billowed, glowing orange along the bottom. The sun was partially visible above the clouds. Six distinct rays shooting from the sun reached toward the ground, forming an inverted fan of light. I walked outside, where light rays—sun swords—surrounded me. It was like being in a tepee encircled with light instead of a canvas tarp.

Orange splotches appeared in a hanging meadow near Fox's den, one large piece topping a boulder, smaller pieces blowing through the grass. Higher magnification revealed hairs waving from the splotches. Horrified, I realized they were pieces of Fox's hide. I regretted telling the class that Fox would be gone when I got home. More so, I regretted saying I would use him for research if he returned. Regret crossed the thin line into guilt.

After realizing that Fox was dead, I kept my eyes on the blowing hide until darkness separated us. I would like to tell you about sadness and loneliness and about losing my fox. But I won't. Because I didn't lose *my* fox. He wasn't mine to lose. And I could not imagine the fox and me as a pair. I was, relatively speaking, too insignificant here. But I could sense our valley, with its bushy, round olive trees, knobby hills, and junipers spilling down the draws, and I sensed that we were all together one fox down, and missing him.

I went to bed thinking that one fewer fox would be sleeping in my valley tonight, and that tomorrow might not be as good as yesterday. How would I go on? Rejoice that nothing was keeping me from focusing on a responsible job? Leave this isolated patch of thatch and cranky magpies? That's what a rational and practical person would do. An image of the

Three Lakes cabin on a grassy knoll above an emerald lake appeared, and I heard tree frogs singing. I couldn't forget Fox any more easily than I could forget those tree frogs at Three Lakes.

I would not be able to share that realization with anyone because I hadn't told anyone he was here in the first place. But on the other hand, no one was going to tell me, *Animals die! Death is inevitable! Nature is cruel!* And I was grateful for that.

DR. AND MR. FRANKENSTEIN

A simple blue flower waved at me, reminding me that one insignificant fox would not be pestering me anymore. Never mind the time; I could sit wherever I wanted. Where I wanted was next to that wild forget-me-not. It had been Fox's seat.

The nylon bottom of my sleeping pad scraped across the rocky ground as I dragged it over to the flower. Clipping the top side straps into the bottom side clips, I transformed the flat sleeping pad into an L-shaped legless chair. Pulling my knees to my chest, I faced the flower. *Doesn't it feel good to be alone?* I asked myself. And since it wasn't a rhetorical question, I thought about it and replied, *Yes, entertaining guests is especially trying for those of us who are particular about where we sit.* But that wasn't really an answer.

You would call the day "cloudless" if you used the description casually. I didn't. You would call the day "cloudless" if you were insensitive to the valley's mourning. I wasn't. Far to the east, barely visible faint streams of clouds hovered above the truncated peak of a classic volcano-shaped mountain. Two clouds, just dense enough to be visible to someone who was grieving, were converging at the same altitude on the opposite horizon.

A lightweight paperback with a deeply creased cover balanced on my thigh. Inhaling its musty smell, I pressed my thumb into its most brutal scar, trying to smooth the rough edge. Dozens of different implements had highlighted its passages; comments filled the margins. Fifteen years earlier I had purchased the book as a throwaway. Now I suspect the dog-eared novel and I will remain together until one of us disintegrates.

I'd found the book at Blanton's grocery in Packwood, Washington, the gateway to Mount Rainier National Park. It was hiding between the bakery and the registers on a circular bookrack missing so many screws that when rotated, it bobbed and dipped like a merry-go-round. None of the half-priced books belonged to the typical grocery-store book genres: no romance, thrillers, or spy-n-die. All the books were pre-owned, seemingly the singular donation of someone's great aunt, long blind or recently deceased. As each book came around, I freed it from its cage and assessed its suitability. I handled all the stained books on the rack before selecting a dark-covered novel half as thick as my ham and rye, and a good bit lighter.

The next day, I backpacked eight miles to one of my duty stations, a three-sided rock shelter perched above the Ohanapecosh River. A great sandbar called Indian Bar split this section of river, trapping twisted, silver fir driftwood and supporting a dense population of pink monkey-faced flowers. An old settler's term, Indian Bar lent its name to both the rock shelter and the surrounding meadows. Indian Bar shelter—a man-made cave—faced a wide-tongued glacier that licked the river's far shore. A snowfield several feet thick yoked the cave and softened the steps for resident mountain goats.

Weeks went by, and despite the desolation—or maybe because of it—I was pretty pleased with the whole situation until the night a couple stumbled in after dark. I was deep inside the candle-lit cave, lying on a wooden plank suspended by thick, soot-blackened chains. A rustling sound called my attention to the front of the shelter, and I looked up from my grocery novel to see a woman step inside, look around, and back out.

Several pages later, loud incomprehensible voices filled the cave; the husband had arrived. He came over to introduce himself, frowning at me and my book. "Doesn't weigh much," I said, waving it at him. The man, who was German, pointed out my uniform hat to his wife to reassure her and unhooked his sleeping bag, rolling it out on one of the lower wooden planks. I jumped down from my perch, set my book on the graffitied and fuel-stained table, and explained to them how I came to be reading *Frankenstein*.

I noted, as they unpacked their food for dinner, that they had divvied up their gear such that each of them had half the essentials: he had all the canned goods, and she carried the only can opener. Expecting that a stove would appear, and that they wouldn't be eating from cold cans, I handed them a plastic needle container—collected from a diabetic colleague—with my stash of dry matches. She transferred a pack of wet matches from a pocket to what I hoped was their trash sack. "You know this is not normal—to pick your reading according to its weight," she said.

I did not know. I had selected my stove, sleeping bag, jacket, and food based on their mass. I dried my own fruit, venison, and tuna and packed my food according to calories per weight. Still, with eleven years of professional backpacking behind me, I refrained from defending myself. My definition of "normal" probably differed from that of a German woman who had been lost, limping, hiking after dark, ill-provisioned, and essentially alone in one of our nation's largest Wilderness areas.

In the morning, the Germans and I hiked into the heath meadows above the snow yoke. Although we stayed on narrow dirt trails, long branches and heavy dew left fuchsia petals clinging to the bare skin above our ragg wool socks. I showed off my wallowa, the single box toilet I'd built to replace the shelter's suffocating outhouse. I'd designed and built the box toilet myself with two caveats in mind: one, nothing was too good for Indian Bar's visitors, and two, Indian Bar almost never had visitors. Creating a wilderness experience for backpackers preempted insurances of privacy; I dug the wallowa into an exposed spot with open vistas. Enchanting scenery surrounded anyone who entrusted his or her naked thighs to my polished pine wallowa seat: wild blue river, mossy cliffs, mountain goats so close you could hear them sneeze.

Years later, the Washington Trails Association reviewed Indian Bar and wrote: "It's also worth noting that the single most spectacular backcountry toilet in the state is found here." Thank you, WTA, *tausen dank*.

The park service did not maintain trails in the subalpine meadows above the wallowa, so we hiked cross-country, edging around an archipelago of waist-high twisted firs. Pointing to a lovely little circle of fir, I called out, *"Krummholz,"* but my companions, upon hearing me use the German term for "twisted wood," did not react. *"Krummholz,"* I repeated, grabbing a clump of short, soft needles. We kept plodding along, and I stopped interpreting for them. Finally, the white corkscrewed bark of a fir with branches all flying off in the same direction claimed our attention. Only a meter high, the fir was probably hundreds of years old. The German man loudly proclaimed some word that sounded vaguely like *krummholz*. I struggled through their German lessons until we were laughing too hard to make any further progress.

Below us, the Ohanapecosh River braided itself around several shoals and curved around an oxbow. We paused to watch mountain goats scuffle down pigeon-blue rocks, and I asked the Germans if Indian Bar reminded them of the Swiss Alps. They said it very much did, and that they lived near the Alps.

"Gesundheit," I said to a chuffing nanny goat.

"Gesundheit," the Germans repeated, trying to mimic my American accent.

They were nicer than I expected, so I identified subalpine flowers as my way of apologizing for spooking them the previous night. "*Lupinus*," I said, pressing one Pivetta between two clumps of purple lupine, "like *Canis lupus*. Wolf. And Lupus, autoimmune disease." I ruffled a clump of short wolf-faced flowers, pestering two torpid bumblebees reclining on the stalk. "People didn't used to like wolves." I waited while the man dug out the close-up lens for an Olympus SLR the woman had been wearing around her waist. "Not sure they liked lupine all that much either."

I told them about Victor Frankenstein because I thought it might help them feel at home. "When Victor is a boy, he and his family summer in the Alps. He calls the mountains sublime. That's his exact word: *sublime*."

"Yes." She smiled. "Two the same, I think—you and your new friend."

"Dr. Frankenstein," her husband added for clarification.

"No, Dr. Frankenstein is not my friend. Maybe someday he will be. I am only on chapter 3." If I had known then that Victor Frankenstein never earns his doctorate, I would have corrected him.

"Chapter 3?" She turned to me, laughing and letting her head fall back. Maybe I was a slow reader; Mary Shelley's archaic vocabulary saw to that. But I don't think the German was laughing at my plodding reading pace, but just to be breathing Indian Bar's wild, clean air.

We waded back downhill through a meadow of tuba-shaped flowers that flexed aside gracefully but too slowly to dodge my eager hand. "Look at its fuzzy tongue," I said, and she poked a finger into the purple penstemon's throat and stroked a thick strip of false anthers. Holding the flower's tongue for her husband, I explained that penstemons belonged to the Figwort family, which was known for weird-looking flowers. After glissading down the snowfield with the German woman's hand on my shoulder, I recited the names of some common figworts: snapdragon, elephant head, bearded tongue, parrot beak, owl-faced clover, monkey flower, fox glove, paint brush.

Next day, I persuaded them to admire elephant-head flowers growing along the Ohanapecosh River. Each fuchsia-colored flower consisted of one tubular petal curling upward like an elephant trunk. On either side of the trunk, broad petals flapped open like fully extended ears. From there we parted ways, they to cross and follow Ohanapecosh Glacier up and over its saddle before descending into another valley, and me to set up a two-door tent in a wind-catcher grove of fir and hemlock not three hundred meters from shore. My most-prized piece of backcountry gear, the tent was a North Face geodesic Ve24, spacious, gold, and so beautiful that when I shook it from the stuff sack, I committed the first deadly sin.

"If you are going to travel with vital items like food and water divided between you, then you need to stay together, not twenty minutes apart." That piece of advice was not my only parting gift. "*Pedicularis groenlandica*," I said, pointing to elephant heads bobbing along the river on their long, thin stalks. Her husband could not have heard; he was already crossing the shoal. "Be careful with that book," she said grabbing both my forearms. "It gives you nightmares." Winking and clicking her tongue, she added, "Big monster."

Frankenstein, which I finished that summer, rode in the trunk of my twenty-year-old Volvo when I left Mount Rainier, and for a long while it seemed that she was wrong about the nightmares.

I HAD BEEN NAPPING and woke to find myself in a darkened laboratory, wearing a white cotton coat, facing a lab bench heaped with bloody body parts and coagulating blood. A year had passed since my Germans had crossed the Ohanapecosh and left me alone in Indian Bar's paradise. Yellow eyes the color of Mr. F.'s monster dangled from a rancid carcass, and the air's green miasma clung to my face. A light ray, filled with dancing dust, escaped through the lone window's thick and dirty glass. With a bloodstained glove, I lifted a test tube into the light, spellbound by the cobweb-like substance swirling in the alcohol-filled vial.

I was extracting the DNA from carcasses for my doctoral dissertation addressing the conservation of bald eagles. After putting away lab tubes and bloody gloves and returning body parts to the walk-in freezer, I went back to my dorm room to sleep.

Frankenstein nightmares woke me.

They were not monster nightmares. Frankenstein's scariest scene occurs long before the monster shakes to life: Mary Shelley's account of Victor sitting for his oral doctoral exams. In my nightmares, I transposed myself into Victor Frankenstein's quaking shoes as they rattle on the dark wood floor and he stands facing the seated Professor Krempe, "a little squat man, with a gruff voice and repulsive countenance." Krempe insults Victor's preparations for his doctoral work, much of which includes reading old and obsolete textbooks. Victor stutters an unacceptable answer. Krempe "slam[s] his hand on the table" saying, "Every instant that you have wasted on those books is utterly and entirely lost. . . . Good God! In what desert land have you lived?"

Like me, Mr. F. suffers arrogant professors, produces chimeras, and lives in a barren landscape bereft of elegant reading material.

Naturally, I admired him.

Unlike me, Mr. Victor Frankenstein doesn't write a dissertation and does not earn a doctorate. While some American universities allow students the option of submitting a project in lieu of a written thesis, Mr. F. lives in Switzerland in the 1800s, and, despite his talents, creating a monster is not tantamount to writing a dissertation. Ingolstadt University does not offer an Ogre Option.

During my university years, if I wasn't in the library or the wildlife genetics lab, you could find me perching on the armrest of a puce vinyl sofa looking out the dormitory window at yellow-flowered foothills and mountains too far away to reach with an uninsured Volvo missing its reverse gear or a broken bicycle lock missing its three-speed red Schwinn. I would reread the merry-go-round bookstand copy of *Frankenstein* from Packwood, Washington, highlighting relevant sections with a thin pink marker. Like me, Victor loved nature, heard his calling before he left elementary school, and failed to receive any advice from his father. As Shelley tells it, "[Victor's] father was not scientific and so [Victor] was left to struggle with a child's blindness, added to a student's thirst for knowledge." The book comforted me when I stood at the crossroads of science and intuition trying to figure out which way to turn.

While on family vacation at a fancy hotel in Thonon Baths, Victor opens the bureau drawer and finds an old, abandoned book written by an unusual natural philosopher, Cornelius Agrippa. Pleased with Agrippa, Victor goes on to read Albert the Magnificent. Albert and Agrippa believed in magic and alchemy—ideas anathema to the academic establishment in Ingolstadt in the late 1700s. Two hundred years later when I entered college, only medieval and Renaissance history students were reading them. A chemistry text might mention that The Magnificent discovered arsenic, or a women's studies class might assign Agrippa's treatise on the superiority of women, but generally the twentieth century's American academy denigrated the pair as madmen, mystics, occultists, and alchemists.

Master Waldman, another one of Victor's professors, wrestles him away from mysticism, introducing him to equally dangerous obsessions: chemistry and math. "Chemistry is that branch of natural philosophy in which the greatest improvements have been and may be made," says Waldman. "If your wish is to become really a man of science, and not merely a *petty experimentalist*, I should advise you to apply to every branch of natural philosophy, including mathematics" (emphasis mine). Victor capitulates, changing his concentration from biological to physical sciences. He lives to regret that decision. In fact, Victor blames his reliance on physical science for his big disaster. I guess we know what he means by "big disaster." Waldman gets one thing right, though. After the "disaster," people all over Europe call Victor some pretty vile names, but "petty experimentalist" is not one of them.

Chemistry and math are fine for people who love chemistry and math, but they don't speak for nature; and neither do magic and alchemy. Frankenstein's apparent dilemma—mathematics or alchemy—was really a trap; Mary Shelley had set him up. Both of Victor's options involved the physical world. Chemistry and math are physical sciences; alchemists and magicians seek to alter physical states, for example by turning lead into gold, or animating cadavers.

I was toying with an option outside the reach of science and the physical world: intuition, the knowledge that comes without conscious reasoning. When I asked questions about Fox—Did he have a personality? Did he care about me? Had he wanted to be my friend? Should I mourn him the way we mourn people?—science and intuition gave me different answers. I couldn't decide between them. Was I being set up too?

The German lady from Indian Bar was right, not only about nightmares, but also that Victor and I were "two the same." Before he designs the monster, Victor is just another confused waif who loves nature, limps through school without mentors, and faces science with naive but honest skepticism. He loves mountains and high-altitude lakes and spends too much time alone (especially after the monster begins offing his friends). In the margins of his books, he scribbles things like "better living through chemistry." He lives to regret that too.

OUTSIDE MY COTTAGE, sitting in my camp chair next to Fox's forget-me-not and missing the fox, I again felt close to Victor. When the blue sky was gone, I closed *Frankenstein* and shrugged a brown Carhartt jacket up around my jaw, pulling its hood against the late afternoon wind. Murders of ravenous clouds were gathering at both ends of my valley, devouring molecules of water as they coalesced. Directly above me, converging clouds were telescoping into a tight circle, spinning inward on me. TBall, freed from the responsibility of incubating eggs, was dive-bombing me along with Torn Tail, the pair apparently unhappy about the lack of egg yolks. For the first time in months, I had skipped breakfast and canceled my morning egg-delivery service.

Fox had left my pasture a mess, crimping my reading meadow's only flower. The forget-me-not drooped, exposing its browning wound. I remembered Fox brushing his muzzle against it when I read aloud to him. I cupped the inflorescence in both hands and unfolded the petals with my thumbs. The adulterated stem, already shriveling, would sacrifice its lone flower before the end of the day so that the main body of the plant could continue living.

Doing nothing, I stayed at the rendezvous site past 4:15. At 5:00 p.m. the earthbound cloud vortex was trying to suck me down with it. Even the magpies were sheltering. I needed to learn more about how Fox had lived. Although I was afraid of what I might find, I decided I would explore his den site. But not now. Not in a cloud vortex.

EVENTUALLY, I EXPLORED the area around the den, poking around longer, and looking more carefully, than when he was alive. I expected to find remnants from a short, staid life. Instead, a wonderland of natural art objects greeted me, funnily arranged as if to be aesthetically pleasing. They whispered stories to me under cloud-covered sky: segmented deer vertebrae, a garter snake's shed skin, grouse feathers spraying from the base of dried yarrow, and green-tinged lacunae mottling an elk's scapula. A large trophy, the elk's scapula suggested that the den was a hunter's home, one whose life, though short, was not without glory.

Arranged on his well-kept lawn—not a speck of scat or a whiff of decay—mementoes from his visits to my house saddened me: a piece of hand-cut deer hide, a plastic seedling tub, a shard of pottery with part of a blue donkey's face. I was less sad when I convinced myself that he had staged his memorabilia with a little bit of whimsy, creating a place where he enjoyed spending time. Maybe he liked the way those objects looked. Maybe he liked the way it felt to be around them. Like the feathers, sand dollars, and dried mushrooms I stuffed into glass and wood boxes and placed on my letter desk, and the colorful beach pebbles I poured into glass test tubes stopped with cork. I think he gathered scraps the same way I did: absentmindedly. Which is to say: instinctively.

Picking up a hefty white chicken feather, I thought of Fox rustling someone's rooster. While two ravens waged an acrobatic attack on a bald eagle, I sat in a sandy pit above his den boulder recalling my own rustling adventures from my early twenties. East front of the Rockies. Buck mule deer. Spectacular scenery. Evergreens speckling rolling hills beneath a banded flattop mountain. Guys from Dupuyer tied my buck to the roof of the jeep lent to me by a male nurse from the Glacier County IHS hospital. Someone I met at the Dupuyer diner brought me home to her family for the night. I stayed over with new people a lot when I hunted. And I hunted a lot. I never thought of them as "strangers," but of course stranger is a relative term. You have to categorize some people as familiar in order to categorize others as strangers.

Fox's teeth had scored the biggest bone at the site, an elk femur. The rest of the carcass, mud mired about two hundred meters away, belonged to a bull who died before Fox was born. I remembered watching Fox gripping the femur with his teeth, choking up, and swinging it around like he was a big leaguer. How could I complain about my handicaps when a runt fox could bat a long bone?

I was hiking home when a fox darted in front of me and crouched behind a boulder not much higher than her shoulders. After making eye contact she ducked back. Her fur was like a cinnamon mink, homogenized and subdued, just slightly paler than rich. I designated the cinnamon a vixen because she didn't identify herself as a male. Besides, avoiding people was a decidedly female trait. She-foxes rarely took risks simply to assuage their curiosity or ward off boredom. I imagine that a population of foxes whose vixens took to socializing with people would dwindle to extinction. Also, she had an aura of feminine vanity. She was stouter than Fox, with a shorter, finer muzzle. She looked to be more symmetrical and unblemished, which might have been due to the distance and the lighting. Perhaps she chose not to tramp around unkempt. Then again, this was just one encounter, and I had seen Fox hundreds of times by now, in wind and rain and snow and desperation and fear, and, frankly, well . . . he was not a perfect specimen. On a good day, he was merely disheveled. When wet, he looked like a dirty dishrag. If you stood on his north side during a strong north wind, he looked like a Chihuahua suffering from chronic Montezuma's revenge. The vixen ran into a thick clump of bunchgrass ten meters away. I sat on a rock and talked softly, but she never exposed more than her muzzle.

No matter. I did not need another fox to entertain me. I was still deciding whether I needed the first fox. During the previous week's field class, my students—essentially my peers—had decided that the only acceptable reason to associate closely and regularly with a fox was to objectify it, to use it, to turn it into a research subject. I implied agreement and then tried to make the implication a reality, imagining myself as a scientist coolly assessing tagged or caged foxes. I imagined filling out and mailing in even one of the applications for university positions awaiting me on my desk—real jobs in real towns—and relocating to a place where my friends would be humans and not foxes.

If I really wanted a study subject, then one fox would be the same as any other.

On the back patio a few days later, while enjoying the retreating sun's glance across my legs, I caught movement near his den site. Looking through the spotting scope, I saw animals proceeding toward the rock where I had last seen Fox alive. Four fox kits, maybe five, rolled and jumped around his boulder.

Three of those kits would make it to the beginning of winter. One grew a tail permanently kinked at ninety degrees about two thirds of the way from the base, and another sported a tail so insubstantial that a musk-rat's could put it to shame. In the middle of all that confusion of kits, one furry orange animal was dancing on a boulder. I don't ever need to be happier than I was at that moment when I realized Fox was alive. On the hillside where he was dancing, rivulets rained down from a carnelian cliff and flowed through round-stemmed sedges, not so different from a stretch of the Wonderland Trail that I used to cross on my way to Indian Bar. Those subalpine meadows spread out in my minds' eye, and I re-membered bending down to pull salamanders out of ice-cold brooks.

When it was too dark to see Fox, even through binoculars, I sat back in my chair, and imagined him dancing all the way back to his den. I had just learned for certain that one fox was not the same as the rest.

ENDLESS POSSIBILITIES
FOR MISCHIEF

At dawn the fox opened his eyes into fur that was soft, fine, fragrant, and someone else's. A foot smashed into his windpipe, diverting his attention from the pain shooting along the side of one ear. Kits had pinned down all four of his legs. A quick body check revealed more unwelcome news: if persistent tiny feet kept pushing, they were going to invert both his elbows. This was not how he liked to greet the day.

When the kits pounced on the mink-colored vixen, she shook and howled. They shed off her like fleas on a dead skunk. She had a hackle-raising scream; he had "qwah." After a few serious head shakes, the hot fur entangling his eyelashes drifted slightly. The paws clinging to his jowl hairs dislodged, too, but they took with them more fur than seemed appropriate. A tiny clawed hand brushed against his eyelashes as it reached up to pull skin from his forehead down to his cheek. Blinded again. *Off plan!*

How often was he waking up with the feeling of trotting into a windstorm on the river's sandy bank and discovering small claws stabbing at his face? How long had he been waking to the sting of yanked-out hair? Tightening his lids against kit drool, he heaved his torso under warm, wet weight. There was only one question worth answering: How to stop this assault?

Wings stuttered over the melee. His friend Round Belly was approaching. He wondered if she had quit a screeching match with the girl in the blue-roofed house to come and rescue him. She flew back and forth over the kits, lightly scraping a claw across their ears. Unable to resist a play fight with a harmless bird, the kits rolled off Fox and freed him. *On plan!* Now he would spread them out in a sand patch and drop in a couple of live grasshoppers for entertainment. Then he could leave them and find himself some sun. He turned the pudgiest kit toward the sand and it flopped over, landing not a toe's width closer to the mark. Another kit, a female with a muzzle soft as a bald caterpillar, would crawl into the sand pit with just a light push. Except she didn't. His next push was a little harder. Maybe too hard. The little fox rolled into a dirt-and-gravel chute. *Weasel pee!* With no neck and legs too short for her rotund body, the rudderless kit was helplessly sliding down the bald chute. Leaping over the top of the rolling kit and digging into the hill with his hind feet, he held his front paws out to arrest the runaway.

He turned uphill; kits were peering over the edge. Scooping the yipping kit underneath and up, he curved around the small zaftig body, reached above her, and pulled them both up. She wiggled one arm free and raked his muzzle. Uphill, the magpie was teasing the other kits with long, steady calls.

When he was young, his mother would sit on her hind legs, swatting magpies. One time, a bird she knocked down sank into its broken wing. Hopping around in a circle, it tried to shield the injury from his littermates. They flashed their shiny fangs and tore the bird into pieces so small no one would bother to eat it. He hadn't ever attacked Round Belly, even though she had followed him around all his life. When he finished pulling the rescued kit up the hill, Round Belly, the biggest magpie he had ever known, was waiting at the den, eating bugs and getting even bigger.

Fox always kept a neat schedule. Now that he was juggling four kits, I didn't expect him to visit again. Certainly not the afternoon following the rock dance.

His nose brushed the weeping stem of his tattered forget-me-not; scuff-marks ran the length of his muzzle. Bald spots and kit licks had left his coat tufted, as if shaved by a remedial barber. Was I flattered that he had missed me? No, he was giving me something more important than a compliment: a *purpose*. Something significant to do besides look for a secure source of income: establish a relationship with a wild animal. I sat cross-legged on the ground with *Frankenstein* on my lap.

"You may bivouac here, Fox."

His forget-me-not had produced three new buds in his four-day absence. He stuck his head under the flower's arched stem so that he appeared to be bowing down under its weight.

The next day at first light, Fox was waiting for the vixen, who had been hunting all night. Just seconds after she breached the grasses, he escaped. In fact, every morning, even after weeks of kit duty, Fox was so eager for freedom he nearly flipped over the returning vixen on his way to sniff out mice, leap through the air, maybe bother some birds. This changing of the guard proceeded on schedule all summer in a most undignified manner, and his pace on egress never slowed.

The first of many days we walked down the gravel driveway and through the pasture, TBall watched me wobbling along through bunch-grasses with Fox alongside, patting soft dirt. Directly above us, dense, disk-shaped clouds were tumbling from a stack. Overlapping, they formed a ring in the blue sky, like cobbles circling a pond. A lonely starling perched on the sagebrush, gyroscoping its head and flashing a bright yellow mating bill. What was it doing here? I told it to lower its elevation. Or its standards. Starlings didn't mate in this high, dry desert.

Poor things, those starlings. Twentieth-century Americans disdained them. Not because their feathers were rippled with a deceptive prism like a black oil slick, but because the birds' ancestors had emigrated from England to North America in the last two hundred years. I had enough to do worrying about my own transgressions to belittle starlings or cast blame on Shakespeareans, who'd carted them to our continent in the 1890s. I had, for one, the Panther Creek Fawn. Besides, time had taught me that there were beings so easily stifled that they were not suited to life on a small, damp island in the North Sea.

WHEN FOX STARTED TROLLING Pillbox Hat Hill in his hunting posture, I returned to a fuel-reduction project I had started in late spring with two meadow patches totaling 320-square feet. After clipping all the vegetation to the ground and raking and flattening the soil, I had started rolling out landscape fabric. The black plastic material prevented sunlight from passing through and would keep the area free of vegetation. Adhering the cloth to the ground entailed pounding four-inch-long staples every few inches. After about twenty hours of labor and a hundred dollars of material, I finished. A few days later, Fox and the kits were in the front lawn diving on voles. They had raked up every inch of the landscape fabric. I tried hard to be mad at them. But I was so happy that Fox and the little ones were having fun. I realized something important about my character that day: I was a forgiving person, under the right circumstances. As I sifted through the shredded plastic, I discovered that the rubber boa was an accidental casualty. Someone's claw had caught the boa while it was sheltering under the tight black blanket.

I was sorry about the boa, but not enough to feel angry with Fox. He was a friend; the boa was only a neighbor.

FOX RAN HIMSELF SKINNY carrying rodents up to the kits all summer. One time he surprised me with a gift of three voles at my doorstep. I could have spent a long time basking in the glory of his adoration, but it turned out I had only an hour. He returned with one more vole, then claimed his booty by clamping the four dead things in his jaws and charging up the hill to the kits. He had figured out that my doorstep provided protection from thieving magpies and had been stashing his loot there so he could continue hunting until he caught a rodent for each kit.

Late afternoon, he would arrive for our rendezvous, sliding himself into the smoothest sitting spot available and leaving me jostling on rocks and bunchgrass in a tippy camp chair. Our seating arrangement was beginning to look less accidental than I once supposed. After I read from *The Little Prince*, he would stretch into one of his yoga poses. Pressing his belly into the gravel and stretching his rear legs back as far as possible, he aimed his paw pads upward. I would squat and perch with the balls of my feet on the ground. One day, as he rose to move into another posture, I dropped to my hands and knees and faced him. Our eyes were level. Believing that I could rise rapidly if necessary, I inched toward him.

Reaching his forepaws forward, he pulled himself closer to me. I shuffled back on all fours. He and his forty-two sharp teeth elbowed forward again; I backed away. He, with his mouth opening wide enough to engulf my entire head, elbowed forward.

"We are playing chicken. If you turn away first, you lose." Fox—who could sever a vole neatly in half with one snap of his jaw—glared. I waited only a few seconds before rolling back on my heels and rising.

We squinted into a speck of blue sky on this overcast day: a sucker hole. Clouds form sucker holes to lure someone, usually a fisherman—that was how I learned it—to come outside. When the fisherman is sufficiently far from shelter to appease the clouds' sense of humor, they close ranks and dump torrents of rain on him. In my own interpretation, when a solid sheet of cloud opens to form a sucker hole, it's as if a big homogenous clump of people in this whole tightly knit human world makes a space to let you and your fox in—and after you accept . . . wham! The big homogenous world of people closes up, casts its forbidding face your way, turns gray, then black, and lets loose the deluge it was planning all along. Sucker! Fox and I enjoyed the sun for about ten minutes before pieces of clouds filled up the sucker hole. "You won," I said. "I am the chicken."

I conscripted the name *chicken* from a game of dare traditionally played with two cars driving directly at each other. Unless one of the drivers swerves, both drivers die in a head-on collision. The driver who prevents a crash by swerving earns the nickname *chicken*. Well, I didn't expect that either Fox or I would die if neither of us capitulated, but still, like the road game, we were playing a game of pride. I liked games, so Fox and I played chicken often. I never won. I would have liked to win, but I knew Fox and his forty-two sharp teeth well enough to understand that he would have liked it more.

Playing chicken forced us to face each other as equals. As a result, our relationship changed. When he'd suffered with mange, or when ranch dogs took a run at him, he seemed frail and needy, so I took charge and became caregiver. But after losing every round of chicken, I realized that we each had strengths and weaknesses. Because responsibilities attach to our strengths, we now had new responsibilities, too. Chasing dogs was still my job; I could intimidate dogs, who were, after all, boxed animals. I could not intimidate Fox. The game leveled the power in our relationship; I lost some, and he gained some. In losing some power, I gained some empathy. I think Fox noticed our power and responsibilities changing too. Playing chicken exposed my puny, flat teeth and general lack of agility, two traits that rendered me altogether incapable of killing a mouse.

So, he caught one for me.

Well, the kits were hunting for themselves by now, and he must have had an extra. In fact, the mouse he brought me looked like a creature he had cached and dug up, so he must have really pitied me. The earnestness with which he attempted to deliver a gift to someone too ignorant to realize its value charmed me. With the dead thing swinging from his mouth, he skipped forward. I tensed. Although I did not want a dead rodent dropped on my bare feet, I tried to stay cool. Among all traits, I most appreciate earnestness.

Sensing my discomfort, he cycled through a series of advancing and retreating moves: two steps forward, one step back. I reversed, pressing my bare heels against the front door. Throwing my arms up to the side, I grasped the doorframe with my fingertips, balancing on my damp toes and feeling like a wilting clematis on an espalier.

Keeping my face beyond reach of sharp and dirty claws I bent forward, pushed my open palms toward him, and said, "No." Not with an exclamation point, because he was standing closer to me than he had ever stood before. Stilling his bandy legs, he bemused himself watching me panic. I remained pressed against the door, my bare feet threatened by Fox in front and sharp-needled juniper on the sides.

Finally, his tiny reserve of patience and humility evaporated. He took his precious mouse away and would bring it to someone more discriminating than I was. He skulked off, stopping periodically to lay the mummy down, raise his head, and stare at me over his shoulder. *Last call! Come and get it!* He had never looked *back* at me before. My inexpressible guilt mushroomed as he padded away.

It wasn't my responsibility to keep Fox from getting his feelings hurt. But it was my responsibility to avoid hurting him. Right away, I started looking for an opportunity to correct my behavior. I figured I wouldn't need to wait long; after all, he wanted to kill mice and I wanted the mice around my cottage killed.

Three or four kits were playing in the woodpile on my delivery drive. I was watching through the bathroom window. Sometimes they scampered over the stacked logs for hours without any adults watching. Fox was upwind, hiding under a pungent sagebrush. When I went out to meet him, the odor of weasel urine overwhelmed me. Nothing on earth smells as bad. Fox's kits probably didn't realize. Their relatively undeveloped olfactory organs buffered the odor. Fox stood up, stretching his neck to get a better look at me, and I figured he needed something more exciting than weasel patrol to break up his day. Back in the garage, I found just the thing: a nervous mouse crawling sidelong against the cement wall.

A mouse in the garage is a mouse in your car. If the mouse is female, your car becomes a mobile maternity ward, a precursor to a population explosion and the end of your sanity. Within a month, mouse bellies are bulging through the upholstery above your head. I knew a woman who drove around for weeks listening to increasingly louder sounds of scratching and gnawing. When she felt one mouse tail too many flicking across her ankle, she jammed on the brakes, got out, and pushed her two-year-old sedan off a cliff.

While shooing the mouse with a broom, I noticed it was hobbled. It limped toward the bunchgrasses, and I scooped a quick ditch in its path. Fox watched the mouse flop into the hole and scratch in umpteen directions. But he didn't attempt to jump what should have been an easy target. I pushed the frantic mouse gently with the broom. Still, Fox didn't move. Pointing vigorously at the handicapped mouse, I called out to Fox, but he refused to budge on his policy of ignoring all my pointed-arm commands. Instead, he vanished.

I dropped a bucket over the three-legged mouse so I could "handle" it later. Everybody did that, and mostly for the same reasons: mice bite us, eat our food, and transmit Hantavirus, which can be fatal. Humans seem to have an instinctive aversion to having mice romping around inside their living space. In fact, civilizations from every continent have idolized foxes because they kill mice.

So, why didn't Fox jump that hobbled mouse?

I had forgotten one very important caveat: foxes *hunt* mice; they do not *attack* them. Hunting an animal is an art; attacking one is just bad manners.

I was a hunter myself; after watching Fox hunt for forty-five consecutive days, I missed playing with my bow and arrows. I found them tucked behind the sofa in the Rainbow Room.

I KNELT NEXT TO a pungent sagebrush to tie my camouflage pant—with full side ammunition pockets—around my boot tops. My legs looked like stubby branched aspen trees. Oak and maple leaves decorated my flannel shirt, which hung half a foot below my belt, so that, altogether, I had composed myself into a temperate deciduous forest, a mixed wood. After buttoning the collar and cuffs to prevent exposed skin from blowing my cover, I retrieved a packet of multicolored camouflage face cream from my bow case. A tube of doe urine rolled out. Tucking it back inside, I pulled out a cordovan armguard. When I'm hunting, the armguard fits snugly over my shirtsleeve, midway between my left wrist and elbow. My arm became a nurse log under an oak canopy forest.

Traditionally, archers carved their arrows from wood. The first archers in my valley carved arrows from bark peeled off old-growth juniper trees. Juniper bark has vertical striations, which lend themselves to strip removal that doesn't kill the donor tree. Ötzi the Iceman, discovered in the Italian-Austrian Alps more than five thousand years after his murderer let him bleed to death, died holding a quiver of arrows carved from *Viburnum lentago*. I wonder if he watched me planting the *Viburnum* in his honor, carefully tilling soil at the end of a row of sturdy Siberian and showy French lilacs. If so, I also hope he knows that I am constantly repairing the deer-fence that protects it.

Curling the fingers of my left hand around the cool metal riser—the midpoint of the bow's front—I extended my arm straight out, perpendicular to my body. My forehead was level with the top of the bow limb; my hips were even with the bottom. The bow, a Hoyt compound, looked meaner than my first bow, a green Bear recurve that Bob had given me (along with the comb) when I left Mount Rainier.

Arrows fit into bowstrings by means of a nock, a deeply grooved chunk of plastic that caps each arrow. When the arrow nocks into the bowstring, it rests lightly on a slim wire stand near the sights. The black metal trigger pull attached to my right palm clipped onto the bowstring, and I pointed my elbow straight back and pulled against thirty-seven pounds until the string skimmed my nose and the bow's pulley held some of the weight. Focusing on a straw bale target, I dimmed my peripheral vision and, holding my breath, released the trigger. The hardest part of pulling that string back and releasing is not holding still but staying quiet. You will want to grunt during the pull, sigh during the release, and howl after the strike. You need to swallow all that.

A golden line streaked twenty-five meters, puncturing a red circle. Bull's-eye. I could have pretended to be a horseman thundering across a steppe behind Genghis Khan; the great Chiricahua chief Cochise moving effortlessly past shadows of towering saguaro; an 1800s voyageur paddling on Lake Kabetogama watching a six-point whitetail buck dappling beneath leaves of big-tooth aspen. I could have imagined myself as any other great bowman. I didn't. When you are shooting a bow, the present moment is perfection: the pull of a single muscle, the silence of a held breath, the sting of the string on my left forearm.

Fletching, either feathers or vanes, encircles the ends of the arrow shaft and stabilizes flight. Ötzi the Iceman fletched his arrows with feathers. Or hired a village fletcher to do it for him. Fletching was an esteemed craft in his day, both in the Alps and throughout the English-speaking lands. If you know someone whose surname is Fletcher, his ancestors finished arrows for English nobility. Today you can stabilize your dart with plastic vanes in every imaginable color. Also in some colors I'm sure you would never imagine.

I fired arrows until smacks from the bowstring left a welt on my inner arm. Now I was just sore enough to be cocky. So I shook off the trigger pull, which was meant to cure a flinch I'd developed a few years earlier. After slipping on a black calfskin hand protector, I released an arrow into the bottom of the bale.

I yanked the arrows, tawny with multicolored vanes, out of the bale target and dropped them into the grass. The next arrow missed the bale target entirely. Camouflage shafts are convenient for hunting because deer can't see them, but they are inconvenient when you lose one—because you can't see them.

Squatting on my heels, I shuffled through tall dry grasses, searching for the arrow. The insulated Carhartt overalls I had changed into dragged their shredded hems behind me in long tails. While crawling on all fours, I looked northeast toward where the far range of snowcapped mountains should have been, and a mound of dry grasses waved through my entire field of vision. The same dry grasses prevented me from seeing the blue river gleaming through leafy cottonwoods. From the elevation of Fox's den, he and I shared nearly the same view, but what he could see from my cottage—unless he could hop up on a rock—was mostly just grass. For the first time I realized that all the times Fox and I had spent hiking and reading together, we were actors in the same play, but on different stages.

Inhaling too much dust and pollen, and barely escaping injuries to my eyes, I maneuvered between stiff bunches of grasses. Forward was not a guaranteed direction. The bunchgrass maze led to dead ends and forced me to back out. A wide, dusty bald spot provided a reprieve until I was jumped by a sagebrush lizard masquerading as a downed twig. Wingless grass seeds attacked me. Because they couldn't fly, the seeds had evolved coats with frills that clasped into hair and hide. Consider the corkscrew-tipped seeds of *Stipa richardsonii*, now twisting into my overalls. Meriwether Lewis called the *Stipas* "needle and thread" grass: thread-thin tails—up to four inches long—and needle-like tips. *Richardsonii* lined the bottoms of my moose-hide mukluks as tightly as if a professional cobbler had sewn them into place. Forgetting about my missing dart, I pictured Fox struggling to tunnel through the debris as he traveled from home to spring to mouse meadows.

A shrike—a gray bandit-faced bird the size of a robin—called from a wild rose that was growing out of the draw. Meat-eating shrikes were not uncommon here, but they didn't get close to the cottage because—unlike TBall—they were clever birds, much too clever to waste time trying to wangle food from me. Shrikes prepared their captured mice by crucifying them on wire fence barbs and leaving their corpses to lengthen into taut red leather. I think they dried their meat to preserve it the way Fox buried his carcasses. Until I saw Fox's trapline baited with eggshell-spiked coffee grounds, I had never known a predator more innovative than a shrike.

Fox was innovative, yes. But not innovative enough to figure out how to traverse a draw filled with tumbleweeds. Fox couldn't fly. And a hundred more such draws furrowed the valley. Hurricane-force winds delivered nature's detritus; steep-sided draws trapped it. Avoiding the draws wasn't a good option; in the open, foxes exposed themselves to trails scoured by predators. When I stared up at the mesa, my mind's eye saw an endless row of perched foxes looking down at their clogged avenues. Countless indignant foxes turned in synchrony and aimed their wizened mugs at me, as if to ask why I hadn't kept their trails clear.

That's how you realize that *Homo sapiens* are holding all the aces. Wind, more than anything else, did not suit Fox. He was jumpy in a ten-mile-per-hour breeze. A fifteen-mile-per-hour wind would rake the meadow, pitching tumbleweeds and jamming them into his den door. I'd seen twenty-five-mile-per-hour gusts curve his sausage-shaped body like a sail.

I hated the wind, too, but at least I could hide indoors. When one of our common-enough fifty-mile-per-hour windstorms hit with gusts exceeding seventy miles per hour, I would lie awake, feeling the cabin shake and listening to thunderous booms intermingling with painful moans and high-pitched screams. Cattle make similar noises during castration when steers bawl high and cows bellow low in response. Wind sometimes sounded like ten minutes of castration cries condensed into two minutes. Anonymous pounding periodically tracked along the roof and bounced down the leeward side. Objects hit the cottage with a thud and a bellow or knocked like hooves along the windward side, repeating at random intervals. My best guess was that cattle from the alfalfa fields, having gone airborne, were crashing into the house.

And my dart? I hoped to be buried with one of my arrows. After forty minutes of unsuccessful searching in the tumbleweed-packed draw, I realized I was not going to be buried with *that* one.

I tossed a bone-colored tumbleweed skeleton up and out of the draw. It was as intricate as coral and as wide as a grizzly bear's head. It flew from my fingers, soaring like a paper kite. Without waiting for it to land, I grabbed another, snapping it into so many small pieces that a fox trotting down the slough could crush it into clay. I kept grabbing and tossing until I could see bare ground. The list of services I provided for Fox now included slough cleaning, weed pulling, dog chasing, and buck bouncing.

And soon it would include shooing cats.

. . .

A FERAL CAT'S menacing shadow stretched toward the cottage. Cats are killing machines. They tear baby foxes from their dens and eat them alive. Okay. I only have proof that that happened once. But how many times do you need to watch a feral cat chase four tiny kits into their den? How long do you have to wait after the bloody cat emerges before accepting that nothing bigger than a beetle will be following it? How much do you owe the vixen who returns in the evening and finds that her babies have been reconstituted into cat shit? I hated feral cats. They ran riot on my property, jumping birds and pulling cottontails from their hiding places. One of them ate on my back steps, replacing the birds and rabbits with piles of offal. The whole area looked like an unlicensed abattoir. I could not bring myself to shoot the cat because it was just this side of pitiful. (And because, well . . . it was a *cat*.)

Fox perched far to the side of my front steps, facing the cat and cowering. It wasn't a big cat, but it competed with Fox for food—invertebrates, rodents, birds, and rabbits—and I expected that it understood, instinctively, that this land didn't have enough resources to allow both it and Fox to earn a decent living here.

Fox's ancestors may have made their way here thousands of years ago, following people of America's first nations as they trudged through melting walls of ice. But never once in all that time did they make the acquaintance of a single house cat. Pointy-shoed ladies carted cats to this continent from England. Cradled in the ladies' warm laps (or some other equally embarrassing conveyance), cats arrived only recently. According to my county's published history, our first non–Native American settlers, a few hundred gold miners who may have owned cats (or not), arrived in 1864. Because cats were relative newcomers, their prey—birds, lizards, and rabbits—may not have evolved avoidance strategies. Cats, I believe, enjoy a better living than honest predators have a right to expect.

Twisting toward me, the cat shadow extended its head. Then the cat cried out.

"Fox, make noise. Go on." Silence. Not even a breeze in the dry grass stalks.

I told Fox to hiss and spit. The cat hissed and spat. Fox alternated his gaze between me and the cat. I wanted him to chase the bully, stand up for himself, learn to fight, so he'd be ready when I wasn't around to protect him.

We waited for what seemed like forever, but Fox, clearly petrified, chose to exercise the better part of valor. The feral cat may have out-weighed him by a dozen pounds—it was hard to tell with its skin so ruched and the fox's so taut. "Yes, black is very slimming, Fox," I said too softly for him to hear. "Surely this is a very fat cat under all that black." Fox held his weak card close to his chest, by which I mean he withheld his breathy "qwah."

The cat was waiting for me to leave so it could jump him. In fact, it could easily kill him. One trait alone, the flat-face profile—the missing muzzle—that makes cats so apparently cute also gives them an unfair advantage. Biting down on a victim's neck, a cat exerts the full force of its skull, whereas a fox's long muzzle attenuates the force of its bite over a larger area. Power is equal to force divided by area. Cats have a more powerful bite because their force spreads over a smaller area. In a battle between that cat and Fox, Nature intended the cat to win. I did not. Slip-ping a matte green predator whistle between my lips, I blew one long shriek, the cry of an injured rabbit, meant to attract coyotes. The two predators scattered in opposite directions. I expected Fox to sulk for a while. Ten minutes later he was sniffing out voles in the front meadow. The cat didn't return.

And so, Fox added another tick to the tally of advantages he gained from our alliance: sunshine. I freed him from the confines of a nocturnal life. Instead of tucking into a dark, damp hole to hide from marauding dogs and feral cats until sunset, he romped through the pasture, harassing rodents and dazzling me with his acrobatics.

If you were to come by around 4:15 any summer afternoon, the sight of us might bring to mind a couple of middle school truants playing hooky. One is reading something completely irrelevant to any responsible line of work, and the other—who should be nocturnal—is sunbathing and massaging his belly on the warm, gravelly driveway. Fox and I, complicit in each other's monkey business, avoided our less enjoyable tasks—educating college students and young foxes—by playing chicken, reading nonsense, and sprawling in the sun.

But you didn't come by, or if you did, we hid.

Not always successfully. Marco Antonio (the dog-owner) popped over with his camera one morning. "Did you see it?" he asked as he skidded down the cobblestone hill separating me from the back trail, "that little white animal?" Marco's voice jarred me from deep reverie, and I muttered an acknowledgment, if not an answer.

Marco Antonio ignored my lack of enthusiasm. "There! There!" he shouted, pointing the camera with one hand and poking my shoulder with the other, "Coyote!" Out of the corner of my eye, I watched Fox making a getaway across the wet meadow, skipping through the wild rye.

Marco pointed again. Fox kept running until even a close-up lens couldn't distinguish him from a Daniel Boone hat. "Come back here," Marco Antonio pleaded, passing me the digital camera. The sun's glare completely obscured the screen.

"Great photo." I nodded exuberantly to add some authenticity to my lie. Meanwhile, Fox slowed to a walk.

"It keeps wanting away from me." Gazing at the disappearing fox, he called, "Stop!"

"Remember that night I called you about the dogs? They were running down that little white animal. Not that one specifically. Not that one at all. But one just like that." I handed back the camera.

"It will come back?" Marco Antonio looked down at the camera, leaned toward the fox, who was now a half mile away, and depressed the magic button. "I think this photo is much better."

In the LCD screen, there was a tiny smear where a fox should have been. "Yes. Much better."

Satisfied, Marco Antonio checked out my odd paraphernalia. A hand spade and a covered red Folgers coffee can rested against my boots. I had been collecting fecal samples.

"You are collecting. Something now special."

I nodded. The red Folgers can contained fox feces, deposition, time, and location known with approximate accuracy thanks to my Garmin wrist-GPS unit.

"It's a ball cactus to transplant to my garden."

Scat contains sloughed-off intestinal cells from which scientists can extract DNA. I was collecting fox shit to justify spending time with Fox, following up on suggestions made by the River Cabins students who knew I had interned on the Human Genome Project in Los Alamos while I was a doctoral candidate. Because I didn't have a lab, I planned to hand the fox scat over to someone who did. Finding takers would have been trivial relative to the work of collecting and labeling the scat. DNA lab monkeys always wanted more shit. On university campuses all over the United States, labs were extracting DNA from scat because no one in authority could say no to shiny new technology, profuse government funds, and cheap graduate student labor. If you thought of all the reasons why you might want to know someone's DNA, and their family's DNA, and their neighbors', and if you never stopped to think about the reasons why you did not *need* to know any of that, or about better ways to employ students and money, well then, you might just go ahead collecting shit and extracting DNA.

In the red Folgers coffee can, cable-shaped fox scat was waiting to have its DNA extracted so a laboratory could identify the number of foxes that shit around here and their paternity and other odd and esoteric facts. I didn't need to gather facts; I studied biology. Facts stuck to me like metal shards to a magnet whenever I was in their vicinity. Then I would try to find uses for the self-adhering facts.

Nothing could be more important than the fact that Fox ran from Marco. I knew then that he was not habituated to *people*, but to *me*. Why? Did he hang around me because I provided egg yolks? Protection? Because he sensed endless possibilities for mischief? Or was it possible to think we might be friends?

Nothing tumbling out of that Folgers can could answer those questions. I'd be better off spending my free time cleaning tumbleweeds out of sloughs like some kind of fox social worker.

LIME GREEN OAK leaves decorated the shaft of my bow, providing great camouflage until the day that deer would discover that oak doesn't grow here. I aimed the target-tipped arrow at a fist-sized pinecone tied to a juniper branch. I watched it fly past the cone and skim the tops of feathery bunchgrasses. I found it—blaze orange vanes encircling the nock and fluorescing with gaudy pride—waiting for me near a gopher mound hidden under salsify seed heads. Playing games is more fun when you don't lose the pieces.

Overhead, a soaring golden eagle, sister species to Mongolia's wedge-tailed eagle, reminded me that until the fox came out to play, I could be Genghis Khan. I raised an arrow to salute the eagle, and to being me. In the background far away, a Harley was publicizing its legally unique sound. The biker, gripping black leather gloves on handlebars, would be wearing a full-face helmet with UV shield; he would be fat, bald, and gripped in the arms of his passenger: a grandma with scraggly bleached blond hair and harsh blush worn too high. As the sound tailed down valley, I wondered who that biker was pretending to be.

MEADOWLARK

Fox had just caught a rabbit but dropped it as soon as he saw me dancing across the pasture in my cactus-crushing Wellies.

I had my eyes uphill, on the hound across the gravel road. Maybe it was on a leash or lazy or mired in quicksand—but that dog never moved from its one spot, a half mile away and an unimpeded line of sound and sight to my front door. I sang over Fox's head, Elvis's song about a hound who can't catch a rabbit. Fox pranced a horseshoe pattern back and forth in front of me. Ignoring Fox, I jumped right into the third iteration of my musical complaint, reminding the hound dog that he hadn't ever caught a rabbit and would never be a friend of mine.

Fox didn't like being ignored. He snatched up his rabbit, squeezing it in the middle and leaving it sagging from either side of his jaw. It looked like the toothpaste tube my fist had wrapped around that very morning. Bending down until my face was an arm's length from his, I placed a hand on each knee. Fox leaned in. "That rascal with the slobbery flews," I whispered, pulling the skin on either side of my mouth and shaking my head to imitate hound flews. "He'll never kill a rabbit."

Fox dropped his rabbit and said, "Qwah."

Standing up, I crooned about the dog whining all the time. It was a pitiful rabbit specimen, but I couldn't stop in the middle of the chorus. The sheriff picked up the abandoned dog a few days later.

We were not trophy hunters, Fox and I. But we gathered our share of mementos. The Boone and Crockett Club wasn't sending judges over to measure the four-by-four mule deer rack hanging above the sofa between photographs of a Grand Teton moose exiting a foggy pond and animal pictographs carved into sandstone. I shot that mule deer in the dawn following a full moon. The night before, I'd tromped four miles along a snow-packed ranch road listening to my footsteps, scouting for hoof prints, watching a bright orange dome fill the horizon in front of me. The entire horizon. Right to left. Nothing but moonrise. I could feel earth's round ball melded under my mukluks. Of course, a full moon seen along the horizon is the same size as every other moon. (So say physicists.) The size of the moon glowing before me was an illusion—*magic!* My mind playing a trick on me. Here's what I learned from that trick: when you are walking alone on the prairie, and unless you are a physicist, how the moon feels, looks, and acts is more important than its approximate size.

I sliced the buck from sternum to pelvis, yanking out the lungs with two bare hands. Pulling the legs, I tilted the 200-pound body. Cavity blood and wiggly, pungent guts spilled onto the snow. I set the heart aside. It had one neat hole—right through the middle. My beautiful rifle, my 06 had done that at two hundred meters offhand with snow covering every scraggly knee-high rabbitbrush on the mesa and a golden eagle passing overhead. I left the buck and headed toward the nearest gravel road. Ranch hands sledding up the mesa saw me and finished the gutting. I spent the night in a wallpapered room with a shag carpet and a chenille bedspread while my buck hung from its hind legs in their outbuilding.

I had bacon and black coffee for breakfast. My harvest—the buck and a doe from later in the day—barely fit into my forest-green Volvo sedan. Carrying a buck propped up in the passenger seat and a headless doe in the back, the Volvo sputtered down a gravel road to a mom-and-pop butchery.

Feather-shaped Lombardy poplars, too tall for their width, lined the drive to the house. Of all trees, I most distrust Lombardies. Pop was waiting outside in dark green coveralls. After throwing a padded cloth over the buck's head to protect the antlers, he hugged it under the front arms. Distracted by the naked and punky-barked trees and searching out an escape route should they succumb to their natural inclination and topple over, I ignored Pop's mutterings. By the time I got over to the buck, it was on a wheeled cart. Pop had his hand looped around one of the buck's legs and was tapping the hoof with a finger. He was pissed.

Right away, I realized the problem. My blood drained away. The buck should have had a carcass tag tied around its leg. It didn't. I pleaded. Pop sucked in his lips, holding up one hand to stop his son from opening the shop door. If he called a game warden, I would lose my hunting privileges and my beautiful .30-06 bolt-action. If he didn't call, and a warden raided the shop, he'd be out of business and worse.

Pop disappeared while I was tearing the car apart like a border guard stopping a van on the Canadian crossing. My head must have been under the front seat when the boy came out and grabbed the doe from the back. Mom, wearing a dress, came out with a tin, offering me a cookie.

Pop was in a better mood when I returned days later with coolers to pick up the meat. I never found the tag.

That's enough reason to mount a four-by-four on a suede pedestal and hang it on a wall the color of prairie rose.

When Fox scored his big trophy, I saved only two feathers. The first thing I recall about that day was watching him through my spotting scope. He was at the far edge of the alfalfa field, a good quarter mile away. Low cloud cover kept the sun from his eyes as he ran a beeline to my cottage without stopping to set down, nibble, or adjust his precious cargo. All the while, he was hustling at a speed that kept me from identifying his prize.

He stopped two meters away from me, a meadowlark's entwined legs dangling from his jaw. He dropped the lark. Walked right past it and sat as I turned to face him. No one likes a dramatic fox, but I had expected a little more animation for such a huge milestone. "It's a miracle," I told him. Then louder, with arms raised and fists clenched in the victory salute, "A *miracle*!" I repeated.

Fox was talented, but he could not fly. I hadn't thought he could take down a robin-sized bird. The spring bluebird carnage I had once accused him of perpetrating had turned out to be the work of kestrels, North America's smallest falcons. At one time, kestrels were hardworking, respectable raptors who earned their living killing insects and hunting BB birds. When the valley people lined the roadways with bluebird nest boxes, kestrels went on the dole. Now they eat subsidized bluebirds morning, noon, and night.

Tennis Ball and Torn Tail swooped in and began tearing at Fox's unguarded kill. The twiggy legs and curled knuckles of the abandoned lark reached skyward. I jumped into the fray when more magpies arrived. As is the case with all animals we dislike, there were too many of them. Thousands probably. The magpies swirled around me in tightening circles, leaving me in a vortex of yellow feathers. Fox ignored the pilfering magpies and my energetic attempts to scare them off.

The magpies retreated to the blue steel roof and lined out, hanging their long toes over the edge and tipping toward me. I brought out a refrigerated raw egg, nesting its white shell in a wreath of blue fescue. "For you," I said to Fox, backing away, maintaining eye contact, and trying to ignore the wretched, random cries of the roof-thumping magpies.

Snatching the egg in his teeth without breaking the shell, Fox disappeared into the vast rolling north meadow below Pillbox Hat Hill. He returned nearly to my doorstep a few minutes later.

Surrendering the lark's loose remains to TBall and Torn Tail, I nested another egg. Fox ran it back to the north meadow. The Egg Games had begun.

After he left for the day, I decided to take a couple of minutes and hunt up those two eggs. I suspected he was watching me search and understood that I had picked up the gauntlet. Thirty "couple minutes" later, I still hadn't located any evidence of an egg internment. Another twenty minutes and dusk prevented me from seeing cactuses underfoot. I headed home.

The next day, I left an egg under his forget-me-not. Running the egg through the spring seep while flushing red-winged blackbirds from the cattails, he disappeared in the hummocky meadow above my well. When he returned to my front pasture, I headed out to find it. Dry and rocky, the meadow couldn't support tall grasses, so tiny flowering plants—some not tall enough to shade a weasel—were flourishing in the sunshine. Taking in a panoramic view, I saw that the flowers' arrangement followed the paths of wind and water, and that the meadow's contours directed these paths. When I crouched down for a closer look, I saw that every bump and slope in the meadow, no matter how slight, steered the flow of water, creating distinct garden eddies, some no bigger than my hand. Wind influenced the shape and size of every plant growing in the eddies. Miniature ferns fashioned their own windbreaks by growing no taller than their windward-side neighbors. Lycopod, a moss-like plant with cylindrical branches, covered the ground like a net made of pipe cleaners. Phlox leaves spread out like shrubs, spiky, out of control, tall as toads. Squatting on leafless stems less than an inch high, walnut-sized blossoms of bitterroot had dried and faded into paper-thin bowls. Some of the dried blossoms, having blown off their stalks, were cartwheeling into rivulets too shallow to hide a robin. I picked up a bitterroot bowl and held it gently. When I pinched its central tubule, shiny black seeds spilled out, freckling a cutleaf daisy's white face.

If I hadn't lost every round of chicken, I might not have devoted so much time to searching for Fox's elusive eggs. But I was now determined to win the Egg Games. And if I hadn't kept playing the Egg Games, I would have missed the miniature world I was discovering by crawling around on all fours with my face snuffling in dirt. Losing could not have been more enlightening.

The next time he ran off with a game egg, I brought out the big guns: leatherette-barreled Bushnell binoculars, older than me and almost as wide. I decided to record his movements. Leaning on the window ledge with a pad and pen and watching Fox trot off with the egg, I wrote "SH FT JUNPR E Well > 45 DOWN" and included a diagram. *How hard could it be to find a freshly buried white egg in dark soil?* Tearing off the notepaper, I headed out to the SH FT JUNPR east of the well and turned downslope at forty-five degrees. It turned out to be the wrong short fat juniper. I would find that egg tomorrow.

🌱

Not one to waste a calm, clear day, the fox slipped under the skirt of a fir tree and dropped in on a party of cud-chewing does. Weak buck scent wafted above the resting animals. The buck had pissed and gone, and the cud-chewers turned out to be asleep, so he headed to the blue-roofed house to bust open an otherwise boring day.

He dug up a previously buried game egg and carried it uphill to a soft hummock. Hurricane Hands was watching as he placed the egg on the ground. She probably wasn't close enough to see it, but even so, kicking up dirt in high, wide arcs—high enough for Hurricane to see—seemed like a good idea. Picking up the egg, he ran off to bury it somewhere else, then headed down to the blaze vixen's hunting ground.

Fox territories operated according to rules. He obeyed those rules just well enough to stay alive—but no better. He was in good shape and well rested; why not trespass into the blaze's territory to toy with a mouse or two? The biggest fox in the valley, she didn't need any more food. Spreading his hind toes wide like a goose foot, he leapt up and sailed through the still air. He enjoyed a soft landing on a good mouse.

Round Belly strutted impatiently while he ate. The girl may have forgotten to put egg yolks out again. If he wanted, he could have worked his way into the dense, prickly juniper, all the way to the bole, stood on his hind toes, stretched his neck, and reached his nose to the bottom of the fat magpie's nest. The same branches had weighed her nest all his life. But he wouldn't mess with a companion's home. And besides, the river reeds still held plenty of duck eggs.

And for the small price of sucking in his stomach and wiggling through a scratchy shrub line, and between the rungs of a wooden fence, he could have chicken for dessert. The fenced area was huge, with horses sleeping on the far end. He headed to a chicken coop that was creaking in the wind, couched low, and waited for the giddy chickens to come strolling out. As the wait got longer, the horses woke, and soon their thick legs and shiny hooves blocked him in. The horses spotted him and whinnied, pounding the ground and filling the air with dust and the smell of manure. *Weasel pee!* The price of a chicken just shot up. One kick from a horse would keep a fox down for a long while. Maybe forever.

The best escape would be a dead run straight toward the sound of Round Belly's screeching. It worked. He ran to the one spot the horses weren't blocking and leapt between two rungs in the fence. Whether she was trying to help him, or whether it was serendipitous that she sat at the edge of a safe route, he couldn't know. But he was in danger and her call was familiar. He crossed the dirt road toward the blue-roofed house, where challenging winds sent him headlong into the sun with Round Belly following. The grass on the hillside was short, soft, and crisscrossed with vole runways. Whenever the breeze disappeared, he waited for his prey to scurry down its path before leaping as high as an overfed raven. And not a single hard landing. Round Belly rested on sagebrush and collected his leftover scraps. Older and weaker hunters didn't leave any scraps behind. They would eat guts if it spared them the energy of a single extra leap.

Several more games left me eggless, so I grabbed my compass and corrected the declination in order to reclaim the eggs. For the next game of hide-the-egg, I followed a transect for a quarter mile. Fox was waiting for me at the cottage when I returned without any eggs; in fact, he was standing in *my* spot on my portico, blocking the door, strutting like a sandhill crane powdered in pink clay. TBall paraded back and forth in front under Tonic, using tommy-gun chatter to warn Torn Tail that the mean girl was headed his way. I yelled at her to scoot. Did they think I'd put out more yolks if they harassed me enough?

"You win," I told Fox. I was crouching close enough to touch him but didn't. You don't just reach out and grab someone because you can or because he's smaller than you. That's one important difference between a pet and a friend. It distinguished Fox from the rubber boa, whom I didn't hesitate to pick up and move to the front steps, where it could discourage mice from drilling into my foundation. "You win," I repeated, and I turned my palms up empty-handed.

I became slyer. Sitting on the camp chair, salvaging buttons from dilapidated shirts, I pretended not to notice him heading north—always north—with the game egg. Still, I never found a missing egg. Two years later, while weeding in the south meadows, I found two of them, only meters away from TBall's nest. I wondered why they were so close to her, and why she hadn't stolen them.

Losing kept me humble. Playing kept me nimble. In *Wind, Sand and Stars*, Saint-Ex writes that during our young adulthood, our future is as malleable as soft clay. Our imaginations continue to shape our future until we grow up, slip into the mold society readies for us, and harden. Once we step out of the mold, our hard clay cannot soften or reshape itself again. In the process of growing up and allowing ourselves to become recruited into this adult-centric world, our imagination contracts.

Like most people, I was born with immunity to overzealous realism. When I was six and seven years old, I staged green army dolls in shrub jungles. Gunners jumped on cobblestones, looking for horny toads to ambush. When I dug my hole to China, a nervy turtle intruded. I double knotted my red Keds as quickly as possible, clamped one hand on each edge of the turtle's shell, and ran it back to the jungle camp. Army dolls dropped from the rubbery branches onto the turtle tank.

I started college. Gibbous-bellied professors with lips like duck beaks scuttled around a courtyard muttering nonsense. Someone's lacquered comb-over flew up into a panache; I felt I had entered the pages of a Dr. Seuss book. Sometime during graduate school, in the midst of all the memorizing and mimicking of facts and professors (respectively), my childhood immunity to overzealous realism wore off. When university ended, I climbed to a podium, shook a hand, answered to "Doctor," and walked away flush with rectifying truths: the jungle was a jade bush, the toads were horned lizards, and, since there wasn't any water anywhere nearby, the military tank must have been a tortoise, not a turtle. At that point, I had almost become what Saint-Ex calls "petit bourgeois," referring not to a shortage of cash but of creativity. Instead of choosing my own path, I stepped into a mold that society had designed for me. Fortunately, I stepped out before the clay hardened. If I hadn't, there would be no going back, because petit bourgeois, according to Saint-Ex, is a permanent affliction. Once you've succumbed to it,

FOX AND I

"nothing within you will ever awaken the sleeping musician, the poet, the astronomer."

Playing hide-the-egg and chicken with Fox awakened my imagination and attenuated my attitude about realism—the belief that only facts matter. Every game forced me to ask questions that have no answers: What is the extent of Fox's personality? What is the depth of our connection? Saint-Ex tells us that it's necessary to ask this type of question in order to be creative. While I am no longer immune to overzealous realism, I am wary of it, thanks to a booster shot from Fox.

As his role in my life expanded, keeping our relationship secret became impossible. When Jenna called, she would ask about the fox before discussing class evaluations.

"Well, I don't know that he's a friend, but I'm not studying him anymore."

"I didn't think that would work." Jenna knew before I did that Fox was my friend and that I could not both treat him as an object and empathize with him.

"I'm writing another textbook for school kids. Natural history. He's helping me write it. I'm using him for the anecdotes."

"Does he know this?" she asked.

"No big deal. I'm not putting him in every chapter. Just a few sentences at the beginning of some, or in material for little shaded boxes scattered about the book."

In other words, I needed to hang out with Fox to catch him in photogenic poses for textbook sidebars. That's what I told Jenna, anyway. The explanation summed up our relationship just fine, highlighting the fact that I was working on a project—a textbook—and not lollygagging with foxes all day. I built up my little alibi until I had quite a nice pile of . . . snow. Except that calling him Fox instead of "the fox" was too much salt in the snow—the fact that I addressed him at all. My alibi was melting away. I tried not to notice.

Copyeditors had just finished with my first book, a middle-school textbook called *Forestry: The Green World*. Chelsea House published it before the end of winter. The book included some first-person anecdotes but generally lacked creativity. Now I wanted to complete a biology-based natural history textbook for middle-school students, one that forced readers outdoors, where they would observe plants and animals with their own eyes. I had taught from dozens of college-level biology textbooks. All of them introduced students to natural history by keeping them inside memorizing facts and formulas about chemicals and molecules and energy. They could have been written by Victor Frankenstein's professors.

If you sat in the Rainbow Room—seven window shades dyed to represent a readily observable natural phenomenon—and thought about writing a textbook that explained natural history, would you start by analyzing molecules? Beginning Abraham Lincoln's biography by discussing his blood type would be equally logical. "Start small," an overused adage, does not mandate limiting yourself to physical smallness. "Small" means "simple." And things you see with a naked eye are simpler than invisible things. Besides, molecules are not big enough to be small. Molecules are minutia.

Minutia do not lend themselves to engaging sidebars.

When I was an undergraduate, I read an essay by Albert Szent-Györgyi, a whole-organism biologist, in which he warned against searching for life by dissecting it into increasingly smaller pieces. He made the mistake himself. Here's what he wrote in that essay: "This downward journey through the scale of dimensions had its irony, for in my search for the secret of life, I ended up with atoms and electrons which have no life at all. Somewhere along the line, life has run out through my fingers."

Szent-Györgyi, a Nobel Prize winner credited with discovering vitamin C, died while I was an undergraduate. A copy of that essay, xeroxed from my sophomore cell biology textbook, traveled with me for over twenty years, during which time I lived like a nomad without any home base or permanent storage unit. I did not want school kids to let life slip through their fingers. I wanted a textbook to open with big and simple images. And then I could parse. Or maybe just stay big.

Every minute I spent observing Fox (supposedly while collecting anecdotes and photographs) increased my admiration for his nonverbal communication skills. For example, I might find myself without his company because he wanted to move *toward an attraction*: a mouse or a mate was calling. Other times he left because he wanted to move *away from me*: for example, in becoming interested in observing one of the omnipresent red-tailed hawks, I had failed to entertain him sufficiently and his attention span had snapped. He could never compete with a diving red-tailed hawk; I'd seen Fox pick up hundreds of rodents but had only once watched a successful red-tailed hunt at close range. I was sitting on the ground when it happened; the hawk's kill sprayed me with robin feathers and created an addictive attachment to the thrill. Whatever his reasons, when Fox left, he signaled to me first, either scanning the ground or turning back and glaring. Yes, a mute fox communicated more effectively than I did. Actions and eyes; subtext without text.

Sometimes when we relaxed, the cinnamon vixen wailed from the den and Fox ignored her, hunkering down tight. But never for long. Many times, he stood poised between my back door and his den with rodent tails swaying from his jaws. Turning his head between the two destinations, he considered his options. Who doesn't face the same dilemma every day? Fox and I were always balancing duty and freedom. Sometimes, he pushed through the problem, choosing to meet his obligations and walking to the den as reluctantly as if mud had clumped up his paws. One evening he responded to the vixen's summons by padding off slowly to the end of my driveway, where he lay down and enjoyed a momentary relief from indenture until she called a second time and he charged uphill to the juniper glade.

Gestures, actions, and facial expressions may be less precise than the spoken word, but they are altogether a more reliable form of communication. Reading to Fox mattered because of pauses and eye contact. Our actions, not our words, built our trust in each other, and we based our relationship on shared activities, not dialogue. In fact, I was more relaxed communicating to Fox than I would have been with a person. Consider how difficult it is to communicate when our tongues send us in one direction and our feet take us in another.

SPOTTED FOXES

By mid-autumn, the fox had entwined his life so tightly around mine that my colleagues stopped separating into two distinct sentences their inquiries about my health and his.

"Fox is good," I'd answer. After exhaling loudly, I'd continue, "*And* I am okay too."

"How are you and the neighbor getting along?" Jenna would ask me, or if was Martha: "How are you and your friend doing?" I ignored the questionable epithets and replied that we were plugging vole holes, packing down gopher mounds, and keeping rabbits on the run. If it was a hot and calm October day, I would admit to nothing more energetic than soaking up sun like cold-blooded sagebrush lizards.

When my colleague Bea emailed from Florida State University wanting more information about Fox, I might reply:

"He wears his coat like a straight-tailed Pomeranian. Alert and thick."

"In quiet, dry snow he leaps often and dives deep. When the rain is loud or the snow thick as cement, he shelters under a juniper canopy."

"He suffers a large potbellied magpie who nests in my juniper tree with unnecessary politeness."

Bea knew about the egg yolks and asked whether they'd shined up his coat.

"Yes. He glows. I need sunglasses to look at him."

I continued disseminating eggshell-spiked coffee grounds to slow the downslope drift of my cottage in the unreliable clay soil. Fox continued baiting his trapline with the grounds. I bragged to Jenna about his new skill.

"Rein him in," she said.

Jenna was divorced and sophisticated by my standards. She was speedy smart because she supervised lots of people and couldn't waste time doling out wisdom willy-nilly. During the three years we had worked together, she advised me about teaching and about dealing with tricky people. I think her soft spot for me came from our shared history of loving and caring for wild land. The federal government had taken hers. "Eminent domain," the government says when they force you to sell them your land. When she lost her cabin in Montana's Bridger Mountains, she lost her marriage. Children hold some marriages together. When the children move on, the marriages disintegrate. Land tied Jenna's marriage together. Forest swaddled her and her husband; they hiked and skied and relaxed. Taking care of the land, bonding over common interests, they envisioned a future. With the cabin gone, the marriage desiccated and blew away. Losing her marriage reduced her income, and she eventually found a new job and relocated to a small city. Lacking ties to the land, her children scattered. Eventually she would leave the state to join her grandchildren.

"You can't let the neighbor run a trapline on your property."

But I could not make Fox, my "neighbor," give up trapping; it was one of his hobbies. Sure, he had other hobbies too: playing chicken and hide-the-egg, spying on me, trespassing. I agreed with Jenna that it seemed like "more than enough," without knowing the requisite number of hobbies due a fox. The rule of thumb, more nefariously known as a para-digm, implied that wild foxes, like other unboxed animals, fulfilled their biological obligations by eating, reproducing, and seeking shelter, and therefore could do without any hobbies at all.

LIFTING THE SHADE, I stared into the eyes of mule deer—looking surprised even after seeing me for the hundredth consecutive morning. They knew me, but with extra sets of eyelashes above and below their eyes and each set two inches long, muleys have a default facial expression that resembles surprise. A yearling buck on the doorstep, pressing his wet nose under soft fencing, was sucking berries off arching snowberry branches that the fencing was meant to protect. A meter away, a fawn was eating the skunk's orange rinds. Adult does gawked at me, some with pregnant bellies dropping into the snow, others with aging backbones poking through their hide.

When the sun was higher, I hiked uphill, shuffling forward through knee-high snow, pushing mukluks as if they were snowplows. Blowing up and aside like goose down, the snow landed on Fox, who was following behind, sniffing for partridge. Indian ricegrass seed heads with ice-coated grains swayed in the light breeze, looking like chandeliers.

A mule deer doe thought she might block my way (everyone knows uphill hikers have the right of way), so I challenged her to a game of chicken. With her twins and my fox watching, neither of us wanted to blink first. I won. Of course, in midwinter at six thousand feet on the forty-fifth parallel, deer blink just to keep their eyelashes from freezing together.

Never mind our peaceful trek, Tennis Ball and two juveniles appeared, landing sequentially in three separate firs. "Foxssss," I whispered, "we've been staked out."

Swooping into piles of snow that shimmered like fish scales, the mag-pies carved elegant scalloped patterns with their wings. I tried looking away, but even now I remember their jeweled shine and beveled tails. Admiring your enemies is a wearying task.

From where we stood, we couldn't see a single road or house. Despite the cold, I felt cozy and safe. I told Jenna that I was observing Fox and collecting anecdotes for my textbook. And when she said, "*Still?*" with her eyebrows rising through the phone line, I claimed to be extrapolating him into The Exemplary Wild Animal.

"That's what you do when you write a textbook, Jenna. Extrapolate. Shave off the outlier elements; mold a specific individual into a model of a generic individual."

To remind me that he was not an exemplary wild animal, or even an exemplary fox, she asked me about his trapline.

Then there was Martha. The first time I told her that a fox was dogging me around, she said, "Right. He's your friend."

He wasn't. I didn't know much about him then, except that he liked to play and win games and had a fast obsession with fat, scab-sucking houseflies. Martha should have been less concerned with his obsession and more worried about my knee's oozing new scab, the result of a slip and roll along a steep trail while I was jogging alone chasing the eagles up the cliff on the day I first met Fox. I could have died. Martha didn't ask how I got the scab. Instead, she pointed out that I'd never had a fox friend (or even a close friend) before, and that my knees, well . . . they were always scabby.

Martha and I had been park service coworkers and neighbors in Glacier Park, where I still owned five wooded acres near her farm. I'd bought the land from her years earlier: green paper cash down from my back pocket; a scrap-paper remit. No interest. A quitclaim deed when I paid it off. Her property ran along the Scenic Flathead River, which was capital *S* Scenic because of an Act of Congress. For seventy years, Martha had been living on her father's homestead along that Wild and Scenic River, with black bears in the apple trees, elk in the hay fields, and nine cords of firewood on the porch. Other than photos of beloved brothers who flew into WWII and didn't fly home, the house hadn't had a man in it in the fifty years since her father died. In those early days before I earned my Bachelor's Degree in zoology, I respected her knowledge about animals above anyone else's. After I finished my doctorate, my opinion of her hadn't changed.

Martha was enough older than me that I treated her with a deference that I think people reserve for their bosses rather than their friends. She knew something about me, and she wouldn't tell for another couple of years. Instead, and in the meanwhile, she said that the fox understood I was different from other people. We were rocking in upholstered wing-backs next to her wood stove that spring I met Fox. I unspooled stories about him while we looked out her bay windows for bald eagles hiding in the snow-topped pines. After pointing to the same eagle we'd been pointing to for fifteen years, she told me to stick with Fox. I listened to the stove burping and spitting, and she interpreted my long silence as ambivalence (which it was). She told me she knew Fox and I belonged together.

Only Martha knew about the times Fox pressed his paws against my window while standing on his hind legs. I was out front pruning caragana the first time. Deer had been browsing on them indiscriminately, and I needed to realign their height and spread so that all of them could enjoy sunshine. A swath of wheatgrass that was too high for Fox to see over blocked his view of me. In his stretched-up position, he looked thin and pitiful, and, I thought, he must have been lonely. I'm sure he was looking for me. I watched him move to a second window. I didn't want to startle him, so I wandered around, picking up interesting rocks and knocking them to make a slight noise. He turned from the window, saw me, and started mousing. That was one of the things I enjoyed most about Fox: being together, while doing separate things.

When I visited Martha at the beginning of my second summer with Fox, she told me he wanted company. I'd been living by myself for what seemed like forever and wondered, aloud, why I never felt alone. If Martha knew, she kept it to herself. Instead, she asked about Fox's little ones.

"Not a single kit made it through the winter. They were tiny. I mistook them for weasels when they were a month old."

"Foxes are small."

"Baby weasels."

"I think that might be what fox kits look like."

"Kits from the alfalfa field den have meaty limbs. They swagger around like young wolverines."

The kits at Fox's den the following year would also end up looking and acting weaselly. They would be wild and squirmy animals. Jittery, out of control, flexible, and fast.

Regardless of the number of degrees *below* zero, Fox bustled around on the dry, calm, sunny days of winter. Wearing every hair perpendicular to his hide, he looked like a giant salsify seed head. When winter wind blew boxcars off the railroad tracks at the foot of the valley, Fox hunkered down, keeping himself dry and leeward in the powder-snow basins above his den. Winter sun melted the snow, packing it down until it was hard and slick as ice. Although foxes belong to the dog family, their bones are less dense and weigh less than dog bones of the same size. Fox's chevron-decorated footpads left a slight depression in the hardpack, too shallow to keep him from skittering out of control when the wind blew. Ballasted with heavy bones, a big belly, and twenty pounds to Fox's six, the feral cat and its unadorned pads tracked straight across the icy snow.

Neither Fox nor I was crazy enough to enjoy sitting still on frigid days, so we ixnayed our reading rendezvous until early March. Instead, if snow had fallen overnight, I was out early checking on tracks. Fox often walked in an elegant straight line, each foot directly in front of, or behind, another. I do something similar when performing the classic kick turn for cross-country skiers. I swing the toe of my right ski up, point it skyward, turn to my right while balancing on the left ski, plant the right ski about

180 degrees to the right, and lay it as near as possible into its own inden-tation. The left ski is then pointing forward, and the right ski is pointing as nearly backward as my ligaments permit. Then I swing the left ski up and around to the right and make a fresh track. Reusing my original two tracks allows me to change direction without further scarring the snow. I don't like messing up the snow and leaving a big oafish sign of my pres-ence. My deep tracks can freeze into an extra mountain for a field mouse to climb, a ridge for an ermine to scale, one extra ditch waiting to turn the ankle of a running deer. I try to be courteous. The tracks we trouble to leave behind tell a story about our character.

In the midday sun you could find me shoveling snow. Monotonous lifting and pushing kept me warm and calm. Of course, by clearing the driveway, I forfeited the chance to show off my Mazda's *let's see what this baby can do* muscle and claim whatever miniscule right to bravado a two-door hatchback might be entitled. Truckers heading down from the mountain—late-season hunters, lion chasers, forest rangers—stared while raising the palms-up signal. *Hey, what? Buy a truck.* Yes, I knew about trucks and snow. Not that long ago, in my twenties and still willing to ride shotgun, my park service friend and I would drive his pickup over oil-slick mud or into cement-like snow with the rear-end fishtailing and the road going one way and the truck going another. From behind the wheel he would say, "Let's see what this baby can do!" We would swerve and swivel, and the mud or the snow filled the hubcaps until we were completely embalmed and stopped dead. I would open the door, jumping out six miles from the nearest anything, and he would say, "Justabout made it." Then he got on the repeater and we would walk out to wherever his friend could meet us.

I am too optimistic to drive a truck. And I haven't ridden shotgun more than a handful of times since.

Besides, a packed driveway freed the wildlife from having to posthole; mule deer pronked higher and skunks hustled faster. Voles scuttled across the dense snow leaving neat, circular dive holes like the tracks of sand crabs on a beach. Refusing to hibernate, voles spent early winter building grassy nests and stuffing them between the root toes of my lilacs. Like all rodents, voles' iron-laden incisors grew constantly. Iron gave their teeth an orange tint, while their perpetually growing teeth gave them a bad habit. They gnawed. They attacked any tree in their sights, sinking those teeth through the bark and into the tree's living tissue. Gnawing this way and that and tilting their jaws, the creatures tested different angles, like apple bobbers at a Halloween party. As the snow piled higher, voles shimmied up trunks, carving trees into totem poles. Lilacs and cherries have thin barks. When a vole eats through the bark, clipping the vein at the soil line, the link from roots to leaves breaks. The flow of nutrients stops, and the tree dies a slow, cold, and invisible death. Meanwhile, voles stayed warm by hiding underneath blankets of snow. I tried to keep the snow blankets away from trees and shrubs to discourage voles from moving in.

In settled snow, I followed tracks to figure out who was moving into the culvert (cottontails) and who was living under the outbuilding (skunks). The culvert extruded on either side of the narrow driveway. I kept digging it out of the snow so Delbert, our UPS driver, wouldn't catch a tire edge. Snow-clogged culverts could also flood a delivery pad that I had constructed near the driveway's end after observing, too many times, Delbert's worried face as he reversed a couple hundred meters back to the gravel road.

Snow drifts pushed against the galvanized welded wire fencing until it popped off the steel T-posts. Aluminum fence posts gripped the wire better than steel did, but heavy drifts bent aluminum posts. Hammering with a rubber mallet usually set them upright again. I also repaired shrub limbs after every big storm. When a large branch ripped under the snow's weight, I cleaved it off and covered the wound with pruning paint. When a small branch ripped, I slung it up with a tongue torn from an old running shoe. When temperatures approached forty degrees, I watered the spruce and re-sprayed anti-desiccant to prevent wind burn and hauled dirt to pack into newly appearing driveway ruts.

In graduate school, I had a car but no land. I changed the car's oil myself. Discovering this, a professor pulled me aside and explained that manual labor was not my bailiwick. Budding scientists do not change oil. They hire people to do it for them. Mortified and out of my element, wearing camouflage to his suit jacket, I succumbed to his conceit, bringing the car to "be serviced," as people unfamiliar with animal husbandry like to say. Until then, I had never paid for an oil change. But I hadn't had a bailiwick before either, and it seemed like a fair trade. Until I noticed my head bleeding from self-inflicted sores. Sometimes I wore liner gloves indoors to protect my head if I scratched. Somehow, I would pull them off, and thin, pale blood would wet my fingers.

People were anxious in graduate school, and not just students. The habits and habitat of modern life are simply not evolutionarily stable. Metal and plastic. Electric lights blotting out stars. Ten-story buildings blocking sun and moon. Cars honking and everything else ringing, beeping, and buzzing until we can't even hear aspen leaves quaking. Think about all the changes that our species has experienced in the last several thousand years. Too many. Too fast.

A person would be crazy if she weren't anxious. Maybe I was the only one in that university town with blood-dampened hair, but I was not the only one with anxiety caused by modern habits and habitats that were not evolutionarily stable. Take an auditorium filled with university professors and doctoral students and pull them outside in groups: the ones addicted to food, tobacco, diet pills, alcohol, marijuana, sex, hard stuff, antidepressants, antipsychotics; the ones who couldn't stop pulling their hair, or picking their face, or cutting their arms. The perpetual psychiatrist appointments, the suicide attempts, the television binges. Maybe I wasn't any better than they were, but I wasn't any worse.

Compared to humans, the natural habits of foxes have been relatively stable for tens of thousands of years. While they've been running and hunting rodents and digging dens, we've been bicycling, motoring, and jetting; eating raw, cooked, and processed foods—foods that last century's citizens couldn't pronounce. We've gone from strolling around naked to wearing Gore-Tex. And there seem to be as many career and lifestyle choices as there are people, while foxes all make their living in pretty much the same way and they haven't changed their diet in a thousand generations. No wonder why he was a calm little animal (when the wind wasn't gale force). Hanging around Fox became my way of relaxing. What can you *do* with a fox? Play. Stretch in the sunshine. Walk in the moonlight. Sit around reading fun books. My scalp stopped bleeding.

On windy days, when white caps rolled in my toilet, I did not expect him and he didn't come. He stayed in his high basin, jumping mice and voles. Still, I continued my habit of using classroom breaks to wander from window to window, anticipating his arrival. Internet classes and discussions with students energized me almost as much as Fox did. An upper-division ecology student wrote about feeding food scraps to a red fox who frequented his Alaskan military base. He was a young soldier then. Now he was a sophisticated college student. Some of our class reading material had instigated guilt about the fox feeding and he was writing to confess. The guilt didn't come from one of my lectures but from researching the issue online for an essay assignment. The student did not cite any specific research, but at that time, you simply had to be an alert participant in American culture to absorb the paradigm. Feeding unboxed animals had fallen out of favor. I didn't know why, and I didn't know enough about his army base to pass judgment. But I did love my students. And how much easier to love a student who took a minute's break from serving his country to pass leftover MRE to a fox?

Nowadays few believe that foxes on Alaskan military bases should eat leftover food. One reason is that it is not natural (at least not as natural as throwing the food into a steel dumpster). In the twenty-first century, everyone wants everything to be natural—with a few exceptions: medicine, transportation, energy, communication, televisions, wrinkles, cell phones, bad eyes, weak hearts, worn knees, small boobs, old hips, indoor temperature. The more we humans pamper ourselves with manmade toys and tools, dressing in polypropylene, Gore-Tex, and nylon fleece and availing ourselves of dentures, braces, statins, vaccines, diet pills, hearing aids, and pacemakers for everyone over the age of seventy-five, the more we demand that unboxed animals stay natural. Like a seesaw with humans on one side of the fulcrum and wildlife on the other, we sink further from a natural life and force wildlife closer to it. Our pursuit of the natural life is as vigorous as it is vicarious.

I wrote back to the student veteran telling him not to worry. "People have been feeding foxes for thousands of years." With tongue in cheek, and because he wrote great essays, I added, "Why do you think foxes are so cute?"

Needing a sidebar anecdote for the textbook I was writing, I pulled my tongue out of my cheek and developed a hypothetical example of Darwin's theory of natural selection. I speculated that foxes wanted protection from bigger animals like wolves, coyotes, cougars, and bobcats. Currying favor with humans could earn that protection. But how to curry favor? Their small size prevented them from offering either protection or portage. They lacked the humility necessary to find useful employment as service animals. Foxes didn't fetch. Do you think they would mindlessly trail sheep around? They would die of boredom.

Cuteness—and their ability to catch mice—may have been their main stock in trade. Perhaps those foxes whose compelling appearance allowed them to ingratiate themselves with people ate better, stayed safer, lived longer. Of course, it was a two-way street. Animals that wanted food and protection needed to change their attitudes toward people. Neither aggression nor coyness would endear them. Using their cuteness as their collateral, the tamest foxes exchanged wildness and solitude for companionship, food, and protection. Eating better and living longer would allow them to produce more offspring. In other words—in Darwin's words—the animals who carried the traits for tameness would experience higher *fitness*. Therefore, members of future generations would inherit the traits for tameness. The cute, tame foxes would become more common than the plainer, wilder foxes.

Coy and skittish, foxes don't often bump into people. If they encounter someone, they might snarl or flee. Most people act the same around wild foxes. As Dr. Belyaev discovered, some small percentage of foxes are genetically predisposed to seek out human companions. I think Fox was one such animal. If a small percentage of foxes seek companionship with people, isn't it likely that a small percentage of people are genetically predisposed to seek out fox companions?

Of course, a predisposition may never reveal itself. We all have genes that allow us to do things that we'll never actually do. For example, genes for intelligence or creativity or athleticism may be of limited use to people who don't have access to basic needs for survival like food, water, and shelter. They wait, these unused genes, packed into our soft, rounded nuclei, tensed and ready to spring, activated only by luck and circumstance.

Chatting about foxes with the Alaskan veteran broke the ice. I began talking to other students about foxes. Red foxes, like people and magpies, live all over the world. My Japanese students, especially fond of foxes, taught me how to say *kitsune*, which is Japanese for *fox*. Listening to stories about thousand-year-old Shinto temples and fox-worshipping monks, I felt my world becoming cozier. Online students shared their stories about wild foxes they'd met as children or young adults, in Maine and Indiana, in villages and vacation cabins; foxes their parents told them to run from. Their interest in the relationship between people and foxes led me to write a sidebar story for my textbook-in-progress, a story that might help them understand natural selection.

❧

A man carries a basket of trout into a stone-cold cave with soot-covered walls. His wife is inside breaking pine branches and tossing them into a mud-walled fire pit when she stops and pulls a branch aside. Two bright pink balls as large as human eyes swell from between strips of the branch's gray bark. Soft and solid, wolf-milk slime is too beautiful to burn. She sets her decorative branch across a flattop rock that holds baskets of drying sorrel.

The man's family sleeps on woven grass mats suspended from wooden beams by braided strips of elk hide. One night a field mouse runs along a ridge in the cave wall, slides down the leather cord, and jumps onto the sleeping woman's head. The mouse collects brown hairs for its nest and leaves sooty footprints across the woman's forehead. More hairs are collected the following night when the mouse returns with its friends and family.

Except for finding the wolf-milk slime, these events are not unusual. At first dozens, and then hundreds, of sooty-walled caves dot the subalpine meadows and harbor warm, long-haired people and cold, pregnant mice.

A white fox vixen with black spots on her midsection paces in front of a nearby hemlock grove. In the hanging valley above her, a lake cupped in white granite tips its outflow into a creek that runs past the grove. The spotted vixen inclines her head to her breast and watches her kits and cousins playing along the creek—black, gray, blond, yellow, blaze, tawny, white—fast foxes leapfrogging over pokey ones. The white foxes, like winter weasels, have black markings.

Meanwhile, in the cave, there is more human hair cradling newborn mice than there is sprouting from human heads. The mice are warm. And people, who were relatively hairless to begin with, are now more hairless. And that is not as inconsequential as it seems. People, even hunter-gatherers, adore their hair.

One day the grove's spotted vixen happens by a cave and hears mice laughing and cave walls howling. People are throwing rocks at mice. (And missing.) She trots to the edge of the cave, presses herself against cold stone, and pounces on the giddy mice tumbling out.

People soon realize that foxes kill mice, so they lure the creatures into their caves by offering them food and protection. By and by, many foxes sleep in many caves, sharing views of sunsets and sunrises and stars with people. And the people are once again, if not hirsute, at least as hairy as Nature intended them to be.

Many generations later, most foxes sleeping near humans are black and white. The other color phases appear on foxes who are too aggressive or too shy to sleep in caves with people. The human population grows, expanding into new territory. The fox population follows the expansion, relaxing onto trees in the little groves surrounding the people's huts. The foxes sleep on the lower branches, and the young soft boughs bend like hammocks.

Eventually, people build sturdier houses, sprinkling strychnine in the corners and setting mouse traps behind refrigerators. They have fewer reasons to protect foxes, and one important reason to kill them: fur coats. Spotted foxes disappear first because they are tamest and therefore easiest to bait and trap. Many more generations later, no one will remember ever having seen or heard about wild spotted foxes.

At least one forest still has hammock boughs. Running alongside the forest is a gorge lined with ash-colored pinnacles, narrow enough that a keen-eyed animal can look across to another forest, but so deep that only birds flying in the gorge can see the bottom. A scientist, panting and dusty, emerges from behind a pinnacle, carrying a metal box with long antennae; numbers flashing on a screen beep and change value with his each step. He faces a ghost forest of standing dead trees whose lower branches are gently bent, hammock-like, their surfaces shiny as if polished from wear. The scientist takes out a notebook and writes that burls, a physiological response to a bacterial infection, have distorted the boughs and caused the branches to bend. In the field research cabin, he takes out his lighter to start a fire in the fireplace. As he builds up the fire, he puts one piece of wood aside. A bright-pink ball, wolf-milk slime, swells from a flaky barked branch. The branch is too punky to burn. He goes outside and tosses the worthless piece of wood into the gorge.

Deep in the forest, too far for anyone to see, one inky fox kit scratches his back against a hammocked branch, crosses his legs, laughs, and sets all the kits in the forest laughing. The scientist hears the noise. Wind. He records some important numbers in his notebook. He will not let his mind play tricks on him.

This is unfortunate. Among all skills possessed by the human mind, performing tricks is the most important.

ELK AND BADGERS

Late April. I dragged storage bins out of the shed, swapping—till mid-September—heavy winter clothes like double-layered wool balaclavas, bibbed ski pants, goose-down mittens, and lined gaiters for light winter clothes like lined canvas overalls, wool ball caps, chopper mitts, and unlined gaiters. I could have pretended that four distinct seasons visited me, but living and dressing for two seasons—like the fox—was simpler.

You might think people would seek out gentler landscapes, places tucked into cozy climates. White sand beaches sprayed between blue water and artistically arranged greenery come to mind. Saint-Ex didn't agree. He'd spent enough time in deserts to figure out that "men attach themselves more stubbornly to barren lands than to any other."

In graduate school, I worked with DNA, a molecule that's shaped somewhat like a ladder. I inserted dye molecules between the rungs to make it easier to see. This procedure is called *intercalating*. The dye doesn't fit well. Edges bulge out, and gaps form between DNA and dye. In comforting habitats, humans can enmesh themselves, snuggle in, and fit securely. But in harsh climates all we can do is intercalate. The stress of this imperfect fit keeps our adrenaline surging. Saint-Ex and his fellow pilots scoped out some of the most popular—and populated—habitats on earth, and yet in the world's harshest places they found "joy that [they] could not possibly know elsewhere." Joy, I'm pretty sure, is an emotion primed by adrenaline.

The desert-like land Fox and I inhabited amassed only ten inches of precipitation each year and was prone to vicious windstorms. Cold and elevated, though not nearly as dry as a true cold desert like the Gobi, our semi-desert frosted over at least once a day from early September through mid-May. Quite a bit of snow fell, but most of it was too dry to ease a dogged drought. You might wring only one inch of water from fifty inches of our driest snow. Wind tossed the dry snow, rearranging it in reckless patterns and leaving behind parched frozen dirt, icy shelves, and waist-high drifts. Clay soil with an embarrassingly high pH hid underneath the snow. Because water couldn't percolate through wet clay or soak into dry clay, plant and tree roots were either desiccating or drowning. Very few plants grew in our alkaline clay, and almost none that did enjoyed themselves.

Before I met the fox, I was planning my escape. Everything I've never had—a home, a credit card, an age- and gender-appropriate job—was waving at me from some imagined city. The cottage was meant to be a way station, somewhere to wait while I tugged on society's skirt and hoisted myself from the wilderness to the real world. I still slept inside a sleeping bag, and like my backcountry cabins, the cottage was small. If I removed all the furniture and shut every door, six Ve24 tents could squeeze inside: four in the Rainbow Room and two below.

After repacking clothes, I sorted old documents into storage bins, dropping university contracts, pay stubs, bills, and anything with my social security number into a bleach bath. Another day, I trekked fifteen miles round trip to offload the incriminating papier-mâché in "green boxes"—our valley's euphemism for "dump site"—because I didn't know that thieves wouldn't steal the identity of one of the few adults in America who didn't own a credit or a debit card.

Behind the cottage, wheat grass was doing what it usually did on windy days: surging up the north hills like waves in a shallow sea. Pointing my face sunward and closing my eyes, I waited, but not a fine hair stirred. The waves of grass rippled, turning into sheets of elk. Scores of shaggy brown necks undulated against the blue sky. The elk herd would be winter-stressed and include tired, pregnant cows. Unless something was chasing them, elk in that condition were no more likely than an ocean to flow three hundred feet uphill. I listened for dogs barking or baying, checked the sky for eagles. Nothing. The silence suggested mountain lion.

Mountain lion?

Big cats were too pragmatic to waste energy running hundreds of shaggy beasts uphill. In fact, I couldn't imagine any wild animal frivolous enough to be droving elk.

He poked his tail up.

"Fox?"

One fox surrounded by a hundred Rocky Mountain elk, each adult outweighing him by a quarter ton.

"Are you insane?" I said in a normal speaking voice, which to Fox, I imagined, sounded quite loud. "Do you know what an elk weighs?" (I used rhetorical questions because Fox couldn't reply.)

About a dozen strides brought him within two meters of me, and he stopped.

"Qwah."

He had heard me speak on at least 380 separate days, usually for extended periods during our simulated conversations, and today, with a curtain of elk legs separating us, *he recognized my voice for the first time*. I picked up a white egg-shaped rock, sat on the back steps, and let our milestone moment sink in: *he was now on the very short list of individuals who recognized my voice.*

I had known for a long while that Fox recognized my appearance; he came around whenever I walked down the driveway or through the north meadow when I made myself large and conspicuous by waving my arms overhead. He wasn't just coming toward someone he recognized as a person. On five occasions he ran away from people crossing my property, including Marco, four of them my size, three of them females, and none of them me. Because Fox made it his business to investigate all the goings-on in his territory, anytime I suspected he was nearby, I made a little commotion by tapping a brownie-sized rock on the wooden front steps and, if he was close enough to hear, he came around. I had always thought I was tricking him. Now that I'm shedding more of my biases about his cognitive ability, I'm thinking that he was coming over for a round of hide-the-egg.

He twisted his torso and gazed up at the previously bald hill now sporting a thick crew cut of brown, upright elk necks. Long elk faces turned in unison and gawked at us. A year had passed since I started reading with Fox; he had become braver without getting any bigger. He used to be frightened by a single mule deer buck, and now he was driving elk. Maybe friendship had emboldened him. I wondered if that was what friendship was supposed to do.

A rust-colored eastern cottontail bobbed up the slope's natural terrace eating soft, feathery grasses, days old. If the enormous rabbit could slip by the feral cat, it could work its way from these north-facing meadows— which would never be fully green—onto vaguely less-brown pastures across the gravel road.

Fox was rubbing his neck through a stand of photogenic wild rye. Braided seed heads darted a couple of feet over his head, creating the perfect picture for a textbook photo. Instead of running for the camera, I waited. All the other photos of Fox had assimilated themselves into my life as though he were family: a leather-bound folder with two photos stood open on the bookshelf, magnetized frames attached Fox's image to the fridge and heater, and two fourteen-by-sixteen-inch wood-framed matte prints hung above the cedar chest in the prairie rose room. Stealing shots for a textbook now felt unnatural. Would you take someone's photo without asking permission? Would you do it if that someone were a friend? In the year that had passed since I'd started reading with Fox, I had become more sensitive without getting more sentimental.

And the photo's caption (there would have to be a caption), what would it say? "Here is *Fox*?" Posing for photographers was never Fox's plan, and foxes, by nature, were planners. That's why a Scottish poet likened man's ability to lay plans with that of mice and not foxes, and that's why the same poet noted that *our* "best laid schemes" (and not those of foxes) sometimes go astray. Using Fox for sidebar photos gave me an alibi for spending time with him every day. It was the one part of my life that was going according to plan. Of course, a bad plan realized is worse luck than a good plan foiled. Now I needed another pretty photo, which would be easy to find, and a new alibi, which would not.

Cascading rocks alerted us to a small band of mule deer lined out and climbing west along craggy cliffs. The cottontail receded into rabbit-brush. Fox followed. I envied his ease of life. Not that he had an *easier* life. Just that he eased into his life. He didn't spend much time alone. He collected all sorts of companions, most notably the magpie Tennis Ball. He also spent time with Torn Tail, the kits, the vixen, and an older male fox. And he had hobbies. Maybe some combination of physiology and genetics had led him to develop them. Maybe not, but, when I met him, he enjoyed more hobbies than I did. I spent more time working for, and worrying about, food and shelter than he did. Instead of hobbies, my free time belonged to unfinished applications for "real jobs" that I didn't want to pursue, located in places where I didn't want to live. My hobby had been worrying. I worried about what I wanted to be now that I was a grownup.

I worried about where to make a real home now that I had overstayed the acceptable amount of time that one should domicile a "way station." The more time I spent watching Fox, the less I worried. As long as he lived here, I wasn't going to move away.

I headed down to a scattered series of boulders and a motley arrangement of holes to see if the old badger had sprung any little ones out this year. Last spring, one young badger had pushed his fluffy head out of the den hole and rumbled like an erupting volcano. Its tiny body would have fit inside my hand, but the clever little animal, a member of the weasel family, didn't reveal any more than the head. I suppose anyone who didn't know that a young badger's body was just a ball of fluff would judge the creature, according to its enormous ears, wing nut-shaped head, and ground-shaking roar, to be an underground troll. But if you knew it was harmless, you would instead notice that its navy-blue eyes were too big for its face, and its smile turned down like that of a sad old man. Despite the droll face, and their friendly demeanor, most everybody chooses to live where oversize weasels are not carving dusty holes the length of size-nine shoes into their lawn. Those of us who have barnacled ourselves to inhospitable places may be trying to avoid people not because we do not like people, but because we love the things that people destroyed. Wild things. Horizons. Trolls.

Joseph Wolf's 1856 painting *Gyrfalcons Striking a Kite* shows a pair of tame, tethered gyrfalcons ravaging a wild red kite. Wolf's gyrfalcons look mean and angry as one grasps the nape of the kite's neck and the other tears into its shoulder. While I studied the painting, one of my favorites, I concluded that, Joseph Wolf, like his friend Charles Darwin, had understood the animosity between wild and domestic animals and was rooting for the wild ones. I wish he were alive today so he could paint domesticated cats in the act of brutalizing wild birds and foxes.

Staring at Wolf's painting at the National Museum of Wildlife Art in Jackson, Wyoming, I felt the kite's pain so keenly, I shivered. I wanted to free it, but after listening to the painting for a while, I realized that Wolf had portrayed it beyond pleading; the kite was dying with its mouth open in a death cry. Standing with my toes on the silver band of duct tape two feet from the canvas and looking at a kite with a face as big as mine, I saw that it wasn't looking at its feathered murderers. It was looking at me and anyone else who might never see a wild kite, but who instead would grow up in a world dominated by humans and their pets. *What have you done?* the kite cries to us.

Perhaps a caged gyrfalcon is as valuable as a free-living falcon, but they *act* differently. Caged animals, unlike wild animals, benefit from our human-centric world and are cowed by us.

I realized that what mattered most to me was not what something *was*, but its behavior: how it lived and what it did.

I shared my revelation with Fox a few days later.

"You know what I'm going to be now that I'm grown up? A verb."

A verb?

"Well, a verb, an adverb. Adjectives are allowed too."

I had been trying to define myself with a noun, a title that identified an occupation, while I should have been relying on verbs. Entitling nouns deceived people. Maybe on purpose. I would rather someone tell me that *he sings* than that *he is a singer*. The latter phrase is trying to nudge me someplace I may not want to go. *He hunts* is a specific phrase, weighted with responsibility; *he is a hunter* implies more than it guarantees. To say, "I teach and guide students" seemed more honest than saying, "I'm a professor." I didn't need to *be*: I needed to *do*. So I began to choose some verbs: write, teach, explore the relationship between people and wild animals. Tend a property.

How often in life do we discover that the source of all our worries is simply a poor grammatical choice?

If Fox could talk, he'd say, *What took you so long?*

"Well, I . . ."

Oh, you're not there yet. If you want to be a wild animal and live the good life, you have two things to figure out.

"What I want to do . . . and . . ."

Habit. And Habitat. Two things.

From the Latin *habitus*, meaning "character," *habit* refers to how we act and what we do. From the Latin *habitare*, meaning "to inhabit," *habitat* refers to where we live. These two variables, which describe our character and our home, apply to every living thing. I should have remembered. When I preserved specimens for herbarium collections at Voyageurs National Park, I recorded both those variables for each pressed plant. Somehow, I had forgotten, mistakenly thinking that I was supposed to choose a profession, label myself with an entitling noun, and follow my career. To wherever.

Ishmael and Saint-Ex chose their habitats first. Then they found jobs that fit. Doing whatever. Do you want a topnotch education? You don't have to live in Boston. "The sea is my Harvard," writes Ishmael, and he goes on to simulate a university life while crewing on the *Pequod*. In *Wind, Sand and Stars*, Saint-Ex writes that he became a pilot because "an airplane is a means of getting away from towns and their bookkeeping and coming to grips with reality." This is no trivial sacrifice. A person would have to really abhor towns to take up cross-continental flying in the 1920s. He flew over the Andes, for goodness sake. But "a man cannot live a decent life in cities," he writes. In the winter a neighbor of mine from downriver rescued me with his front-end loader. There were eighteen inches of snow on my lane. In the summer, a few other people used this road, but in the winter, only me. We lamented that we had so much road to plow and so few houses here to share the cost. When I asked my neighbor if he'd be moving to the townsite like most everyone else, he said, "I would slit my throat before I'd live in a town." Which, when you think about it, is just as likely to be fatal as flying a tin can over the Andes in a snowstorm.

"Men will die," Saint-Ex writes in *Wind, Sand and Stars*, "for a cal-
cined, leafless, stony mountain . . . will defend to the death their great
store of sand as if it were a treasure of gold dust." Not all animals need
space, solitude, and wildness, but all animals need to fight for their opti-
mum habitat, whatever it is. Fox and I spread our toes in the Indian ricegrass and faced the sun, heliotropic, like Darwin's mustards, feeling no
less dependent upon the sun for energy than the plants around us. And
we—me and the fox who now recognized my voice—kept turning.

ELEPHANTS

By early May, we had read *The Little Prince* several times. Since I never bothered with a bookmark, we read freestyle. Most days I did more talking than reading. When my supply of scintillating stories ran out, I brought out a new book. Fox had to listen to me read from Dr. Seuss's *Horton Hears a Who!*, a glossy, red oversize book about an eponymous elephant who hears the peep of an eponymous Who in the thunderous Jungle of Nool. No other book in my cottage seemed appropriate for someone with an eighteen-minute attention span and modest mental acuity.

"Whos are so small that their entire town fits on a tiny speck embedded in a thistle." I held up a drawing of a vulture-like bird with a single flower in its beak. "Black-bottomed eagle. It's making off with the thistle with Whoville inside." Fox tilted his chin up for a view. In the story, the vulture-like bird drops the Whos' thistle into a field with a billion other thistles. The endangered Whos call out for help, and only the caring, observant, and big-eared Horton can hear them. "Horton," I said, holding up another page, "sets out to find the Whos, one thistle at a time."

When the wind wasn't blowing, our valley was well suited to reading alfresco: cozy, well lit, and not too tight. And private. Although several landowners divided the foothills, borders were invisible, structures were scarce, and fences uncommon. You might find a bit of barbed wire wrapped around a few cattle paddocks and chicken coops, a couple strips of post-and-pole-confined mules and horses.

Fox and I followed a party of four resident deer shuffling toward his den. In the dusky light, their backsides formed three white streaks of distinct phosphorescent guidelines: the tail in the center and two lines along the backs of each lower leg. "I wonder if that has a purpose, Fox—all that glowing like highway markers?" I guessed, out loud, that backside markings allowed deer to follow each other and march in straight lines. We stopped speculating about deer when we came to a patch of white sage. After checking that thatch ants weren't hanging underneath, I pruned a bouquet of long, soft leaves and slipped them into my coat pocket.

Phosphorescent white markings on mule deer had a purpose only if straight lines also had a purpose. So, there was our next topic: the essence of straight lines. I didn't care what we discussed. His inability to precisely understand me afforded a limitless number of engaging topics.

The four deer joined a herd line crossing the alfalfa field below us. Walking in a straight line would save deer energy if they were plowing through deep snow because only the lead deer would break new trail and everyone else would use less energy than the animal it was following. But the field wasn't snowy. Maybe the straight line confined their scent and shrunk whatever advertisement they'd be flashing to predators. Maybe not. We didn't need an answer; we really just wanted to stretch and poke around. I squinted, my eyelids fluttered, and the deer became pylons lined up in the seemingly endless emptiness of east central Montana.

Yes, Fox and I were goofing off. We were not doing science, collecting data, or writing hypotheses; he wasn't helping me write a textbook. Instead, we were entertaining ourselves with an endeavor no more intellectually rigorous than playing with green army dolls. Night after night, when more respectable individuals paired up and watched TV or visited movie theaters or leaned on counters spotted with gooey droplets of yellowing cream and called fancy drink orders to a barista, Fox and I spied around.

DAYS AFTER OUR discourse on deer, he disappeared. I sat alone at the rendezvous site. Grief descended on the fourth day. I didn't recognize it. By focusing specifically on one goal—finding the fox—I reduced everything around me to a blur. It's not that hard to do if you are used to looking through a bow sight. Meanwhile, the target image in the center—the lost fox—grew so large that all the images necessary to maintain sanity disappeared, and madness enveloped me.

I walked miles from the cottage along gravel roads until they ended on private land; I followed faint dirt trails until they disappeared into bedrock. Almost four miles from the cottage, a man hoeing a tiny garden outside a single-story modular house hadn't seen a fox. Not even after I asked him six or seven times. Perhaps I shouldn't have been wearing such an old and poorly engineered down coat. While pleading my case, raising my arms and gesticulating, I noticed white feathers raining on me. They were escaping through the seams of my coat and floating around me like I was a crazed cooped chicken.

Every passing truck, either government or civilian, deepened my paranoia that a human predator had taken advantage of Fox's good nature. Federal personnel would be out trapping who-knows-what for whatever reason. Civilians shot anything capable of menacing chickens and anything that looked like it might grow up to be a coyote. Lion chasing, a popular (and legal) habit-forming sport, kept hunters and their hound dogs on the prowl in the surrounding wilderness. A lion hound without a mountain lion to tail is a hound on the trail of a fox. Trucks drove down from the National Forest behind me every day, all with stocked gun racks in the cab and ominous boxes in the bay. And each one could have been holding Fox—dead, caged, or manacled.

Sheets of old snow stretched over the ground like slices of Swiss cheese, pale yellow and rubbery. Round clumps of bunchgrasses pushed up through the snow, cutting out neat circles. It was the ugliest snow of the year, and its inability to capture and hold animal tracks sabotaged my search. After dark, while wondering if it was time to give up, I thought about those double rainbows that had changed the course of our relationship by convincing me that nature's most wonderful gifts are often short-lived. But a rainbow and a fox are imperfect analogues. One is ethereal, the other precarious. I accepted that, but I wasn't ready to live without him. Sitting in my enclosed stairway, the only dark place in the cottage, I decided to ask God for a favor in exchange for giving up some vice.

Rifle casings lined up on the stairwell ledge beside me, all headstamp down so they doubled as miniature vases. Some held dried twigs of red osier dogwood, others one or two feathers: orange flicker, yellow mead-owlark, blue Steller's jay. I handled all of them while considering the deal I could cut. Nothing came to mind. Unless God took a very broad view of "vice," I didn't have anything swap-worthy.

Playing with the stock market? Would that count? In grad school, I ate ramen for dinner and powdered milk for breakfast, skimming my tiny salary to buy shares in companies that published great books and some-times picking up shares of companies whose biomedical research I ad-mired. I still owned the stocks, and the market was kind of like gambling. I could offer that up in a trade. Maybe. But . . . no . . . it wouldn't work. Free-market capitalism was way too complicated to explain to God.

Instead, I reasoned with God, telling him to bring the fox back because he deserved a longer life. Did I believe that God would answer my prayer? Yes, I knew he would. Not because I believed in God, but because I knew that God believed in foxes.

While trolling for Fox by sweeping moose-hide mukluks through the tall grasses, I spotted a new trail. Lined out parallel to Fox's main trail, the new one stretched across higher and dryer ground. In that new trail, in direct line of sight of both my cottage and his den, three thorny weeds stood erect. Last year's Russian thistle, they were enormous weeds relative to the width of the trail, but relative to the billion acres that a less-discerning fox could walk through to get to my cottage, you would think they were three very inconsequential weeds. The thorns, however, produced consequences by any measure, tearing my bare hands to strips as I tugged them loose. After pulling out the old Russians, I sat back on my heels, folding my head down so the cold wind couldn't get to the sweat under my neck. I was sucking air against the stinging torn flesh on my palms when I looked up to see, bounding right at me, Fox—bursting through a sheet of tall, cylindrical ryegrass like a gunslinger through batwing doors.

If I had been a reasonable person, and not teetering on the cusp between despair and elation, I would have known to save up some of this overwhelming joy, store it, use it to buffer myself when the next bad thing happened, because bad things, inevitably, do happen. Instead, I figured that happiness was so resplendent, and the universe so kind, that nothing bad could ever happen again.

IN EACH OF MY online undergraduate classes, I posted a short autobiography. That spring, for the first time, I wrote: "Hobbies:" and then I filled in: "befriending foxes."

"How do you befriend a fox?" they asked.

I now knew for sure I had not chased down our friendship. My attempt to objectify Fox as a research subject had failed; my attempt to extrapolate him into a generic and impersonal animal had backfired. The more I watched him, the more I understood him and appreciated his ease of living; insight became empathy. And empathy, I am convinced, is the gateway to friendship. Do you think I told the undergraduates that? Yes? Then you have never tried to teach evolution to undergraduates. Believe me; they have enough on their plates learning about vestigial tails without contemplating the relationship between empathy and friendship.

"Making friends with foxes is not easy," I told my students. "You need alligator skin because you are going to pull a lot of weeds."

WHALES AND POLAR BEARS

In the evenings, at random and frequent times after dark and before bed, I would take a break from my reading and classwork to wander around the house and look out the windows. I often saw a mouse, squatting on the red brick walkway and pushing fistfuls of seeds into its mouth; occasionally deer, elk, fox, and skunk; usually no one. But I never stopped looking. This night, I was already asleep in my sleeping bag when a bright moon and an inexplicable yearning woke me around 1:00 a.m. Balancing on a white pine stepstool for a wide panorama of the front field, I peeked through the Rainbow Room's green window. Fox.

Last time I'd watched Fox at night, the moon was sickle-shaped, so I'd turned on the porch light before stepping outside. Moths fluttered around my forehead, shedding their creepy brown scales into my fine and abundant hair. Tonight, with moonlight mimicking a bright dusk, I kept the light off as I left the cottage. Moths disregarded me, and the sharp night air sliced through me as if it were obsidian. Bundling my puffy cotton jacket closer, I waited while Fox hunted and the cold sent my upper back muscles rippling toward my spine. Shushing sounds, ebbing and flowing in great waves, marked the path of an invisible Fox stalking mice through the meadow grass.

When he approached the cottage's wooden steps, I joined him and we walked together to his den. A dome of soft white moonlight scrambled all movement and sound around us. When he stopped to stick his nose up, I inhaled deeply, but the humidity was so high that scent molecules stuck to water molecules and sank before they reached me. I couldn't have smelled a skunk unless I'd stepped on it. Trying not to, I scanned the ground looking for undulating white stripes.

Crescendo whistles, high-pitched calls, and long wails teased us. Who was stalking us in this fuzzy-edged night? Maybe it was only wind. Maybe that whirring noise came from little brown bats. We hiked to the last switchback below his den, his shadow longer and more elegant than any he wore in the daytime.

Despite their reputation as provocateurs to insanity and backdrops for witches on sticks, full moons are simply a rare opportunity for a unique kind of hike. Fox and I were not insomniacs; nothing had chased us into the night, and we weren't using darkness to hide from people. After all, we lived where there weren't any people. Or almost none. I just enjoyed the beauty, mystery, and adrenaline rush of hiking under moonlight. You would agree, if you lived in an isolated area and witnessed the full moon the way Fox and I did, as if Benjamin Franklin had not flown his electrifying kite. As if the last century had not turned.

A couple nights later, with the moon round and rising in a clear sky, I was waiting for him outside. He trotted fast and direct to the steps. His wispy, translucent fur was swaying in the moon's light. I stepped away from the door, and four round and fluid kits rolled past me. Fox moved off to the side, leaving me surrounded by little leaping foxes. Close enough to touch, they were tumbling around me like acrobats while my hands sprung up in surprise. I focused on two tussling kits, and everything around them homogenized into a blur.

Riveted, I strained my eyes to watch their undisciplined performance in the moon's light, and my other senses diminished as if I were dropping slowly underwater. Gulping air, holding my breath, I fell into the night with unfettered foxes swimming all around me.

I may have stood still for twenty, forty minutes. Shadows changed direction before I started walking through the front field. Grass eddies swirled in disparate places, fox heads popping out from each one. Moonlight or a wide band of glinting river backlit little pointy heads as they rose. One-two-three-four . . . too fast to count, they came and went . . . yes . . . a head . . . no . . . gone too fast. A head popped out of an eddy, swinging left, right, left again, before submerging below last year's perennial grass stalks. I tried to anticipate the eddies so I could catch a fox head rising, but I missed so often and they moved so fast it made me dizzy, and the night became increasingly surreal.

Rolling back on their hind legs and facing each other, a pair of yowling kits boxed with both forearms. Two more jumped on them, and the fox huddle became a spastic, thrashing mass. When they calmed down, the four enmeshed foxes were throbbing like a single large animal. They dispersed when one took off in bounding leaps. Others jumped up on small boulders before following their den mates on a treasure hunt. Someone dug up one of Fox's cached cadavers and somersaulted around the prize. A snarling, heftier sibling sauntered up, exposing fangs that caused the littler thief to surrender its copped cache for a game of tag.

The foursome, unencumbered by parental supervision, had discovered ecstasy, and they were scampering dangerously out of control. "Fox," I called to my curled-up friend lying near me, "you need to tighten the leash." Wrapping his tail around his shoulder, and tucking his snout into his forearms, he sank to the ground and curled up like a pill bug until he was so round that even an imbecile could see that he hadn't any leash.

When one of the kits rolled or leaped or grabbed a piece of grass or swatted a big moth, I pumped my hands open and closed, spreading my fingers wide like a prehistoric image in a Dinwoody pictograph. The kits charged up and down the sides of the draw like bobsledding Olympiads. I called out to him in a loud voice, "There are weasels in the draw! Wild cats!" But he would not round them up. He would not even stand.

"Fox!" He pretended not to hear. I was a Who without a Horton. The kits needed protection or they were going to get nabbed. At the very least, someone had to watch for feral cats. "Fox!" But it was too late to get him involved; he had already decided there was no point in both of us doing my job.

To my repertoire of memorized scenes—red berries the size of toad eyes; near-frozen cobalt-colored ponds; pond-pocked meadows below fields of tall blue lupine—I added baby fox heads bobbing in grasses on a moonlit night. I would carry it as a talisman the way I carried any other memory. But unlike any other memory, in this image I wasn't alone.

That night, I couldn't sleep; an overwhelming feeling of well-being caffeinated me. I watched sharp-edged clouds transform the night sky into a navy-blue plate of raised-relief Wedgewood. Fox would be watching those stars from his den site on the slope above. I laid my forearm across my desk and swept all the papers from the nascent textbook into a wastebasket. They teetered on the rim, threatening to either fall out and slide across the floor for a second chance or curl into the damp, sticky container and disappear.

I realized the time had come to hit the brakes, stop going in the direction I was heading—academy, textbooks, career. It was time to turn around. Fortunately, when I realized this, I wasn't going fast enough to come to a dramatic screeching halt. Like any animal, my instinct had prevented me from running too fast while I didn't know where I was going. Now I knew.

The previous week, I had walked with a university class through a forest dominated by skinny, weedy lodgepole pine growing from a brown forest floor: all dirt and no detritus. Poor overheated soil kept the pine population down and prevented leafy, ground-covering plants from growing. The community of trees that composed the forest determined its smell, shape, and sounds: its essence. "Communities change," I told the students. "The essence of the forest changes." Hundreds of years old, the trees whose branches we were handling were part of a forest that had not yet matured. "These lodgepole are forerunners, initiating a mature forest that they themselves will not dominate." If nothing interfered, the immature lodgepole forest would eventually grow into a forest dominated by Engelmann spruce, subalpine fir, and whitebark pine. Physical changes would precede the new stage; for example, the exposed soil would aerate and collect nutrients, and new trees would grow large enough to provide shade. Then the lodgepole would die back, become sparse, and we would call this stage of the forest, the one dominated by spruce and fir, "the climax stage."

We found a few dead fire-blackened trees that were spruce, and some—identified by a cantilevered shape and a twinning base—that were whitebark pine. "The forest seems to have almost achieved its climax phase, and then a wildfire—a dramatic disturbance—blew through, and the forest had to start all over from the beginning with the lodgepoles. Avalanches, major floods, logging operations, all these cataclysmic events set the clock back. Hypothetically, this forest is marching again toward its climax." The climax community enjoys near-perfect communication with its physical environment. Because of that communication, few alterations will affect its future. The climax stage is the comfortable and most stable phase. One that is not a prelude to anything, but a culmination of everything.

Like a forest, my life had progressed through several stages and was reaching the climax phase. I knew my relationship with Fox was more important than anything else in my life, and I could see that my purpose would be to tell his story. And purpose, I now knew, was more important than profession.

Funnily enough, for all my worrying and deep thinking, I had changed course because of a physical event—the kits in the moonlight—and the ensuing emotion. Reason and rationality had nothing to do with it; he trusted me, that's what mattered.

And, so, casting reason aside, I forgot to think about this: What would happen when Fox died? How would I replace that relationship? Would my first real friendship be my last?

PEOPLE OFTEN DESCRIBE *Moby-Dick* as a novel about a mad sea captain. I think of the novel as a journal written by a loner who loves nature and wild animals, and who mourns the extermination of the American buffalo. Whose nature (and probably nurture) compels him to live beyond the gridlines. Ishmael leans away from the cultured society and toward the wilder world, staying close enough to people to satisfy his curiosity yet far away enough to avoid commitment. On a ship crowded with people of his own culture, he chooses a Pacific Island pagan as his one friend. Like me, Ishmael thinks that dividing the world into humans and non-humans is irrational; instead he believes that all members of the animal kingdom—including humans—fall into one of two categories, wild and domestic, with some humans falling into one category and some the other. I'd read *Moby-Dick* so often I felt as if I was conversing with Ishmael, a fictional sailor.

"Are whales as intelligent as people?" I asked him.

"A whale is more intelligent than most people. A whale is as intelligent as Dante or Plato" (see chapter 85, "The Fountain").

"Killing a person is murder. What do you think about killing a nonhuman animal?"

"If we kill an animal in self-defense, it is not murder. No doubt, the first man that ever murdered an ox simply to make a soup was regarded as a murderer; perhaps he was hung, and if he had been put on trial by his oxen he certainly would have been. Yes, we murder whales. We murder whales when we kill them just to acquire oil to light gay bridals and illuminate our churches" (see chapter 65, "The Whale as a Dish"; chapter 81, "The *Pequod* Meets the Virgin"; and chapter 82, "The Honor and Glory of Whaling").

"Is it moral to eat animals?"

"It is immoral to eat four-legged animals" (see chapter 65, "The Whale as a Dish").

If I lived on a ship and ate dairy products, I could swap meat for fish and cheese. But I am a landlocked dairy-avoider living in cattle, sheep, and elk country. Replacing mammals with fish of equal quality isn't a viable financial option, which means that eating meat is simply a defense of my livelihood and well-being. When I am an old lady, maybe I will think about Ishmael and stop eating meat. Until then, someone needs to kill the animals that provide my meat, so it might as well be me.

"Your shipmates say that whales are man-killing fish and monsters. It's easy to attribute a nefarious personality to an animal. Do whales have any positive personality traits?"

"In fact, some whales display personalities that match their unique philosophical outlook on life. When facing death, the right whale is practical and resigned. I take him to have been a Stoic; the sperm whale a Platonian, who might have taken up Spinoza in his later years. We whalers have named some whales, not because of their unique appearance, but because of their unique behavior. So there, too, is your personality, in the pragmatism of a dying whale. And, therefore, in the sperm whales, who are ponderous and profound beings, sublime, and inherently dignified" (see chapter 75, "The Right Whale's Head," and chapter 85, "The Fountain").

"It must be hard for your shipmates to look into a whale's eye when they're torturing it. But if they hesitate, if they think the whale might be an animal with feelings, if they're not able to kill these whales . . . well? What happens to whaling? It seems like the economy of the whole northeast coast is betting that sailors will look away."

"Looking into Moby Dick's eyes, I saw a pitiful sight. Nothing but blind bulbs resided in the places where eyes should have been" (see chapter 81, "The *Pequod* Meets the Virgin").

"Did you feel empathy?"

"Yes. When First Mate Flask stabbed a harpoon into one of Moby Dick's festering wounds, I saw the wound burst and squirt, and I recoiled in pain and in synchrony with him, Moby Dick. Another time, another whale, the sun sent shadows of three ships to the deep ocean, and I felt the whale's anxiety. How appalling to the wounded whale must have been such huge phantoms flitting over his head!" (see chapter 81, "The *Pequod* Meets the Virgin").

WE DRAW MINUTE DISTINCTIONS between individual people—the way they look and how they act. When it comes to nonhuman animals, we tend to generalize because too often they all look, sound, and act alike to us. We're just not very empathetic toward wild animals. I've a notion it's because we think we're evolutionarily advanced and more intelligent than they are. Arrogance dissolves empathy.

I live in a harsh land; wind, drought, and extreme temperatures keep me humble. Maybe that's one reason I empathized with Fox and recognized him as an individual, not as a generic fox. I shied away from every adult fox but him. He, in turn, shied away from other people. We had very different personalities, the fox and I. He was outgoing, interacted with other foxes, and enjoyed the company of Tennis Ball. I was always alone, trying to disappear. And TBall just annoyed me. While it is not rare for a male fox to stay with a group after the weaning of the kits, it's not common either. I've seen dens that never housed any adult males, and dens with males who disappeared soon after the weaning. As a male fox, he could live as a loner, but he chose not to. Despite those differences, we both worshiped the heat of the sun and the light of the moon. You will never convince me you need more than that to forge a friendship.

And we were friends, the fox and I. Consider what happened when a five-headed ball cactus stepped between us. Before I dug up the cactus and replanted it along the front steps, the rare specimen had been growing on a steep, rocky slope in the far north fields, and I worried that an eroding cliff would swallow it or that it would tumble under a rock slide. And since I was moving it, why not next to my front steps, where I could admire it every day? Of course, I was planting the cactus right next to the steps where Fox liked to wander, but surely he could maneuver past a little round plant with a three-inch diameter.

He was perusing the front of the cottage, looking tight and acting anxious. I was scraping tent caterpillars off cherry boughs, dropping them into glass jars, and tightening the lids. I thought he wanted company; he wasn't hunting, and he was right next to the steps. He often took the opportunity to curl up and take some sunshine when he saw me sit down to play the role of protector. Fox raised a paw, bouncing it in the air before lowering it with a mechanical hesitation. Hooking one toenail into the edge of my freshly planted trophy cactus, he stared me down. One tiny cactus with spines so slight he could easily have unearthed it and tossed it aside. Instead, he left his toenail hooked into the cactus, refusing to release me from his squinty stare until I was only a few steps away. Heading back up the driveway, he stopped once, to look around his front leg and shoot me a final glare.

I looked for him all the next day. He missed hearing about Horton, practicing yoga in the gravel, and hunting mice in the pasture. Ditto the next day, and then the snow began. Heavy spring snow rose like yeast bread between the bunchgrasses. I couldn't sleep. Several hours shy of dawn, I threw a down coat over my naked body. A ball cactus had upset my friend. For the price of a little discomfort, I could set things right with him. I was bigger, older, and prehensile. Noblesse oblige. After digging up my prized cactus, I jailed it in a clay pot and placed it on the windowsill. Next day, Fox curled up on the vacated spot, staying so long his six-pound body left an impression in the dirt.

I didn't tell anyone about my captured cactus. Who replants in a snowstorm to appease a fox? Looking back, I would say that when a person thinks they are wrong for doing something that feels right, well, then, the definition of *wrong* needs to shift.

When he wasn't around, the potted cactus went outside to breathe some wild air. Most times, it tumbled out of its cell and rolled free. Truth is, like me, ball cactuses do not respond well to captivity. Anemia infected its fuchsia petals, and they paled and pinstriped. In all its resentment, the cactus's blooms came to resemble pink ticking. I have never imprisoned another plant, though I maintain the right to do so someday.

I don't object to the idea of keeping plants confined indoors any more than I object to keeping animals in zoos. Although I'd never been to a zoo, I was hoping to go one day. I knew all about Knut, a polar bear cub in a German zoo whose mother abandoned him. From Knut's story, I learned that polar bears would rather die than be raised by humans. A man identified as "an animal rights activist" claimed that "in the wild," maternal abandonment is a death sentence. This segued into the statement that because wild and abandoned cubs died, death was natural, and therefore allowing little Knut to live was unnatural. It did not segue into the corollary that because nature is highly variable, not all abandoned cubs have died or will die. In other words, the activist assumed that only the most common behavior was natural, and that any behavior that was not average was unnatural.

Somehow, zealots had turned an assumption into a mandate: avoiding unnatural acts was the directive of a zoo. Everyone was too emotional to realize that almost no one believed that assumption to be true. Did *anyone* think zoos were natural? Meanwhile, the same zealots extrapolated all this nonsense into an exuberant epiphany: *Embrace nature and kill the cub.* In fact, activists tried to sue zoo administrators to force them to kill baby bear Knut. I found two actual attributed quotes. One man—identified in the articles only as an animal rights activist—said, "In actual fact, the zoo needs to kill the bear," and, "If a polar bear mother rejected the baby, then I believe the zoo must follow the instincts of nature. In the wild, it would have been left to die." Wolfram Graf-Rudolf, then director of Germany's Aachen Zoo, said, "The mistake has been made. One should have had the courage to put [Knut] to sleep much earlier."

Naturally, abandoned cubs struggle for life and come nearer to death than their cohorts with attentive mothers. Naturally, people help struggling, abandoned cubs. That's what my instinct would tell me to do. I know, because Panther Creek's abandoned fawn tested my instincts. And fox's four kits tested my instincts when they ran wild in the slough while he slept. Our instinct tells us what is natural; our society tells us what is normal—if we let it.

Nature is cruel: that's a trope masquerading as a paradigm, in the sense that a carpetbagger might masquerade as a charlatan.

I read that polar bears would rather be dead than raised by humans. Apparently, polar bears are bound to a higher moral standard than I am. I would prefer being raised by polar bears to being dead. I am so much less concerned with being "normal" than with simply being alive. Besides, attempting to be normal does not seem like a worthwhile pursuit for a busy person. Fox would not approve of wasting time pondering fathomless questions like *What is normal?* Choosing between life and death is a simple matter and always a good investment of your time.

And how could I ignore the fact that a great many of the world's children are enjoying a less nurturing upbringing than that which could be provided by polar bears?

MAGPIES

The fox was sitting on the hillside when he recognized the long tail and bright white rump patch of a female harrier. She was flying fast over the alfalfa field below him and banking sharply. Eager to snatch voles, she slowed and dropped. Now she was flying too low, as if the air weren't getting heavier and sinking around her. Having sensed the dropping air pressure, the fox, wary of the weather's fickle nature, waited for the tempest from his new den site. Closer to the blue-roofed house, farther from the eagle's nest, the new home nestled into the same cliffs as last year's. But this new den offered a better view of the river's big bend and a flashier facade: a rock terrace instead of a dirt patio. On the sunset side of the terrace, a cove of junipers horseshoed around one den door and opened toward the river. Despite surrounding a sumac bush and two rocks that were big enough to stand on, the cove had room for the vixen, three kits, and a trio of uninvited deer. Before the optimistic harrier finished circling the alfalfa field, the sky filled with sleet, hail, snow, sunlight, rain, and, finally, after a roaring wind, more sunlight.

Near the den site, the kink-tailed kit was crouching under a maple-leafed currant bush watching Hurricane Hands use a pathetically long tool to rearrange a pile of dirt. The other kits chased each other to the big flattop rock above the main den site; the rock sheltered the kits like a roof when they hid underneath it and supported them like a patio when they sunbathed on its heated surface. A raven flew by carrying part of a bluebird in its beak. Landing near a toad-shaped boulder, it joined more ravens, all croaking and bursting into leaps, not even the highest of which could have topped a standing elk's head. If ravens were already meat-drunk from feeding on the riverside elk carcass, it would be too late for him to wiggle in for a bite.

Instead, he bounded down to the rabbit fields, where sprouting grasses were glistening under melting snow. When he arrived, deer were scattered on both sides of the cattail-clotted creek that bisected the field. Busy eating, they bent over like pea vines, aiming their trespassing rumps in every direction.

When deer ate in that disorderly fashion, they hesitated to reorganize and move on. Instead, and despite the fact that grass tasted like air, they would keep eating until they bloated and their droppings covered the ground and emitted copious amounts of methane. Meanwhile, having all those hard-hoofed feet around would make it difficult for him to chase rabbits. Not that he couldn't catch a rabbit in the shrubs, but they'd be harder to see and would taste like sagebrush. Getting rid of the deer before they destroyed the rabbit field would require prodding, persistence, focus, and bone-hard self-esteem. No amount of clapping from Hurricane Hands could accomplish that.

At the edge of the field, a pair of does in the shadow of a creaking cottonwood were grooming each other's necks with their teeth. He crept up so close that he could see that the deer's legs were covered with ticks. When he leaned in to touch a whisker to the young doe's ankle, she flicked her heel back as if he were no scarier than a bug. *As if!* While the doe sucked grass, the fox watched the underside of her throat. The loose skin under her jaw rippled like high water in the creek. He moved closer under one of the doe's front knees and stared where her nose hit the ground. The ticks were sucking blood so fast, her leg looked blurry. The next time her tongue slipped out, he tapped one of his long black whiskers against her lower leg. The deer didn't even flinch. *On plan!*

Now that he was invisible, he slunk over to the deer farthest from the downhill run and watched the herd gobbling grass like it was sweet, dried huckleberry. He bounced behind the last bloated deer and brushed his tail against her flank. She jerked her head up, her eyes popped open, and she galloped down the hill, pushing all the deer in front of her off his rabbit field.

He was having a productive afternoon when, overhead, a red-tailed hawk screamed and a white-headed eagle dove toward the field. The eagle hustled away, and another red-tailed joined the chase; shadows criss-crossed the rabbit fields. Before the commotion ended, the fox escaped into the brushlands. A spotted robin that had crouched in sagebrush to consider that morning's hard rain was too small a meal to exchange for a wet tussle with a pungent shrub. He might return when the bird was drier or fatter.

He was on his way to his favorite slough for a quick meal when he spied another harrier. Cruising slowly, swooping low, and occasionally disappearing, the harrier had the same idea as he did—pilfering voles. He shot his white-tipped tail straight up to alert Round Belly that he needed help.

🪶

The magpie known as Tennis Ball to the girl and Round Belly to the fox thrust her head out from the opening of her nest, a big, dome-covered bowl in a short, twisted juniper. Three years old, its lower lip was receding, and its roof overhung far enough to darken the interior. The round-bellied magpie emerged from the nest sphere's single entrance wondering about egg yolks that might be nearby under the tall, naked-legged juniper.

After flying past a row of lilacs, she circled the juniper but found nothing underneath. She wasn't surprised. The appearance of yolks had always depended on the unreliable mood and manners of the person in the blue-roofed house.

The juniper's middle branches were shaking under the weight of a twittering mass of waxwings vainly flashing red-and-yellow shoulder brooches. If she landed on a branch below them and pushed off forcefully, the branch would bounce upward and whip those little birds right off the tree. But the round-bellied magpie, a matriarch, had no time to lark around.

Heading toward the river, she spied white-headed eagles standing in a flat, open field near an elk carcass. They were waiting for a golden-necked eagle to finish feeding, and she decided to join them. Her torn-tailed mate, already on the sidelines, recognized her unique wing stutter and looked up as she landed.

They were still waiting when a flock of magpies from the far-away willows arrived, fanning out and circling the carcass. Someone would have to fly up to meet them. The visiting magpies were not aggressive, but decorum dictated that someone acknowledge them. She and her mate had always upheld decorum, but it was becoming tiresome. When no one flew to the task, she and her mate rose as they always did. She thought back to the days when his tail was elegant and full and life was less exhausting.

When the golden-necked eagle retired to a wooden telephone pole, everyone jostled for a bit of the elk carcass. Waves of sun and snow washed over the mob of scavengers. A huge and noisy band of ravens, each bird twice her size, arrived, and the round-bellied magpie decided to settle for bugs. She jumped on the sway back of a white-tailed deer who was meandering across the field and picked ticks off its back. A fawn glanced up. Its sharp upturned nose, oversize eyes, and rounded forehead reminded her of the fox.

With the round-bellied magpie still on its back, the white-tailed deer meandered with its herd alongside a slough. Overhead, a harrier's shadow drove a juvenile robin into a wet sagebrush, where it shook a slow vole from under the shrub. The vole scurried in and out of bunchgrasses and through the fox's favorite vole slough. The harrier followed the vole, dipping and rising with its prey. The matriarch knew that if the harrier had an easy time hunting the slough, it would return. She decided to make its hunt a little less easy. Leaping from the deer's rump, she exposed her white belly to the owl-faced harrier. Announcing herself that way, like a big, bright target, was inherently dangerous. Anyone would think she was crazy or brave. But flashing her white breast didn't just attract predators; it also sent a distress signal to her friends. She was not crazy or brave; she simply believed that she had more friends than enemies.

A small pack of magpies joined the matriarch, and they chased the panicking harrier until it turned sharply and flew off into the hummocks.

🌱

On a warm day, in early afternoon, the fox, having clipped a mouse in half, gagged on the head-end and dropped it into a buttercup. Nursing females left a sticky residue on his tongue and he avoided eating them. Eating only what you wanted to eat was one of the advantages that came with being fast, and clever, and not a deer. Magnificent hunters developed picky palates. Besides nursing females, big, belligerent males tasted foul, and he preferred a vole to a mouse in any case. Besides, a vole's plump body would be free of rubber or plastic. Sometimes he would pick up a junked mouse, wait until the Alfalfa Flat foxes were asleep, and leave it outside their den.

Today he was chewing the best bits off a vole while the parts that he didn't favor slid down the flat blades of grass between his forearms. When he got up, Round Belly finished off the meal. Then she entertained him, twisting and twirling in midair. Flying was a neat trick, but he wouldn't trade teeth for feathers. He ate voles; magpies ate scraps. Sometimes it seemed that a pied bird's life was nothing more than a series of hard landings. She was still engaged in aerial acrobatics when he headed to the blue-roofed house to sleep in the sun. When he hunted voles and Hurricane walked alongside, the round-bellied magpie never joined them. Ever since the day he brought Hurricane a meadowlark, and she had screamed and flailed her arms at Round Belly, he had known that she and the magpie were enemies.

It was early evening when the fox, running along a ravine, heard the rustling and clicking of partridges. They shot out from under a sticky current bush before he could grab one. The covey left a single bird behind, exposed but for a thick currant branch reaching across its back.

After shifting her weight and lifting one scaly foot forward, the young bird froze. The fox steadied himself to wait until the bird ducked or took another step. A long wait was fair price for the occasional wild chicken. Not so long ago he had waited until the sun had moved from one side of his face to the other for the chance to drop a white-feathered rooster.

🌱

The round-bellied magpie was flying after a red-tailed hawk when she looked down on what might have been a rotting pumpkin: orange, dirty, and round. But the slightly fetid smell bothered her, and she flew closer. It was instead a feral cat creeping through short grasses, heading for the fox, who was still hunting in the ravine. She had known the fox since he was a suckling. He had grown to become a reliable source of food scraps for her. A hustler's life lacked routine, but not responsibility. She watched as the orange cat melded into the dirt behind, downwind, and a few steps away from the fox. From that position, the cat was invisible to the fox, and ready to jump him, pin him down, and bite through his skinny neck. The magpie landed in the nearest saltbush to watch.

✦

I carved little depressions in the dirt with a stone and scooted yolk-filled eggshells inside them. Earlier that morning I had added the egg whites to a mix of black cherries and melted chocolate, saving the raw yolks for the animals. The cherries were from a package of frozen cherries, and the chocolate was Baker's, semisweetened. I had pulverized Quaker Oats into oat flour and puréed the chocolate-cherry batter with a handheld mixer. After combining dry and wet ingredients and adding sliced almonds, I poured my cake batter into a glass baking dish.

Gin was overflowing today with stocky gray birds flicking yellow-banded tails. Their head feathers were combed up into topknots. If the birds wore nametags, they would read: "*Bombycilla garrulus.*" If the nametags were in English instead of Latin, they would read: "silky-tailed chattering birds." According to the Audubon Society, the common name was Bohemian waxwing. They were eating juniper "berries" and chattering. I was enthralled with their appearance. They were almost as elegant as Hungarian partridges and large enough to enjoy without binoculars. They would not stay long and might not use this migration route again. Waxwings were as fickle as they were beautiful.

You cannot welcome waxwings into your home as guests and allow a magpie to drool egg yolks on their fine, feathered crests. What to do about TBall? I Grinched the yolks. I remembered when thirteen Hungarian partridge fell asleep under Tonic, each bird laying its head on the thigh of another so that the covey formed a perfect wreath. Determined to protect the birds, I'd had to Grinch the yolks then too. And there had been other times. Maybe TBall was not complaining because I had grabbed the yolks back but because I did it so often.

Gray clouds puckered into a sucker hole. They didn't fool me. But the risk of being miserable in a squall paled next to the pleasure of standing underneath an ephemeral shower of sun-dappled snow on a summer day and looking through to the blue-sky backdrop. I ended up tromping around on the north hills chasing a feral cat. Fox was hunting far ahead of me, with the omnipresent Tennis Ball following closely behind him. Calf-high sprigs of perennial grass were so reddened and sore from frigid, sunny days they practically squeaked in pain when I stepped on them. Feeling their anguish, I stretched my stride to its limit as best I could.

❧

Only one thing mattered to the Hungarian partridge trapped in the fox's glare—in order to survive, she would turn herself into stone. She did not breathe or blink. Standing stationary was not good enough. She needed to become as inert as granite. The wind whiffled through a rotting thatch ant nest, sending fine spores floating her way. One spore landed on the thin membrane that separated a maroon eye-ring from a gray eyelid. Blinking at the spore, the partridge flinched; and the currant branch no longer separated her from the fox.

❧

The round-bellied magpie wrapped her claws around a dead branch, balancing precariously as she monitored the cat's movements. The cat, crouching, her mouth agape, readied to spring on the fox, who was watching the partridge. When the partridge bent forward, the fox pounced. The magpie darted at the cat's back. The cat had a split second to decide whether to defend itself from the magpie or kill the fox. Glaring through the matriarch as if she were an icicle, the cat focused on a sharp, orange muzzle.

The muzzle turned into a magpie. The cat spun halfway around and hooked a set of claws into the magpie's soft breast tissue. Pinned on her back, the matriarch aimed her beak into the cat's eye. The cat inserted a second set of claws below the first. Just as her beak reached the cat's eye, the cat pulled its claws sideways, ripping the round-bellied magpie with such force that guts sprayed upward. Blinded by a warm gush of her own blood, the matriarch bled out quickly.

🌱

The fox, who had darted out of the ravine at the commotion, ran uphill on the grassy slope, stopping at a boulder a safe distance away, his appetite now vanished. The cat took a couple steps backward, dragging Round Belly's carcass off the dirt and onto a rock slab. Watching her carcass flap from the cat's jaw, the fox felt the way he had only felt on those rare occasions after eating something wrong, the bad mushroom, or the butterflies with too much elk droppings on their feet. Times like that, too dizzy to stand, he had lain down and waited, overheating and shivering in alternating spells. Turning away from the remains of Round Belly, he could see a long stretch of the river far below. Magpies filled the cottonwoods along the far shore and faced the little island, a haven he imagined to be calm and sunny and free of predators. But he would probably never go now that Round Belly was gone. The last time he was egg hunting along the shore he had looked downriver and felt too small for the journey.

Round Belly had provided him with a carefree life that his size and silence would have otherwise prevented. When he was still a kit, before he met the girl, Round Belly was the only one who had protected him, staying close and diving on anyone, even his siblings, when they threatened him.

🌱

On a jagged rock slab jammed under a dead sagebrush, a cat crouched with magpie guts spilling over its front leg. As I approached, it swayed into the bunchgrasses, weighed down with hairballs and a tattered wing hanging from its jaw. The rest of the carcass stayed behind on the rock. Uphill, Fox was staring at the mutilated magpie and shaking. From underneath the rock, an army of ants was streaming up, over the edge, and across the rock face. They crossed lines of fresh, wet blood and crawled over the pink flesh and white tendons and into the ripped upper arm. I looked at Fox just long enough to realize that the shredded magpie was TBall.

I tripped home between bunchgrasses and cacti, skipping too fast to pick up a pencil that ejected from one of my pockets. A chocolate cake was waiting, and the more distance I put between myself and the carnage, the faster my appetite would return. Never mind that TBall belonged to my community and was Fox's friend, she had suffered horribly while a putrid mass of fur and rotting claws had slowly ripped her to death. Yes, she was a seemingly omnipresent and grudge-bearing creature who squawked too much and too loudly. But the real reason I didn't like her was that she harassed Fox. And now, too late, I knew I had misjudged her.

I remembered something from late March, when magpies were fortifying their nests for spring broods. It had been horrifically windy, so the birds had toiled when the wind waned and stopped when it waxed. Except Tennis Ball. She had stayed busy through any gust, the better to obstruct the devil when it came looking for idle claws. Flitting around on the ground, TBall had picked up spiky, small-leafed saltbush twigs that had blown off winter-killed plants. When a gale shushed a twig from the bird's beak and sent it cartwheeling, the magpie had stood steadfast with piercing black eyes and wind-whipped feathers, gripped the hard clay dirt, and waited for another twig to blow by.

SPOTTED OWLS

Soon after Four-Kit Night, I began trading in Fox currency, which is to say I reassigned my desires and the prices I was willing to pay for their fulfillment. The incident made me think back to a simpler time in my life, when I was a young ranger in Mount Rainier National Park's Wilderness and only windshield glass, painted steel, and Michelin tires protected me and everything I owned from the world. During my park ranger days, the spotted owl war divided our community. It started when an organization nominated spotted owls and their habitat—old-growth forests—for protection under the Endangered Species Act. Because so many local jobs involved harvesting timber from the old growth, some people believed that placing spotted owls on The List would decimate the economy. And so it was that everyone in our community aligned him- or herself with The Listers or The Loggers.

One night, in the middle of this fighting, I swung open the bathroom door of a bar in Packwood, Washington, and in place of the toilet tissue found a handwritten sign with a question, "out of toelet paper?" And an answer, "wipe your ass with a spotted owl." More disconcerting than the misspelling of *toilet* was the implication that our need for toilet paper justified destroying old-growth forests. I liked toilet paper as much as any semicivilized person, but I would rather have wiped my ass with poison ivy than with tissue paper made from a 400-year-old tree. I was just a blue-collar ranger and didn't have a college degree, but I assumed that wasn't really the choice anyway. I assumed we could figure out how to have toilet paper. And birds. And trees.

We had put a man on the moon, after all.

Then I went to graduate school and learned that "we" had not put a man on the moon. Rocket scientists did that. And from what I'd been able to ferret out about them, they were engaged in projects for which they were more highly remunerated than toilet paper designers. Projects like designing rockets.

So it fell to all of us using the woods to think about what we wanted and what we were willing to tender. Non-loggers—backpackers mostly—favored listing the owl and protecting the wilderness it lived in. They felt that loggers were encroaching on the wilderness. (Owls thought the same thing about backpackers.)

Spotteds are as wise as any owl, but most people don't think so because they are hornless, and cartoonists don't have anything around which to loop their tiny eyeglasses. Like all members of the charismatic owl genus known as *Strix*, spotted owls are dish-faced and round-eyed. Three species of *Strix* shared the Wilderness area I patrolled: barred, great gray, and spotted.

You would be thrilled to emerge from a tent in the Wilderness and look into the eyes of *any* dish-faced owl. In fact, you would be thrilled just to realize you were camping in Wilderness. I know I was. The loggers with whom I shared the woods felt the same way. Although I was a backcountry ranger with the National Park Service and loggers worked for the private sector, our habits were similar. We both worked in the woods, avoided civilization, and dressed and groomed so oddly that from a distance our genders defied classification. We did not have college degrees.

Our jobs required a little supervision and a lot of muscle. No one would mistakenly call us "well paid," and still we would not trade our quality of life for more money. Which is to say, loggers weren't crazy people. If the salary for cutting ten trees matched that for cutting ten thousand trees, loggers would rather . . . well . . . it's obvious, isn't it? We all wanted a good, honest life in the woods.

I wanted that life after leaving the park, but when I'd earned my doctorate, I felt that acceding to a brass badge, a starched uniform, and unhelpful policies was too much to pay for the privilege. I wanted to manage my own land, not someone else's. I wanted to sink into land and wrap it around myself. And I wanted the land to reside in a special place, somewhere with an equitable distribution of power between people and Nature. A place where sometimes Nature would refuse to let us boss her around. And where wild fawns wouldn't die slow painful deaths after domestic dogs bit chunks out of their thighs.

Four-Kit Night taught me that we need to choose our desires carefully. A man with emeralds isn't rich because of the intrinsic value of emeralds. He's rich because of *your* desire for his emeralds. The joy that I experienced on Four-Kit Night was a product, and it had a price. If I wanted to buy more experiences like that, then I would need to pay for them by giving up a city job with a decent income and health insurance (and money left over for emeralds). How much did I want to live here in isolation, with foxes? What was I willing to pay for it?

In July, for the second birthday I would celebrate with the fox in my life, my friend Mike Higham drove down from Canada to visit for a week. His ancient Volvo sedan winced down the driveway and onto the front field and rolled to a stop in my garden, just inches from the front steps.

I tried to explain his mistake as he stepped out of the car.

"Ahhhh. This is a garden." He slid his sunglasses up and looked down at the cheat grass seed heads clinging to his socks. "And the difference between your driveway and the garden is . . . ?"

251

"The driveway gets driven on."

Because he still looked confused, I added, "By *design*. The driveway gets driven on by design. Not by accident. The garden is here." I waved a hand at the Volvo. "I am going to plant it . . . someday. Probably. The pasture is . . ." I spun around to look for a landmark. "Well. It's the part that I won't plant."

"And yet, garden, pasture, driveway . . . they all look the same."

Regardless, Mike's car needed to move. Whether it was the shiny body, noxious chassis, or rubber tires, Fox did not tolerate automobiles in his territory. Mike backed down the drive with his arm hanging out the window swatting dried husks from last year's black henbane. In another month, scores of henbane blossoms would burst open, and I would learn what a hearty weed could do with nothing but gravel and deer piss for sustenance. Helga, a colleague working upriver in Yellowstone National Park, dropped by to stash her station wagon behind my cottage. She asked why my driveway's location kept changing. I was kicking clay onto the wagon's obtrusively glossy rim when Helga answered her question by informing me that I camouflaged my driveway to discourage visitors. I did not deny it. Even Mike couldn't distinguish between driveway and pasture and he had a doctorate in botany.

The next morning, Mike and I motored into the Beartooth Mountains searching for sights to photograph and rocks to collect. Riding shotgun in a private rig without an actual shotgun racked across the back window was a new experience for me. Unless I was hunting with someone—and I usually hunted alone—I always took the wheel. Relinquishing control was uncomfortable, but the scenery eventually alleviated my distress. A wooden platform that our electric cooperative had built onto a retired telephone pole to stop ospreys from electrocuting themselves with live wires supported an overflowing nest with a Canada goose head popping out. Three great blue herons kited above their riverside rookery—dense and pointy-topped spruce trees near an island in the river. Black moose legs rushed through a thick clump of gray-barked fir trees, followed by a brown baby moose with a panda-marked face that made its eyes look as big as saucers.

Poplar seeds that resembled cotton balls covered the black highway. They swirled ahead of us, floating several inches into the air and making me feel as though I were riding through clouds. Mike stopped to photograph an elegant whitetail doe, and I woke from my passenger's trance, slipped out of the Volvo, and headed for the scree.

He caught up with me while I was bending over small boulders. "Searching for a party favor," I said, "for Fox. For my birthday."

"Noted," said Mike, tightening the chest straps on his capped Canon. "What are our specs?"

We climbed far up the alluvial fan until the only remaining road sounds came from Harleys. With our ankles turning this way and that, our toes sliding and wedging themselves under motley-colored granites, we lifted, examined, and sorted like two Hortons in a clover patch searching for Whoville. We did not settle for the first best rock; we held out for the last best, the perfect rock among hundreds. The one we carried a quarter mile back to the Volvo was a slightly concave surfboard when viewed from the side, an isosceles triangle from above.

Back home, we positioned Surfboard Rock so Fox could rest on it while admiring his forget-me-not. A Hungarian partridge hen held her breath as she watched us wedging small stones and clay underneath the seesawing rock. We pretended to ignore her but heard the covey shuffling across the brittle grasses into the septic ditch where they could hide and heat themselves between rocks and thistles. We celebrated my birthday with watermelon and Fox, the former uneaten by the latter. "Happy birthday to us, Fox," I said, and I spit out a watermelon seed. Fox balanced on Surfboard Rock, daring anyone to say otherwise. Mike stayed inside. After witnessing Fox flee from Marco Antonio, I didn't think he would tolerate another person. Mike didn't mind; he was, by nature, accommodating.

We had met a couple years earlier in Yellowstone, while I was waiting up late in a lodge for a policeman to return my stolen spotting scope. I was prepared for a hassle because I knew they would want to keep it in evidence for a while. Mike offered to sit up with me and wait, and we started talking. He was a botanist by profession and a photographer by passion. Bizarrely, because he was good-looking and compassionate and funny, he had never married and had lived alone most of his life; as he explained it, his mother's disdain for him had tainted his ability to interact with women.

The next day, we were all of us busy because it was cool, clear, and calm, and any other summer day might just as easily pelt us with hail or fry us with rays and leave us as deflated as slow worms on a hot rock. It's good to get outside before the day's heat, especially if you like watching damselflies. You can lure the beautiful creatures by spraying water and wetting down any surface, but especially one without vegetation. That's a trick I learned while fighting wildland fires in Minnesota. Damsels love freshly wetted black ash. I often dug fire line with nothing but damselflies to distract me from blisters bleeding inside my ten-inch White's. Some days I mopped up knee-high smoldering ash pits with nothing but these bright turquoise insects breaking up Nature's grayscale wasteland.

I was spraying down Fox's birthday rock with water when a damsel came to my distress, crooking her six angular legs and landing on his rock like a Mars rover. Twisting her thin, straight body and large, oblong head, she explored miniscule pools pitted into Surfboard's broad top. Pausing occasionally, she turned herself into a series of turquoise sculptures. An hour passed before she tired of posing and I moved to the white-leafed sage—hip-high and barrel-tubby—for another show: red ladybug beetles spinning around white velvet branches. The beetles were chasing the aphids. Somersaulting over each other in their panic to escape, the aphids piled up into green grape-like clusters. Also in the audience: sturdy thatch ants who decided I was a bigger and easier target than the ladybugs. When they hustled for my Wellies, I retreated faster than General Custer at Little Bighorn. During this performance, Fox was excavating a hole near Tonic that would become his grouse-hunting blind.

Fox arrived for our rendezvous, and shortly afterward Torn Tail appeared, taking his usual perch on Gin and looking more forlorn than you might have guessed possible for a scrawny, ripped up, black-beaked scavenger. After considering the bird, Fox and I faced each other.

"Maybe I should have been putting out more yolks?" Truth is, we were all three of us missing TBall.

With the light still good, I spent an hour watching a skunk churning the soil. Every few minutes it advanced, its wide, flat body undulating and its thick tail erect but for the lolling tip. Who would pass up the rare chance to admire a skunk tail brushing the air with a big question mark?

So, this was what we did with our time. And people wondered how we stayed busy without televisions.

MY LEGS SWUNG OUT of bed and hit the floor before I realized that a howl had woken me. Trailing behind on the whiplash, my head righted in time to spot through the window a kink-tailed kit with its head thrown back. Cracking open the dawn, the hooligan was yipping long, loud, and high. Shoving my bare feet into Wellies, I ran out of the house, the unfolded rubber pinching my calves. I almost tripped over the kit before I stopped running.

"Hush." It hushed. I checked around and convinced myself it wasn't in any danger. "Go on." It went. Its tail waved high, and I could see that someone had taken an irreplaceable bite from its white tassel, leaving only a few wispy strands on the right edge.

When the hooligan called reveille again the next morning, I reported for roll call. After satisfying itself that I had responded appropriately, the kit moved on. At sunup the morning after that, it screamed again. Yipping at dawn became a regular and yet unpredictable event. I felt like a hoodwinked townsman in Aesop's fable listening to a shepherd boy call "Wolf!" So the next time a hooligan cried at dawn, I hesitated by the window instead of running outside. A wounded tail, kinked like the neck of a trumpeter swan, poked out of the short grasses. That was enough to remind me that the lives of young wild animals skew toward disaster. I ran out the door. A great land baron steps up when an earnest young fox calls for a fire drill.

Emergency preparedness training wasn't their only hobby. The hooligans stole things. Pretty much anything they could carry off: melamine plates, plastic planters, plant tags. And even some things they couldn't carry off. After spotting a bright red line writhing through the grasses, I intercepted a role of flagging in mid-hijack.

Two years before Fox arrived, a vixen had given birth in a den adjacent to my backyard parking pad, not twenty-two meters from the bathroom window. When they were a month old, the kits played and wandered a few meters beyond the den. I got a great view by pulling off the window screen and kneeling on the toilet. Every evening, the vixen returned from hunting and stood straight-legged and stone-still while the four largest kits jumped underneath her and nursed. Night after night, four stocky kits finished nursing and ran off, leaving the fifth and unfed runt bumping its head up against the vixen's underside trying to coax milk from her empty teats. Night by night the deflated runt shrank, flattening further into the ground. One morning nothing remained but orange fuzz and four fat survivors. They squealed and ducked into one of their two den holes, keeping their distance from me. But not their secrets.

The mother of the frisky foursome was relatively bold and unafraid of the cottage, often hunting in my back meadow. The vixen from Fox's den rarely came outside in daylight, didn't hunt on my property, and never traveled with Fox except the one time she and Fox ambushed a small black feral cat below Pillbox Hat Hill. I was watching with binoculars. The cat was ambling slowly into a juniper's shadow. I would have sworn no other large animal was around, when the vixen, like a phantom, appeared in front of it. She swatted her long arm across the cat's face. Fox emerged from the uphill gully, a couple of meters behind the cat's tail. He chomped through the cat's shoulders, crushing its windpipe. I imagined hearing a gurgle and a loud escape of air.

With the dead cat hanging limp from his jaws, Fox watched the vixen run the fastest route to the den area. When she was out of sight, he came right to my cottage. He wasted an enormous amount of energy by loping past me with his dead cat's tail swinging from one side of his jaw. The route brought him farther downhill and about fifteen minutes out of his way; he lost both distance and elevation. But he achieved his purpose: flaunting that dead cat to impress me.

Of course, I don't *know* why he ran past me. Not because he was a fox, but because he was an individual. I don't know what motivates all *my* actions, let alone someone else's. I'll never know, for example, why anyone treats me the way they do. I certainly couldn't discover the truth by simply asking. People use words to communicate, and, knowingly or not, those words can be false. So I interpret what people say by watching what they do. Otherwise, if I'm relying on people's words, I am always getting tricked. Fox was easier to understand than people because he couldn't use words to deceive me.

WITHIN A WEEK, Jenna's university program with the University of Montana Western would bring me deep into Yellowstone National Park— three hours deep and seven days away from Fox. I became sullen as my field trip approached, wading through seas of tall grasses, first with him in my wake, later with me in his. I hiked to his den, where Fox looked down on a thin band of clouds floating below us, parallel to—and just above—the river. Enjoying their carefree existence, the surviving kits tussled on the long flat rock that topped their condo complex: one adult, three kits, no discipline. When I said goodbye, a cluster of tiny clouds floated in the sky, like an archipelago in a crystal-clear ocean.

Driving to Yellowstone, I practiced saying, "My best friend is a fox."

I know man's best friend is supposed to be a dog, but only because people pull the French philosopher François Voltaire's quote out of context. He never actually said, "A dog is man's best friend." And, anyway, long before Voltaire, Middle Eastern girls were befriending foxes. In the Levant, the region that today encompasses Israel, Jordan, Lebanon, and Palestine, 16,000-year-old graves cradle the bodies of girls, dogs, and foxes. A series of 8,000-year-old graves discovered in northern Israel tell a similar story. The dogs were working animals and dependent upon people. Not the foxes. Anthropologists figured that out by examining the bones and their stomach contents. Like their owners, the dogs ate grains, something they would never eat unless people were feeding them. The buried foxes remained true to a wild diet. It seems the dogs were pets and property; the foxes, I suspect, were friends.

"Nature has given the dog to man for his defense," wrote Voltaire, "and for his pleasure. Of all the animals it is the most faithful: it is the best friend man can have." When I met Fox, I couldn't admit to knowing anything about friendship. Now I know this: Voltaire has low standards for a famous guy. Defense and loyalty? A best friend should give you something money *can't* buy.

I planned to wait for an appropriate moment to announce, "My best friend is a fox," and while the students were cocking their heads in the classic pose of canine inquisitiveness, I would confuse them by adding that I was the loner who didn't want a friend, and he—the fox—was a bon vivant who dogged me around until I gave in. I would explain that Fox was a wild animal—not a pet—and that he chose his own companions and lived as independently from me as any one of them did.

. . .

"MY BEST FRIEND is a wild red fox."

They stared as if I were wearing cropped green jeans trimmed with orange ribbon. Apparently, the moment was not appropriate.

In hindsight: Everyone assumes that if your *best* friend is a fox, your *only* friend is a fox. And that was not the sort of thing anyone should have been bragging about. I could have denied his existence or our relationship, but what if the knowledge that his friend was a person was a source of pride for the fox? What amount of ego could justify an omission that might supply a modicum of satisfaction to a powerless tiny animal like Fox?

When Saint-Ex was dying in the Sahara Desert, foxes comforted him. He befriended them. Though he could have eaten one to save his life, he understood that we should not eat our friends no matter the temptation. If Saint-Ex wouldn't eat a fox to save his life, I wouldn't disown one to save face. I'd rather have people ridicule me for having a nit's wit than a snake's tongue.

Before meeting Fox, I avoided humanizing wild animals, an attitude I picked up in my scientific training and in my professional life as a ranger. I passed that attitude on to my students. The summer before I met him, I brought students to the National Museum of Wildlife Art in Jackson, Wyoming, on a cold summer day: windy, thirty-four degrees, and drizzling. In other words, too nice to let a museum enshroud me, but my contract said otherwise. We entered the museum, and a painting of swans accosted us. It was loud and mislabeled.

An artist had painted the swans with bright orange bills and curvy necks. Their eyes cast demurely downward as if admiring their own reflections. They were mute swans, *Cygnus olor*: classic, elegant, and European. Mutes populate the pages of *Grimm's Fairy Tales*, floating in castle moats with their wings arched up over their backs. Lovely. And silent.

The plaque read: "Trumpeter Swans (*Cygnus buccinator*)."

You'd think a wildlife artist would know the difference between a European mute swan and a native trumpeter swan, especially since the museum specialized in *native* wildlife. Trumpeters are stockier birds with black beaks. Instead of classic curvy necks and downcast faces, trumpeters hold their bills perpendicular to their tall straight necks. They float with their wings gripping their flanks, whereas mutes keep their wings ruffled up in an alluring pose. Instead of Ss, mutes are plumb-necked Zs. And they aren't silent; they sound like a honking car rodeo. Almost no one finds them as attractive as mutes. Sometimes trumpeters swished over my head when I skied. Sometimes they flew close enough that I could touch one with my raised ski pole, close enough for me to realize that their wingspan exceeded my height. They weren't just bigger than mutes; they were bigger than everything—they were North America's largest waterfowl. And we almost exterminated them.

Two hundred years ago, anyone floating the Mississippi River or fishing Chesapeake Bay could have watched trumpeter swans flying overhead. Between 1850 and 1880, the Governor and Company of Adventurers of England Trading into Hudson Bay (later shortened to Hudson's Bay Company) collected eighteen thousand swan skins—almost all of them peeled off trumpeters—and turned them into women's fashion accessories. Americans coveted the feathers but not the bird; landowners killed them and restocked their ponds with silent, beautiful European swans. By the time the Great Depression descended, fewer than a hundred trumpeters survived in the United States. Now that they are no longer harvested, trumpeters number in the tens of thousands. Some of that increase is due to reintroductions, including in my own valley. Most of them winter in Montana, Idaho, and Wyoming; we could see a dozen from the museum's rocky parapet.

The artist had confused mutes with trumpeters. Fortunately for my students, my doctoral degree and I had come prepared with *facts*. One of Montana's most famous wildlife artists, Mr. S., was outside lecturing in the sculpture garden, and when he paused for questions, my hand shot right up. I shook my little facts out like loaded dice on a craps table, ending with an emphatic, "So! Those are *not* trumpeter swans in your painting."

"Oh, no, they are," he replied calmly after a split-second pause. "In fact, they're *vain* trumpeters, and for that reason, they are *pretending* to be mute swans."

Naturally, I thought he was a jerk.

Graduate school training had led me to believe that understanding animals required gathering facts and creating objective and quantifiable data. Nothing more. I lost my imagination and ignored the importance of intuition. I thought it made me more professional. It didn't. Never mind that Mr. S. was an artist and I was a biologist; lack of imagination is not a career choice, it's a personality crisis.

Three years after I sauntered away from Mr. S., I was heading back to the museum with a similar class to show my students what a trumpeter swan looks like when it's putting on airs. Some of them would accuse me of fitting Mark Twain's definition of a *nature-fakir*: "a person who knows more about an animal than the animal knows about itself." I was fine with that. After all, there was a fox sunning above the Yellowstone River who knew more about me than I knew about myself.

SAND DOLLARS

I finished presenting the last slideshow of our weeklong field class. Thirty-five miles upriver from my cottage, I was anxious to go home. While our cabins were tucked into a damp green oasis, Fox had been suffering in an alarmingly dry August, and I was worried. Outside the auditorium, the sweet odor of rotting fruit wafted off the canker wounds in the cottonwoods. Cow elk meandered through the parking lot with their noses in the air, acting disaffected while their calves tried to nurse. Under a lamplight, Yellowstone's Mammoth Subdistrict Ranger was waiting for me. "Wildfire . . . fifty-mile-per-hour winds . . . road closed . . . evacuations likely."

This was not my first evacuation. In 2003, I had evacuated those five wooded acres next to Glacier National Park that I had purchased from Martha. No one expects a place called "glacier" to burn. Like International Falls, Minnesota, but a few thousand feet higher, Glacier's northern boundary follows the forty-ninth parallel. Annual snowfall on my parcel averaged thirteen feet. The year of the evacuation, I had been skiing in

Glacier on the Fourth of July. Then it got hot. Weeks passed without rain. Inside the forest, sparks from multiple sources exploded into wildfires. I stored my skis on July 8, and twenty days later, with the Robert Fire advancing toward my property, officials issued evacuation orders.

Robert was only one fire in a complex of wildfires that bit 136,000 acres and some outbuildings out of the Glacier National Park area. I didn't have a house on my land, but if I did, I would have been able to rebuild it in less than a year. If I lost the western red cedars on my property, I wouldn't see them restored in my lifetime. Of course, old cedars—several hundred years old—can handle themselves in a wildfire. Ancient cedars might even benefit from a wildfire if it burned away the pesky underbrush. My red cedars were about eighty years old and living at the eastern extent of their natural range. They loved humidity and shade. If wildfire removed the forest canopy, sunlight would heat the soil, drying it out and killing the red cedar embryos. Seeds that survived the drought wouldn't germinate until after pines and firs grew up, branched out, and shaded the forest floor.

Someone started the Robert Fire. Law enforcement officers didn't charge anyone, but they assigned the cause to either arson or human error, something like a four-foot log left burning in a campfire circle with a two-foot diameter. I would be more forgiving if Nature had started the fire by throwing a lightning bolt and cracking open one of those Douglas firs that were so tall I couldn't see the crown with my head tipped all the way back. Manmade fires demoralize me. They remind me that we are too many people living in too small a space and that I share the planet with bad people for whom we will never have enough space.

On the Robert, managers steered the wildfire away from private forests and cabins using an aggressive technique known as back-burning— fighting fire with fire. To get the back-burn started, helicopters dropped fuel-filled Ping-Pong balls that ignited when they hit the ground. The backfire was meant to produce an updraft that would pull the fire away from private landholdings—including mine. Backfires are dangerous. If the management-ignited fire blew in the wrong direction, the Robert would have incinerated a great deal of private property. Back-burns are also dangerous for firefighters. I'd been a buck firefighter under Ping-Pong balls in Hells Canyon, Idaho. I thought I might die. As the balls were dropping, a few went astray, wind and mass being what they are. We had to run after the wayward balls and beat out the flames and then run back uphill to the safety of the rocky ridgetop. On the Robert, the back-burn worked, and my little cedars survived.

Facing my second evacuation, I checked into a motel in Gardiner, a hamlet straddling the Yellowstone River. The next morning, I was sitting at the counter of a diner, scraping my fork across a plate of cold scrambled eggs. Our county undersheriff lumbered in wearing a radio that was crackling barely audible commands. Keeping his head down, he pushed through the kitchen doors to gossip with the cook, emerging with a piece of flakey toast, no plate. He told me the blockade might open for an hour or two before noon. His free knuckle rapped alongside my coffee mug. *Let's go. Cowboy up.* I was too exhausted to eat or cry.

Getting to the barricade quickly might give me time to pack and do the fire chores: sliding furniture away from windows, unlocking doors for firemen, drenching wooden steps, running soaker hoses. Packing. Contacting Helga about her station wagon still sitting at the cottage.

I used the motel's landline to phone my friend Mark, a wildlife photographer in Gardiner, and he picked me up from the diner. Mark's son and his girlfriend, Lori, both offered to help me move. Leaving my hatchback behind, we drove to the fire blockade in Mark's truck, not knowing whether the road to my house would be open.

For several miles we followed the river's canyon, white water to our left, a rocky ridge and Dome Mountain on our right. Above the summit, a column of white smoke streamed into the sky, curling upward until it was twice the height of the mountain. Dense brown clouds surrounding the white pillar were rolling upward and punching into the bright cobalt sky. Crossing a bridge put the river on our right, and I could see the hillside above my cottage. When a narrow stream of black smoke shot up, I figured that structures were burning and I started to cry.

I've seen enough crown fires that I can't remember the first one. Like so many park rangers from around the United States, I'd served on a fire crew in Yellowstone during the infamous summer of 1988. Now I was staring at billowing gray plumes that were rising and expanding at a speed that exceeded all my expectations of physical reality. Like the fear small animals have of shadows passing overhead, my fear of great uncontrollable forces was primal. Worse, distance had muzzled the inferno. Silent enemies are more frightening than those we can hear.

"Two hours. In and out. Houses on your lane are burning." The uniformed official manning the roadblock slapped Mark's truck and waved us through. Everything I wanted to save fit in either Helga's station wagon or in Mark's small truck. We grabbed my .30-06, slides, skis, books, Remington 20-gauge, Pivettas, Moss tent, several pairs of moose-hide mukluks, a Model 19 .357 with a crosshatch pattern carved into the wooden grip, four sleeping bags and a bivy sack, a bear on skis given to me by a fellow ranger at Mount Rainier, two bows and a camouflage quiver with arrows, my North Face Moraine women's internal-frame backpack. I did not own anything heavy or fragile. No TV, stereo, cell phone, or desktop computer; no dishes that cost more than a dollar, glassware, or pottery. Very little jewelry.

My grandfather's ring, gold, scored, and inset with a diamond, circled my middle finger. I pushed it there when I was twelve and never removed it. My grandmother had given it to him the first time he went to jail. She died about two decades before my birth, so I can't ask her for the details. I loved the ring because I loved my grandfather, and I loved my grandfather because he was the only adult who held my hand and sang to me and took me to Disneyland. Or maybe because he was the only adult who held my hand. He drove me around on the back of his Harley and in the back-seat of his T-Bird. I especially loved chasing horned toads up the brick wall of his house. He sent me birthday cards signed with an X. Not the letter *X*, the figure X; that's how people sign when no one has taught them the alphabet. I don't know much about him, and he didn't know much about me. When I was twelve, my father told me that he died in prison and when I put up a huge fight about going to the funeral, he taught me a new phrase, "potter's field."

All the furniture except the bed and the two second-hand sofas folded or doubled as packing crates. For the first time, this paucity of belongings embarrassed me. Mark referred to the cottage as a "starter home," imply-ing that a real home was in the works or at least in the realm of possibility. It wasn't.

Shallow home is a better description of the cottage. Like a sun-bleached sand dollar, I left just a little dent in my substrate. Have you ever tried to pull a sand dollar from the beach? As soon as you lift it out of the mire, a water vortex obliterates all traces of the spot where it had settled. Begin-ning in college, every place I lived had been tentative or uncertain; I be-came stuck wherever a disinterested tide left me. But a shallow home is no home at all. So why didn't I dig in, mark my territory, and transition to a forever home? I had so many reasons. As soon as I talked myself out of one excuse, another one advanced forward. Either I was waiting for some-thing (like a real job) or someone (like a real relationship), or I didn't need a forever home after all. And even if I did need a forever home, I didn't deserve one anyway.

We finished emptying the cottage with time remaining on our two-hour allotment and fire fuming above the back hills. Mark took photos. The fire's visual impact must have been astounding for a professional art-ist. For me, the fire produced a more visceral reaction. I had spent enough time on the land to recognize that fire and I were so much alike—fueling ourselves with carbohydrates, exhaling carbon dioxide, consuming oxygen, releasing water—that we threatened each other.

Carbohydrates are composed of nothing more than carbon, hydrogen, and oxygen. Those odd and noncaloric ingredients turn into sugar and starches when plants cobble together water and carbon dioxide. The sun powers the entire process.

If my God were physical instead of spiritual, it would be the sun. If trees had a god, it, too, would be the sun. And for the same reason. The sun warms and feeds us, providing fuel for all the work we do and for every intricate task our cells perform. Every time a plant cell creates a carbohydrate, the sun adds a little spark of energy to it. Pairs of carbon atoms hold the energy. They act like two kids stretching a rubber band between them. Each carbon holds on to one end of the band and pulls. In the case of a tree, they might hold that taut band for hundreds of years. When a wildfire attacks, billions of carbon kids let go of their rubber bands all at once. *Zing!* Energy explodes into the atmosphere.

Mark and I could feel the heat as we walked up to Helga's wagon, my ride back to town. I opened the door and it sank toward the ground, threatening to fall off. Above us, wind was spraying flames sideways across the hillside. A long line of black smoke trailed behind the blaze so that it looked like a fire-breathing dragon was scrambling in and out of the dales.

Only days earlier, our natural history class had visited Grant Village interpretive center, where we had picked up brochures from the Department of the Interior that opened with this line: "If variety is the spice of life, then fire is the very life of variety." It also stated, "Fire is the great recycler." This made fire sound like a good thing. Well, better than a fire-breathing dragon anyway. Most fire ecology websites or books will explain that combustion mineralizes nutrients and transfers them from living tissue mass to dead tissue. Mineralization is primarily the work of animals. Animals mineralize nutrients by excreting their food. Elk pellets. Night soil. Bear shit. Buffalo pie. The food they eat is living tissue—biomass—and the substance they excrete into the soil is dead tissue—necromass. Fires are so much like us they can perform the same task, consuming biomass and spitting out the raw minerals.

Living things need nutrients that are in limited supply. Unless they're recycled, we'll run out. Phosphorous, for example, is a critical component of DNA. Tonic and Gin were absorbing phosphorus from the soil and using it to build new cells. If they were caught in the wildfire, the phosphorous in their tissues would be "mineralized," or recycled, into the soil and absorbed by their surviving offspring. Someone studying Gin and Tonic with an objective eye might conclude that the old junipers were unproductive and that combustion would be a good, fair death, like pneumonia to an old man.

One ridge beyond my cottage, a cumulus cloud swelled above a fire plume. Mark and I watched hopefully as if a rainstorm was thinking about rescuing us. In reality, the fire was burning through a mature pine forest and creating its own weather. As each tree succumbed to the fire, it released an amount of water equal to about half its weight. The resulting steam column rose about six miles before condensing into a cloud.

When Lori came out and reminded me to check the front door one last time, I hurried toward the cottage but detoured at the steps. Running now, I picked up a soaker hose and dropped it off between Gin and Tonic. When I returned to the vehicles, Lori was tapping her watch. She was smart. And she taught school. She must have already known about fire convection columns, the cumulous clouds forming above them, and how the fire threatening my land was simply, and importantly, recycling water. But she was too polite to lecture us. Our planet exists inside something like a sealed terrarium that prevents water from entering or leaving. So, we've got a limited amount, and we have to share. If you are a gamer, think of water as a zero-sum competition. If one player gains a unit of water, another player needs to sacrifice a unit.

It's true that wildfires recycle water. So do pandemics. If a virus wipes out a portion of my county, dead bodies will surrender their water allowance to the terrarium's atmosphere, where it will be available to other living things. This type of recycling is not analogous to tossing an empty pop can into the correct bin. Fire robs water from one forest and gives it to another. Like Robin Hood, but without any morals.

Lori shut the door to Helga's wagon, and we took off. I told God not to let the fire recycle Gin and Tonic. They were the oldest living things I'd ever loved.

I didn't love the cottage, but if it burned down, I could never replace the time and energy I'd devoted to building it. Finding and buying raw land had been a monumental task. I began by visiting the county plat room to see who owned what. While there, I read well reports and recorded the depth and head pressure of all the extant water wells. I drove around and checked out the land with good wells, and when I found parcels that looked inviting, I visited the owners. In fact, I visited the owners of the land I ended up buying multiple times before they gave in and agreed to sell. Then I got a loan from a farmer's bank.

Learning graduate-level physical chemistry was easier than developing raw land. My original loan only covered land; I needed another loan before I could start building. With one room on each level, my floor plan was too odd to qualify for a Fannie Mae. I found a mortgage broker who helped me score a construction loan even though my salary came from guiding backcountry hikers—a part-time gig with no health insurance. The search was slow, but I finally found a wonderful contractor who was willing to build a hobbit hole in an isolated area. Meanwhile, an affluent city, sixty miles west, was paying laborers more than I could afford, so skilled workers were hard to find. Next came improving the well, testing the water, filing water rights. Then the hard work began: choosing the size and aspect of the house and driveway; designing the floor plan; selecting wall colors, light fixtures, and appliances. The nearest Home

Depot was more than two hundred miles away. The builders and I haggled over window placement in the Rainbow Room. I wanted windows spaced unevenly so I could gaze on certain peaks while standing in one spot. Before transferring from construction mortgage to home mortgage, I needed a home inspection. And a new mortgage bank.

Some jobs were emotionally taxing: driving sixty miles to the contractor's house to ask why he hadn't painted the downstairs yet; finding out that he was waiting for me to change my mind about "pink walls"; explaining again that the color I chose was rose adobe, *not pink*; dealing with a well-drilling team who didn't want to finish the project because my place "looks snaky." Do you know what kind of men work outdoors in an isolated area downriver from a place called Rattlesnake Butte and *don't* bring guns to work? The kind of men who cannot legally carry guns. The kind of men convicted of domestic assault.

As you might imagine, there were not too many single women developing raw and isolated land.

I trundled home several days after the evacuation. My cottage was smoky but unharmed. All three kits had survived the fire and were roaming around looking for things to steal. The vixen stayed hidden but caterwauled sporadically. The smoke cleared in two weeks, and a high-pitched wail and a kink-tail poking through wheatgrasses signaled the commencement of fire drills. The great land baron, humbled by wildfire, ran out to renew battle with runaway dogs, feral cats, and slough-stuffing tumbleweeds.

Fox was missing.

A firefighter stationed half a mile down the road to log and orient the arriving mop-up crews didn't *think* any of their heavy vehicles had run over an adult fox. I froze. He rephrased his words. "No. We'd have noticed. No one ran over a fox. But a scrawny fox—"

"Yes! That's him!"

"Real scrawny? An adult? Headed to the river one night."

I started toward the river.

He called after me that he was sorry. When I turned around, he shrugged and shook his head as if to say, *It's a fire. Animals die.* I shuffled toward the river with my muddy-feet walk. He would have been right if he had said, "It's a fire. *Wild* animals die."

If I had owned Fox, if I had licensed, collared, tagged, or leashed him, then firefighters would have tried to save him. But if I owned him, how could I have called him my friend?

After bushwhacking through thickets of delicate red willow, rubbery coyote willow, and fragrant wolf willow, I reached the river. On the far shore, Cloud Catcher Mountain rose three thousand feet above the water, its wide alluvial fans spreading into sagebrush steppe. A white disk-shaped cloud was hovering between its twin peaks, rocking like a meniscus in a glass. Fox could have fled to safety with the vixen and the four-month-old kits, but I believe he waited for me. I imagined him upright on his hind legs and pressing his nose into my front window like he used to do. I could see him standing with his ears drawn back until his ankles shook and then skipping backward to regain his balance. His last memory of me was an empty house. But what could I have done if I had seen him? I couldn't have taken him away with me.

When I headed home, the white disk cloud was still rocking between the peaks, unable to generate enough energy to splash over either one.

Purple-tinged bird droppings speckled Surfboard Rock. Birds were taking liberties they wouldn't have dared a month earlier when their faith in Fox's hunting prowess kept them off his pedestal. He wouldn't even let me touch the surfboard. One day rain was pelting down so hard that mud splashed into the air. I was putting a plastic tub outside for Delbert, our UPS man, and Fox, sheltering under Tonic, was watching me. When I got too close to the surfboard, he abandoned cover and pounced on it. I stood under the portico watching rain drench him until the concave pits on his baby boulder turned into little pools. He wasn't going to let me grab that rock. It was his second most favorite.

I had stolen his first favorite right out from under him. The limestone block, a fairly well-formed rectangle, had been performing an important function: decorating the dirt path between the driveway and the front steps. Like most limestone, it had solidified under a shallow sea, in this case, 350 million years earlier. Partially embedded crinoids and brachiopods made the surface rough and uneven. Fox was always rubbing his fuzzy butt on it and—I imagined—wearing down the raised clam shells and other Paleozoic fossils. Soon after we met, when I was still impatient with his company, I caught him scratching his stomach on my precious specimen. So, I got a wild hair and yelled at him to scoot. Footprints in the dirt betrayed him; he was sneaking back when I wasn't looking. *Foxes do not need bidets*, I thought to myself when I brought it inside, *and anyway he'll never notice*. Now the sedimentary sample reclines indoors on a felt-covered pedestal and serves no purpose at all. When your friend is gone, you remember these slights and ask yourself what difference one more fuzzed butt would have made to a 350-million-year-old rock. You don't answer the question because it's rhetorical.

Since then I have realized that massaging himself with that slab—the only one in his home range with a perfectly rough surface and a shape that fit his body—put a little well-earned joy in his life. And now I was serving penance by scrubbing bird droppings off Surfboard Rock, like a monk in a Japanese fox shrine.

Well, the shrines are not really *for* foxes. They're *for* Inari, a Shinto and Buddhist deity whose close relationship with foxes begins around 700 CE. I learned about Inari from my Japanese students. I told them about my best friend; they told me about Inari foxes. Foxes are Inari's guardians, messengers, or servants; the relationship is as fluid as a fox. Some of the fox statues that monks wash are human-sized. Holding their heads and tails erect, the foxes wear red ceremonial capes and guard the temple entrances. In his 1894 book, *Glimpses of Unfamiliar Japan*, Lafcadio Hearn writes that hundreds of stone foxes reside in shrines to Inari, "the God of Rice." Shrines and temples in larger towns might have thousands of carved fox figurines, some small enough to hide in tiny crevices. Fox icons—and often real foxes—appear in thirty thousand Inari temples throughout Japan, a country the size of California. In other words, if we distributed the temples evenly throughout the country, one would appear every twelve and a half square miles. Fox images are everywhere in Japan.

And why not? If you follow the Shinto belief system and immerse yourself in nature, you'll see a lot of wild animals, but none more charismatic and strikingly beautiful than a red fox. And in the days before pesticides, none more useful. Imagine wrapping your blistered hands around a wooden hoe shaft as you toil in your vegetable field. Gazing downfield, you spy onion greens slipping into the dirt. An underground vole is sucking on the bulb, siphoning your crop as you watch helplessly. Foxes arrive and rescue you from starvation. They are glorious animals and you adore them.

Hearn interpreted the personalities of the Inari fox statues: "Whimsical, apathetic, inquisitive, saturnine, jocose, ironical; they watch and snooze and squint and wink and sneer; they wait with lurking smiles; they listen with cocked ears most stealthily, keeping their mouths open or closed. There is an amusing individuality about them all, and an air of knowing mockery about most of them, even those whose noses have been broken off." If he had written *even those whose voices have been broken off,* he could have been describing Fox.

From Hearn's writings I learned that foxes can be supernatural and convey prayers and wishes to Inari. Shape-shifting foxes trick, deceive, or enchant people for both good and bad ends. Their most egregious crime is "taking diabolical possession of [people] and tormenting them into madness."

If you want to believe Shinto stories about foxes shape-shifting and communicating with gods, well, then, you need to take it on faith. But as for foxes spreading a little inspiration, casting spells on people, and chasing mischief, well, that sounds right to me. Country people living with foxes would have plenty of stories to tell, all of them springing from the natural behavior of foxes and people. Consider a farmer shambling home from the rice field, exhausted and hungry, when a bright red fox leaps through the field, stops, and gazes at him. That night his wife gives birth to the son he's been praying for. He'd seen dozens of animals that day— sparrows, squirrels, beetles, frogs, flies. But he *remembers* the fox. And so it goes, his story entwining with other villagers' tales of fox sightings coinciding with momentous occasions. A woman discovers a fox den and forfeits her chores to spend days, then weeks, watching foxes play. The tales spread and become part of the cultural folklore.

Hearn writes that Japanese country people, "like the peasantry of Catholic Europe," make up myths for themselves. If I lived in an age when stories depended upon word-of-mouth instead of books, Fox and I might have become a myth. Our story, like any traditional folklore, would be brief and symbolic: *Once upon a time, a girl who needed a friend grew up believing she was a magpie. From the magpies, she learned to allow ancient memories to command her attitude toward people. She adopted the magpie habit of taking whatever was offered to her but would not acknowledge or deign to rely on the giver. A wild fox pursued the magpie-girl, and she fell under his spell. From the fox she learned the purpose and the responsibility of friendship. He helped her choose a path for her life. But when a great wildfire came, she left the fox to die. Realizing her wrongdoing too late . . .* Well, and then they would end it with a few words. Maybe, overtaken with grief and guilt, she would (figuratively) stab her beak into her breast and tear her flesh out like the mandarin duck hen in Lafcadio Hearn's folktale; or she would revert to her magpie personality; or figure out how she can find another friend; or learn what to do if she doesn't find one.

275

While I was hosing down the surfboard, rose-colored clouds spilled slowly across the mountains, like a can of tipped paint. For thousands of years, Japanese faithful have maintained the Inari-temple fox statues. As long as I lived here, I would be cleaning this rock and planting and tending a little crop of forget-me-nots. Just as I finished cleaning Surfboard, the clouds burst and flew apart. I watched the rose-colored pieces spread, trying hard not to blink and miss something now that I was watching for both of us.

I began mourning him by doing things that he would have done. My anger did not dissipate. His death was intolerable. Chimerical images I had carried as talismans couldn't help me because my mind was numb. My body was exploding from the inside. It is impossible to function when you feel your insides pushing against your skin and nothing gives way, not for hours, or even days. With so much anger trapped inside me, my adrenaline surged. Physiological reactions followed: rising blood pressure, rapid respiration, hyperglycemia. Some people might eat or drink to tamp surging adrenaline, but the advantage to being athletic is that you can rid yourself of anger and excess adrenaline by simply pushing your fist through a wall. Fortunately, the cottage had very little wall space and lots of barbells. I pumped iron.

Flushing away the adrenaline left me calm but dazed. In March, a large skunk was sleeping in a mixture of scree, juniper berries, and old leaves. A tiny skunk waddled around the adult while rocks clattered underneath its feet. When the adult didn't rise with my calling, I brushed a branch through its long hair and realized it was dead. The baby could not understand why the adult was so quiet, why it wasn't getting up. Even the mating flickers on a nearby juniper's crown stopped dancing to peer over at the bewildered baby skunk, one of nature's most forlorn sights. Now I was that low-slung baby skunk toddling down the slope. How did Fox die? What were his last moments like? If the fog would clear, maybe I could see the answers. All I could do was gather as many facts as possible and wait. If I was lucky, my mind would perform tricks.

❦

Never dammed, channeled, riprapped, or straightened, everywhere the Yellowstone River runs, it runs wild. Curving into its muddy banks like a giant salamander, it is the longest free-flowing river in the United States. Elliptical islands swell between the river's braids, creating logjams that trap small plant debris like branches, twigs, and leaves. The river knits the debris into raft-like mats. At the right moment, in some nuanced mood of current, she sets the rafts free.

Today a shaking fox reclines on a raft moored to an overhanging willow. Earlier in the summer, a cat killed one of his friends. His other friend is missing. After watching and waiting for several days, he has become increasingly disoriented as the smoke and the noise have grown heavier and louder. His eyes and throat sting, his tongue is gritty from panting in the hot smoky air, and still the girl hasn't appeared. How could she have abandoned him in the middle of this catastrophe?

The bowline, a tangle of clematis vines, surrenders to the tossing river, and the fox sails away. The day is hot, the ride is rolling, and the fox is hungry. His raft hits a barren pebble island and leaves him marooned. With deep channels of fast water on all sides, the hungry fox on the island of sand and cobbles is dying. The fox has always loved sunbathing, and now with sun covering him, he is warm enough that he could be happy forever. But the sun keeps heating until it is no longer warming but stabbing. He's burning hot, and the heat moves inside him, gently pushing his consciousness out of its way. In lucid moments, he sees other foxes, the magpie, and the girl. She is sitting in front of him, talking and pushing brown hair away from her eyes. The evening sky is pinking. Her long, feathered tail fans. It isn't the girl after all: it's the magpie. She lifts off, flying past the den cove with long fingers strumming the air. Watching her fly, he is unsure . . . person . . . magpie. Then he is certain. They are so similar—the girl and the magpie. In his exhaustion, he can't waste energy separating them into two.

In the end, the sun bursts through his tiny body and seeps into the cobbles below him.

I knelt next to Fox's birthday rock, stroking its rough, rounded edges and picturing "F-O-X" carved on top. The owner of a monument factory seventy miles away said he would engrave Surfboard while I waited. More than halfway there, I realized my idea was ridiculous. *F-O-X on a rock?* The one thing he never wanted to be was just another fox on a rock. But friends are not flawless. If he knew anything about me, he knew that.

Worse luck, I am only human; ostentatious grieving is our touchstone. Maybe wild animals are too genuine to grieve ostentatiously. After he died, I decided to grieve with a little less culture and a little more wildness—like an animal. This meant, of course, almost not at all. I soon came to understand the self-serving nature of human grief; my sadness was nothing compared to his. I had lost a friend; he had lost his life. He died too young, too happy, too ambitious. How could I wallow in a shallow pool of misery when his misery was infinite? Regardless of where Fox ended up when he died, he would rather be here, pushing his nose into that blue forget-me-not, leaping on a vole, sunbathing on a boulder. He would want to be alive. I want that, too, but I won't be so patronizing as to pretend that I want it more than he does.

FIELDS OF DUN AND GUNNY

A flock of bluebirds pushes against unyielding wind. Sinking slightly, the birds slip under the current and advance steadily until the wind finds them again. Gut punched by one gigantic gust, the flock back flips, rights, regroups, carries on. Above Gin, my favorite juniper, they hover and rise like a cumulus cloud. Before the next gust strikes, they flatten into a cirrus sheet, tip their black beaks toward the tree, and descend. Within seconds, the bluebirds infuse the entire juniper. Their quivering turns the flame-shaped Gin into a propane pilot light, an image more comforting this chilly spring day than tiny birds, blue or otherwise.

I wouldn't mind being alone with bluebirds, but the red-winged blackbirds swaying on cattail heads can't resist a following wind. They push off and end up layered between Gin's braided branches. Robins sheltering in pea shrubs wait for a lull, and then they flee to take up widely separate perches in Gin. Perhaps they'd been arguing. I can't hear anything over the cackling of red-winged blackbirds. *Why do different species of birds huddle together?* I never answered that question because it has no answer.

It's the wrong question. Lots of wild animals are less finicky about whom they socialize with than we are. The right question is *Why don't people socialize with animals?* And by "animals," I mean unboxed animals. Like the little prince's fox. Like my fox. Animals that are as free-living and independent from us as a meadowlark is from a wren. Maybe we like pretending that they are not very human. Or that we are not very wild.

The dry meadows are covered with clumps of dun bunchgrasses poking through soil the color of a gunnysack. Today, I've been outside so long that my lungs have synchronized to heave between gusts of wind. I keep squinting to wring wind tears from my eyes. I'm thinking about a fox who's been dead for two years now and who wanted to rub noses with the only blue flower in this endless field of dun and gunny.

There isn't a clipboard to shield me from the wind today because I am not counting birds or doing science. It's not that counting is bad. Numbers provide the raw material for statistics that enlighten us about how average animals behave. Of course, I am not just talking about wild animals. Most of us want to understand how all average animals behave, including people. Society sets parameters for "normal" behavior based upon what it perceives as "average." And it never hurts to know what the rest of the world is up to. Don't discount the value in that. But don't confuse normal behavior with natural behavior. If people need to stay under the bell curve's peak to be "natural," then we are, all of us, and everywhere, dun and gunny.

This reminds me of Martha's secret. I share a curious worldview with Ishmael, Saint-Ex, and another million or so people (in this world of seven billion). By instinct, we perceive a world dominated by Nature, its wild animals, plant life, and nonhuman elements: sand or sky or sea. We don't purposely ignore people; we just have trouble focusing on them. As Martha would say, my first family was everyone who lived outside—squirrels and lizards and ducks. Sometimes I push human faces to the far background. Finally, Martha told me that some of the time, I don't see people because I'm communicating with other animals. Or staring at clouds. And when she thought I figured it out, I think she said, "*Most* of the time, you don't hear us." Something like that.

If Martha had read *Moby-Dick*, she would have recognized my personality in the novel's last scene. *Pequod*, the busted whaler—now nearly vertical—is sinking. Tashtego, the Native American harpooner, is drowning in a shark-infested sea and will soon join all of Ishmael's compatriots. Something Tashtego is holding, part of the ship perhaps, inadvertently traps a sea eagle. During the entire tragedy of the *Pequod*, Ishmael, who is off the ship and watching from one of the smaller whaleboats, most keenly perceives the trapped bird. The sea eagle panics, struggling to free itself while slowly submerging to its death. How is it that in all the infinite, gray depth that surrounds him, while he's listening to his shipmates' screams, Ishmael writes, finally, about the suffering of one anonymous hawk? "And so the bird of heaven, with archangelic shrieks, and his imperial beak thrust upwards, and his whole captive form folded in the flag of Ahab, went down with his ship, which, like Satan, would not sink to hell till she had dragged a living part of heaven along with her."

I suspect that Ishmael wasn't quite tame. Neither are most foxes. Foxes are genetically predisposed to be wild and shun people and our contraptions. Through Dmitri Belyaev's research we learned that people can tame foxes. Fox was not typical for his species, and I am not typical for mine. That's what the statistics show anyway. Mostly what makes me atypical is that I live alone, far from any town or city or suburb. Fortunately, I have access to books that let me connect with people whose spirits transcend time and place. People like Saint-Ex and Ishmael and Mr. Frankenstein. Of course, we all carry genes that never matter, those that predispose us but don't commit us to any specific behavior. Sometimes, without the right circumstances, genes aren't enough to determine our behavior. Sometimes we do what we want despite our genes.

Fox and I first came eye to eye when a housefly distracted me from counting birds in the very same juniper I am looking at now. It was a warmer day, and yet I wore more clothes. Today I'm wearing Carhartt overalls and a red river-driver shirt because I value my time and don't mind being chilly. Piling on enough clothes to stay warm takes too long. Even if I live another sixty years, life will be short. I can't waste time wrapping up against inevitable wind.

Before I met him, I hadn't thought of a red fox as one of life's necessary accouterments. I was plodding along, somewhere between birth and death, and, like you, trying to do whatever people of our age and culture were supposed to be doing. I experienced my share of life's requisite calamities. Some left scars. Overall, my life was not especially wanting. Not especially anything except uncertain and sans Fox. Today, my relationship with him so thoroughly defines my life that all my previous years on earth seem like nothing so much as impoverished by foxlessness.

I finally figured out that the fly on my knee—mesmerizing Fox on one side and me on the other—was not the centripetal force that pulled Fox and me together. Not really. At a single extended moment of time, we both stared at a black fly sucking blood from my scab and saw an ornate creature dancing on a crimson pedestal. We both dismissed the inherent danger of breathing within striking distance of someone's hands or fangs and watched the dancer twirl blood like it was a silk scarf. I doubt there was another individual in the valley that day who would have done the same.

I've stopped planting forget-me-nots and keeping Surfboard Rock clean for Fox. I prefer bright red yarrow and purple Russian sage, so I've let them crowd out his favorite flower. Some days, cherry-red bird droppings coat Surfboard. My concern is with foxes now, not with Fox. That's part of his legacy, and legacies are the point of friendship. I keep the draw clean so foxes can travel safely from ridges to river. I fight tumbling, tall, and thorny weeds aggressively.

If it weren't so windy, I could sit at the old rendezvous site. I've stopped throwing my camp chair on hard clumps of spiky weeds, stopped asking permission of the land to seat me. I'm here for the long haul, so I find a comfortable spot and make myself fit in, like Fox used to do. Life on the land is not a way station while I wait to entangle myself in a more appropriate career. Wild lands and quiet spaces are not my escape; they are my home base. Sporadically, I retreat to field classes, surrounding myself with people and enjoying a reprieve from natural space. I know there are people who do the reverse, and people who have not yet decided which is home and which is holiday. However we choose, let's not fuss about it; we'll bump into each other in the coming or going. I trust we'll be cordial.

During the fire, I evacuated my entire cottage in two hours. It will never again be that easy to move. The cottage is deeply rooted. Like Fox, I have marked my territory. Remember when I became indignant over the suggestion that fox ("Foxie!") was a pet, and I told you that hanging around a fox was not the same thing as decorating a terrier in tartans or teaching a parrot to solicit crackers? Here's why: When you spend time with your pets, they become more like you. When I spent time with Fox, I became more like him. Monkey saw; monkey did. And like Fox, I have filled my home with objects of personal value. After replacing my young cherry tree (times three), I began large landscaping projects. Because builders are erecting houses at a never-ending pace and traffic on the gravel road is sure to pick up, I am planting long, deep hedges that will soon be ten feet tall and will form dense screens even after autumn's leaves drop. I ordered furniture built and delivered by Amish folks in the Midwest, and, for the first time ever, the furniture is too big to fit in the hatchback.

I've become more like Fox in other ways, too, because in order to find friends who are like Fox, I have to act like him and not like a magpie. I've stopped trying to disappear. We had been opposites that way, the fox and I. He wanted connections. He wanted to matter. And for no reason other than that it felt so much better than being alone, he often liked to have someone at his side when he padded under the full moon's light or stretched on a sun-warmed rock. Accidents of birth didn't handicap him. So I've had an oral surgeon remove the frenum between my front teeth and stitch up my gum. I decided to visit the Everglades, and the first person I asked to join me said yes. Now Jack and I chat on the phone all the time. I've been corresponding with Chun and Doug, a couple I met in Yellowstone, the ones who recommended *Downton Abbey*. They asked me to meet them in Mount Rainier. It was terrific fun, and now we're planning our next vacation together.

I've committed myself to a full-time university job and will not look back. Jenna wrote a letter of recommendation for me. Almost every day I study, discuss, and write about natural history, not from a college campus, but from a country cottage or an outdoor field site—a virtual campus, an online community. I teach biology, a discipline with beautiful edges, sharp as obsidian. But that eloquent precision is not enough to satisfy me. I like to keep my thoughts so fluid that the real world and the imagined world swirl together until it is just as easy to separate them as it is to combine them.

IT'S NOVEMBER, and the low-elevation rifle hunt is open. Mule deer are frantically dodging guns, hormones, and trucks. They are not successful. Yesterday I drove thirty miles to town along a blood-splashed two-lane. Now a cold north front is driving more deer down from the high country, and I wander around my property, waiting to warn them off my favorite shrubs. It seems like there are hundreds of them in the back pasture, though I count only fifty. They have come to build their first winter trails across my property. They move slowly, but I am patient, steering them around my shrubs and trees before they entrench a trail. Once their route sets, this herd will march unwaveringly upon it for the next six months. In one winter, fifty deer that look like hundreds can carve a canal into a meadow. The herd tumbles down my back hill, skidding on fresh snow and meandering toward my steps. They are pretending not to notice me and expect me to return the courtesy. I don't. Because they move as a herd and the young rarely nurse this late in the year, I am having a hard time picking out the family units.

Clouds shape today's sky. They cast it gray and flash blue sucker holes from time to time. The edges of one sucker hole roll upward as though someone has punched a fist through the clouds from below. Before the day ends, I'll stand under it and pretend to be shocked when clouds sear the hole shut, turn charcoal black, and hose me down. Acting the fool for anxious clouds is just one of the roles I sometimes play because I live in country where the sky dominates land, buildings, roads. Other times, I decide to wear Gore-Tex and act like I don't care.

Tennis Ball's nest has not had any occupants since the fire. Once round and bigger than a basketball, it is now cascading though the juniper and will soon disappear into the duff. Iridescent blackbirds built a hand-sized nest several branches above it. For two months this spring, they sat in her juniper and rattled like maracas, pausing only occasionally to emit an unsettling sound like someone blowing bubbles into a glass of water.

If new magpies move in, I suspect they, too, like Tennis Ball, will dislike me. Many magpie generations ago, the first humans they saw were ruthless. And it will take too many more generations of human kindness and egg yolks before they learn to trust us again. When I came along, trying to make friends with them, I was too late by a hundred years. Despite the egg yolks, I really wasn't all that nice to Tennis Ball. It wasn't conscious, but in hindsight I understand that I couldn't like her because she was too similar to me. She reminded me of my worse traits. She couldn't change her druthers, but I can change mine. Not because I'm better or gifted, but only because I'll live longer. It's not practical for a short-lived bird to change her personality.

The herd places its collective lips on cold, wet grass shoots, rolls their eyes upward, and navigates across my artesian spring's runoff channel.

One little buck, about five months old, stares up at the cottage's blue steel roof, searching for something besides old grass. I wonder if he'll get enough to eat. While his sloppily assembled herd shifts past my outbuilding, he and one adult doe linger behind. I watch through the glass door.

A sizeable gap separates the little buck and adult doe from their herd. Staring at me, he dawdles too long for the impatient doe. She gives up waiting and pushes on to catch up with the others, now across the creek. He continues staring at me from five meters off. Now and then, the doe stops, turns her head 180 degrees, and looks behind at the little gray buck. He still has not eaten, but his stocky well-proportioned body alleviates my concern; he is finding food somewhere. For now, while I stand behind the glass storm door, he only wants to watch me. I wave my right hand in front of my face to signal that I am watching him, too. Then I open the storm door, step outside, raise my arms over my head, and clap, curious whether sudden movement will spook him. It doesn't.

His little horns have not begun to sprout, but his brow line has darkened. Without moving his legs, he bends his neck to nose a Townsend's solitaire off a sagebrush, but the bird, holding fast, flicks a wing into the buck's cheek. Jerking his head up, the little deer looks straight at me, wondering if I have witnessed the insult. Doe and herd are half a mile away, white tails flashing as they line out across the alfalfa field. I wait. He won't stop staring. Fifteen minutes later, when the solitaire flies away, I tell him, "Goodnight," go inside, and drop the violet shade over the glass.

ACKNOWLEDGMENTS

I am happy to acknowledge specific individuals and organizations for their contributions to the manuscript. I am indebted to: my friend Jack, who followed Fox's story from the beginning and made sure I didn't give up; Verna Macpherson for wisdom and countless days in Yellowstone and the Grand Tetons; Mary Carparelli for friendship and refining my ideas about Fox and myself; Martha Sloan for prodding me toward a deeper understanding of myself; the Museum of Wildlife Art for welcoming me over the years; Nick Flynn, Steve Almond, and Deirdre McNamer for offering creative advice; Amanda Fortini, Tim Cahill, and Tessa Fontaine for inspiration and commentary; Barrett Briske for copyediting; everyone at Spiegel & Grau for working hard on and believing in the story. Dawn Hill read and critiqued the entire manuscript. Without the generosity and kindness of the Pirate's Alley Faulkner Society, Rosemary James, Joseph DeSalvo, and Andrei Codrescu, I would not have met Celina Spiegel. To Celina, I am indebted beyond words; she alone is the *sine qua non* for *Fox and I*.

ABOUT THE AUTHOR

Catherine Raven earned a PhD in biology from Montana State University and degrees in zoology and botany from the University of Montana. She is a former national park ranger at Glacier, Mount Rainier, North Cascades, Voyageurs, and Yellowstone national parks, and her natural history essays have appeared in *American Scientist*, *Journal of American Mensa*, and *Montana Magazine*. A member of American Mensa and Sigma Xi, she is the author of a middle-grade textbook, *Forestry: The Green World*, published by Chelsea House. You can find her in Fox's valley tugging tumbleweeds from the sloughs.